Correct cd.
7/99

THE UNITED NATIONS

Also by Evan Luard

BRITAIN AND CHINA
NATIONALITY AND WEALTH
CONFLICT AND PEACE IN THE MODERN INTERNATIONAL
 SYSTEM
THE CONTROL OF THE SEA-BED
INTERNATIONAL AGENCIES: The Emerging Framework of
 Interdependence
TYPES OF INTERNATIONAL SOCIETY
SOCIALISM WITHOUT THE STATE
A HISTORY OF THE UNITED NATIONS: Volume 1, The Years of
 Western Domination, 1945–1955
A HISTORY OF THE UNITED NATIONS: Volume 2, The Age of
 Decolonization, 1955–1965
THE MANAGEMENT OF THE WORLD ECONOMY
ECONOMIC RELATIONSHIPS AMONG STATES
WAR IN INTERNATIONAL SOCIETY
THE BLUNTED SWORD: The Erosion of Military Power in Modern World
 Politics
THE GLOBALIZATION OF POLITICS
THE BALANCE OF POWER
THE CONCERT OF EUROPE

Also by Derek Heater

CONTEMPORARY POLITICAL IDEAS
BRITAIN AND THE OUTSIDE WORLD
PEACE THROUGH EDUCATION: The Contribution of the Council for
 Education in World Citizenship
CASE STUDIES IN TWENTIETH-CENTURY WORLD HISTORY
CITIZENSHIP: The Civic Ideal in World History, Politics and Education
THE IDEA OF EUROPEAN UNITY
AN INTRODUCTION TO INTERNATIONAL POLITICS (*with G. R.
 Berridge*)

The United Nations

How it Works and What it Does

Second Edition

Evan Luard
Revised by Derek Heater

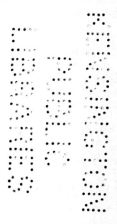

MACMILLAN

First edition 1979
Reprinted 1986, 1987, 1989, 1992
Second edition 1994

Published by
THE MACMILLAN PRESS LTD
Houndmills, Basingstoke, Hampshire RG21 2XS
and London
Companies and representatives
throughout the world

ISBN 0-333-59362-6 hardcover
ISBN 0-333-59363-4 paperback

A catalogue record for this book is available
from the British Library.

Copy-edited and typeset by Povey–Edmondson
Okehampton and Rochdale, England

Printed in Hong Kong

Contents

Foreword to the First Edition

This book is an attempt to take a fresh look at the United Nations and the role which it plays in the modern international political system: to describe the way it operates today, and to examine the reforms needed to make it a more effective force in modern world politics.

Many people feel that the UN has failed. It has fallen down, they say, in its central role of keeping the world's peace. It has become little more than a debating chamber, dominated by very small nations, where hotheads angrily abuse each other, and where nothing effective ever gets done. Others feel that, though we have a UN, the existing organisation is largely irrelevant to current needs, and is of little importance in relation to more potent factors in world politics – superpower diplomacy, the multinational corporation, regional communities, such as the EEC, international political movements or terrorist organisations. Others again merely take the UN for granted as a fact of life, necessary but of little importance to themselves, about which they think as little as they decently can.

Though their views differ widely, these groups have two things in common. First, they mainly possess only the haziest notion of what the UN actually is and what it does in practice. This book is therefore designed partly to help correct this widespread ignorance. It aims to provide an up-to-date description of what the UN is, how it works, and how it has evolved over the years – including what takes place behind the scenes, as well as what is visible to the naked eye. It seeks to show how its role is changing with changes in the world about it.

The critics are also agreed in feeling, with some reason, that the UN, in its present form, is inadequate to the world's current needs. The book therefore seeks to examine some of the changes which have affected it – the influx of new members, many of them very small, the role of great power diplomacy in diminishing its role, the prevalence of internal rather than external conflict in the modern world, the inadequate peace-keeping capacity, the disordered state of the finances, the poor morale of international civil servants, the chronic political conflicts, once mainly between East and West and now mainly between rich and poor, among others. Finally, it seeks, on the basis of this survey, to consider the changes that could be made in the system to make it a more effective force in world politics.

In some ways the UN is now coming into its own again. There is increasing recognition of the need for serious negotiation among the world community about world problems – North–South issues, nuclear proliferation, the sea-bed and the international environment, as well as more immediate threats to the peace. Demands for UN peace-keeping forces are again widely made: three are operating at present in Cyprus, Sinai and Syria, and others have recently been called for (in Namibia, Rhodesia and Lebanon). There is a new willingness to look to the UN for solutions to major problems, or at least as a forum for discussion. It thus becomes all the more important for a fresh look at the organisation to see how it can be made better adapted to meet the growing demands that are made on it.

It is thus hoped that the book may be of interest to the general reader interested in international affairs, as well as to students having a more specialised concern with international organisations. To those who care about world politics nothing can be more important than the state of its main institution for the discussion of conflict. This book is intended to provoke thought and discussion about the body's future. It is hoped that, together with its companion volume, *International Agencies: The Emerging Framework of Interdependence*, it may serve to provide a general survey of the institutions of contemporary international society.

The author wishes to thank the Fabian Society for permission to make use of a passage from his pamphlet, published under their auspices, entitled *The United Nations in a New Age*.

EVAN LUARD

Foreword to the Second Edition

Since this book was first published the United Nations has undergone a number of changes, assumed new commitments and found itself working in a remarkably altered international environment. The need for a revised edition is therefore evident. Very sadly the death of the author has necessitated the involvement of a new hand in the task of revision. I have attempted to retain as much of the original text as possible. The reader will notice three kinds of changes. The first are small matters such as using more up-to-date examples and altering the tenses of verbs. The second change is the deletion of substantially outdated matter and the interpolation of new paragraphs to take account of recent events. Finally, I have replaced the eighth, concluding, chapter completely.

These revisions have been undertaken in order to preserve the usefulness of a book written by a fine and dedicated politician and scholar. He had an intimate knowledge of the UN, serving as a delegate to the General Assembly, 1967–8 and as a member of the Secretary-General's Committee of Experts on the Restructuring of the UN's Economic and Social Activities, 1975. He was a prolific, though careful and lucid, writer on international relations, most particularly international organisations. Students of the United Nations are especially indebted to him for the two volumes of *A History of the United Nations*, covering the first twenty years of the life of the Organisation. It is one of the many sadnesses of Evan Luard's early death that he was unable to complete this projected magisterial work.

I am most grateful for the kind help I have received from the Librarian of the United Nations Information Centre in London and from Professor Hans Singer of the Institute of Development Studies, University of Sussex, who made many useful suggestions for improving Chapters 6 and 8. Neither, of course, is responsible for any remaining errors and omissions in the text.

DEREK HEATER

THE UNITED NATIONS SYSTEM

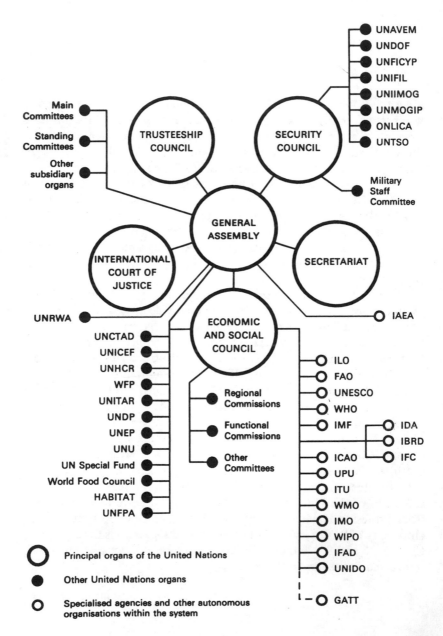

Introduction: Has the UN Failed?

THE UN'S CHANGING ROLE

Governments, in all countries and of all political persuasions, continually affirm, in as many as possible of their public statements, their undying devotion to the United Nations and all its purposes and principles. They continually express, as often as they decently can, as they have done for the past half-century, their determination to uphold its objectives, to strengthen its effectiveness, and to love, cherish and preserve it in every possible way.

But there has been sometimes a tone of desperation in such statements. The words become an act of faith, an incantation which all feel obliged to pronounce, but in which they no longer feel any great confidence. The paying of such obeisances is regarded as a necessary formality, but there is little inclination to take them too seriously: still less to act upon them. The underlying presumption has been that the UN is 'ineffective'. It has contributed little to the solution of major problems in recent years. In a word, it has 'failed'. It must continue to exist, of course, like the House of Lords, the Daughters of the American Revolution and other decaying institutions; but little account need any longer be taken of it in the everyday policies of governments.

In some ways this general attitude of indifference, even contempt, was more disturbing in the 1970s and 1980s than the hostility which prevailed in earlier years. Previously there was, among some, downright hostility to the UN and a wish to see it destroyed altogether. But there were at least many others who retained a burning faith in its potential, and were therefore prepared to give it a significant part in policy making. Recently, until the revival of support in the late 1980s, there have been fewer in either category: few who retained any faith in its capacity to forge a substantial change in the traditional conduct of international relations among states; just as there were few who wished to abolish it – for why abolish the totally impotent? It has been regarded not so much as the sinister instrument of hostile and seditious forces, as the feeble mouthpiece of ineffective

1

busybodies; not as a threat, but as an irrelevance. The main exception to this prevailing attitude has been the Heritage Foundation in the USA. This body, bitterly antipathetic to the UN, had considerable influence with the Reagan government.

These feelings derived from a number of sources. Partly they were the result of wholly unrealistic expectations. The child who expects her new doll not merely to talk but to answer all her questions correctly, the driver who expects his new car not merely to go at 100 miles an hour but to turn all corners automatically will (unless they have bought unusually advanced models) inevitably feel cheated and disillusioned. Similarly, those who have traditionally regarded the UN as the modern manifestation of divine providence, a holy and impeccable supreme being, which can be called down from the skies to wave its magic wand and produce peace at a moment's notice, are inevitably disillusioned when they discover it is composed of frail and mortal human beings, representing conventional and conflicting states, with the same weaknesses and inconsistencies as their predecessors over generations. Those who thought it only required the Security Council to meet and pronounce on every act of violence in any part of the world to produce instant concord have felt deceived and tricked when they find that even the most skilfully worded resolution is not invariably instantaneous in effect. The syllogism is simple if crude: the UN was created to assure peace; peace has not been assured; therefore the UN has failed.

Even among those whose standards are somewhat less exacting, the sense of let-down remains. Consciousness that the UN has failed to bring solutions to any of the main conflicts of recent years (the Middle East and Vietnam, Bangladesh and Biafra, the Dominican Republic and Yugoslavia, Ethiopia and Rhodesia) creates a feeling that it is an increasingly marginal force in modern world politics. The real solutions, the serious negotiations, it is felt (on these, as on East–West relations, strategic weapons, or monetary and trade policy) are undertaken elsewhere, between the great powers. The UN, on all these matters, seems ineffective and irrelevant. It provides, it is said, only words but not deeds; it is a focus for propaganda rather than for serious discussion and debate; it is dominated by a majority of very small, irresponsible nations who use their votes to steamroller through unrealistic resolutions; it flounders in endless and insuperable financial difficulties; it is a costly, inefficient and time-consuming bureaucracy.

Some of these criticisms are downright untruths. It is not the case that the UN provides only words but not deeds. Even in the peace-keeping field, the most difficult of all, the UN has established several major peace forces, which have done much to maintain or restore peace in four important conflict areas (the Middle East, the Congo, Cyprus and south-western Africa), has established observer forces in a number of other cases, and has, elsewhere, successfully mediated in disputes which might otherwise have led to war. In the economic and social field, the deeds are even more manifest. Leaving aside the World Bank, which had 78 billion dollars of loans outstanding in 1989, leaving aside the other specialised agencies (a vitally important and growing part of the UN system. which spend over two billion dollars a year in essential services), extensive programmes of economic and technical assistance are provided by the UN proper. The United Nations Development Programme (UNDP) which is run and organised under the UN, spends about 700 million dollars a year on worthwhile programmes. Even more important, the UN is now increasingly called upon to perform a whole range of new and important programmes, in areas where world-wide action is essential: on the environment, population, disaster relief, refugees, narcotics control and many others. These practical programmes have in many cases been outstandingly successful. Though sometimes ignored altogether in assessments of its activities, these are the areas of UN activity which today are developing fastest and are perhaps most valuable.

Some of the other criticisms contain a core of truth. The UN has a cumbersome and sometimes irresponsible Assembly; is bureaucratic; has financial problems. The fact that the criticisms are made at all, however, and that so much is made of them, again shows the unrealistic standards which are created for the UN, and for the UN alone. It is recognised that national parliaments waste much time in idle debate, childish antics and sterile altercation; but this causes little more reaction than a shrug of the shoulders, and the assumption that this is a normal fact of life. It is accepted that in almost every national administration in the world there is inefficient and wasteful bureaucracy (and in many, dishonesty and corruption as well, happily virtually unknown in the UN system); and this too is taken for granted. It is known that national and municipal governments have their financial problems; and this is regarded as inevitable. It is only because many people have, if only subconsciously, a conception of the UN as something above and beyond reality, as a mythical Utopian entity that should be free of all mortal failings, that they condemn, with such violence, inadequacies which elsewhere they would accept as inescapable,

The UN, indeed, as has often been pointed out, can never be anything but a mirror of the world as it is. It merely gathers together the multiplicity of individual national states with all their imperfections. If the states are bellicose, the UN will be full of bellicosity. If the world is a world of cold war, the UN will be a system of cold war (as in its first fifteen years). If the world is one of rich/poor confrontation (as today), so will the UN be also. If the world is beset with nationalism, so too must the UN be. If there are conflicts and disagreements among continents, races or ideologies, these will be manifest in the UN as well. It is no use blaming the UN, therefore, for deficiencies which are those of the world it reflects. The UN is as good or as bad as the nations which compose it.

When all this is said and done, however, it remains true that, for a number of reasons, the UN does not today, especially in the peace and security area, perform the role it was expected to play when it was founded. This is only partly for the institutional reasons, sometimes quoted, which have been operative for many years: the failure to create, as originally intended, a powerful Security Council force, the use of the veto, the 'by-passing' of the UN through agreements outside it. These are themselves reflections of tensions and hostilities, which would have made it difficult for the UN to perform effectively and to maintain world peace in any case. Even if, for example, a Security Council force, as envisaged in Articles 42 to 49 of the Charter, had been created, even if the veto had been used more sparingly in the early years, even if every major issue had been brought first to the Security Council before discussions began elsewhere, it is unlikely that, in most of the situations it has confronted, agreement would have been easily reached on effective UN action to keep the peace. Here, too, the difficulties were symptoms, rather than causes, of the UN's failure to play a more dominant role in world affairs. The difficulties have been those of world politics as a whole, which no international machinery, however perfect, can automatically dissolve or spirit away. And recent fluctuations in world politics have been mirrored in the varying capacity of the UN to cope with the problems.

Let us look at the developments of recent years which have affected the UN's capacity.

TRENDS IN MODERN WORLD POLITICS

The underlying factors which have prevented the UN from performing the role which many originally envisaged for it are of a number of kinds. First, the world has become smaller. The Charter was based on the assumption that though, on matters *directly* affecting themselves, the permanent members would be able to prevent UN action through the use of the veto, there would be a wide range of other matters, for example affecting other parts of the world, in which they would normally be able to agree on the action required because their own interests were minimal. The common belief that the founders of the UN assumed 'great-power unanimity' is an absurdity: the cold war had already begun at the time the Charter was signed and few were so naïve as to think that there would not be serious disagreements on many of the matters which arose. They merely assumed that where there was such a direct conflict of interest the UN would be helpless. At least the disagreements should not be allowed to destroy the Organisation. What is true is that they underestimated the scope of these great-power conflicts. The shrinkage of distance made the disagreements far more universal in impact than expected. There has been no part of the world, however remote, which was not regarded as essential to the interests of some or all of the great powers: over Iran as over Hungary, over Lebanon as over Angola, each felt its interests involved, so that the Organisation was split fatally. Over Vietnam, the world's most important trouble spot for nearly ten years, for that reason the UN was almost totally inactive. The entry of China has only increased the difficulty. Until the mid-1980s there were few threats to peace, wherever they arose, on which there was not a major conflict of interest between two or more of the permanent members; and this often prevented effective action being taken.

Second, a very large proportion of conflicts in the modern world, are, at least nominally, internal problems. Most wars in the contemporary world are civil wars rather than international wars (or at least begin as such).[1] But the Charter reflects the assumptions of sovereignty. Article 2(7) of the Charter was inserted to prevent interference in matters 'essentially within the domestic jurisdiction' of a member state. This provision can be, and is, used to prevent UN action over civil wars, unless the government concerned actively demands it (as they did, unusually, over the Congo, Cyprus and Angola). On these grounds such major conflicts as those in Biafra and Bangladesh (until it became the cause of international war), not to speak of lesser wars in Laos, Sudan, Burma, Chad, Burundi, Ethiopia, Lebanon (1975–6) and others (in other words most of the main conflicts of recent years) were not discussed in the UN at all. It seems reasonable to forecast that conflicts in the next decade or two will continue to be predominantly of this type. In that case, it is pleasing to predict that the involvement of the UN in helping to end or reduce conflict in Afghanistan, Angola and Namibia in the late 1980s may foretoken a more active role of the organisation in civil wars with international implications.

Third, the existence of spheres of influence and regional organisations has weakened the UN as a universal force. During the period of the cold war the West did not attempt to interfere in eastern Europe, even over the events in Hungary and Czechoslovakia. The Soviet Union was prepared to accept US dominance in Guatemala and the Dominican Republic and, ultimately, in the Cuban missile crisis. The Nixon and the Brezhnev doctrines, in different ways, were designed to underwrite this world partition. The growth of western European and Chinese power, the increasing resentment in Africa and Latin America at great-power interference, and the increasing reluctance of US public opinion to accept a continuing role for the US as international policeman, bring about a world of increasingly self-sufficient regions, each determined to regulate its own affairs, and each reluctant often to allow outside intervention, even by a body such as the UN. Regional organisations, such as the Organisation of American States (OAS), the Organisation of African Union (OAU) and the Arab League often feel they wish to handle 'family quarrels' themselves. In Europe the emerging European institutions (the Conference on Security and Co-operation in Europe (CSCE) and the European Community (EC)) have in recent years developed peace-keeping pretensions.

Fourth, a considerable number of the major issues of the modern world are questions of human rights, whether the rights are those of individuals (say, in South Africa, or China) or of large minorities (such as the Christians in southern Sudan or the Kurds in Iraq, the Tamils in Sri Lanka or the Palestinians in Israel). The UN is a body of nation-states, however, each concerned to preserve national sovereignty, and each having probably at least one such skeleton in its own cupboard. The assembled governments in that organisation, therefore, however much some are genuinely concerned over particular human rights issues, are usually reluctant to interfere too blatantly in the internal affairs of another state. Thus the provisions of Article 2(7), excluding questions of domestic jurisdiction, are not only widely invoked by the government accused in such cases, but are often interpreted with sympathy and understanding by fellow-members too. Where the violation is a particularly gross one, and where there is a large number of nations which feels racial solidarity with the oppressed group (as over South Africa), such objections may be overcome. In other cases, however, even where basic political rights are denied (as in the many states condemned for human rights violations by, for example, Amnesty International) they are held to make any action by the world body inadmissible. Here again, therefore, the UN is made impotent.

Fifth, some of the great powers have explicitly opposed a strong UN role. The Communist countries in general, as a permanent minority within the organisation, and one pathologically suspicious of all external interference, were always apprehensive that the UN might be used against their interests by a hostile majority (its Afro-Asian majority as much as its former Western majority). For this reason they were consistently hostile to any steps which might have the effect of strengthening the Organisation. They opposed increases in its budget or in those of the agencies. They opposed 'strong' candidates for Secretary-General. They were particularly unfavourable to any extension of the UN's peace-keeping role, and to anything else which looked even remotely 'supranational'. China too, though seeking to win support and goodwill among the developing countries, may resist giving the UN strong powers. There have been times, most recently during the presidency of Ronald Reagan, when the USA made it evident that its support for the Organisation was contingent on its support for American interests. She succeeded in reducing her financial commitment to it and suspects the Afro-Asian majority there for their anti-American sentiment or for 'politicisation'. Britain and France have sometimes seemed little more positive. With the ending of the cold war around 1990 the 'Big Five' (that is, the permanent members of the Security Council) became more enthusiastic and less obstructive in their policies towards the UN.

Sixth, the increase in the number of very small members, exercising equal voting power with the very largest, perhaps as much as anything threatens to weaken UN authority. States with a population of over 100 million account for about 60 per cent of the world's population, yet they wield only 11 votes in a General Assembly of 175 members. This anomaly lessens respect for UN resolutions. It arouses resentment among larger powers. And it makes the greatest powers of all particularly chary of giving any effective authority to the world body, or at least the Assembly. The effect of this is seen also in the Security Council. Not only may the ten non-permanent members represent small populations compared with the five permanent members, but those 'Big Five' no longer represent the reality of world

power: Japan and Germany almost certainly have greater claims to
that status than Britain and France.

Seventh, the development of great-power politics has served to
downgrade the UN. During the cold war US–Soviet summit meetings
by-passed the UN system. Increasingly, in economic matters the
powerful groups, notably the Group of Seven (G7) and EC, make
important decisions outside the UN context.

Eighth, the glaring economic disparities between rich and poor
countries create wholly new pressures and tensions, which increasingly
become the most important of all. But the UN has not yet found the
means of resolving them effectively. Thus to the rich countries the UN
begins to look more and more like a begging-bowl, with ever more
onerous demands directed towards them from which they are therefore
inclined to shy away. To the poor, it seems to provide the only
available means of bringing pressure to bear on the rich, yet fails to do
so effectively. Either way, images of the UN's proper role increasingly
diverge and become the source of more and more misunderstandings.

Ninth, the major problems to be confronted are no longer only those
of peace and war. A whole range of new international issues has
emerged, which were scarcely thought of when the UN was founded,
but which now occupy a central place in international politics. The role
of the multinational corporation, the pollution of the international
environment, the depletion of world resources, the problem of
terrorism, the relief of debt for poor countries, the world population
problem, the ownership of deep-sea resources, these and others like
them become the key political issues of the international community.
But the structure and procedures of the UN have not always been
adapted sufficiently to deal adequately with this type of question. And
so, here too, the Organisation increasingly seems to some irrelevant to
man's major concerns.

Finally, and perhaps most fundamental of all, the old Adam of
national sovereignty will not go away as obligingly as the UN founders
fondly hoped. Indeed, nationalist feeling, in some parts of the world at
least, is more powerful than ever. Governments strongly influenced by
these sentiments do not easily respond to the urgings of an organisation
which in any case has no ultimate means of enforcing its wishes. Most
governments support the UN where the UN view is identical with their
own. So the West could make a virtue of supporting the UN in the
1950s, when what the UN wanted was what the West wanted (except
perhaps on colonial issues); while today the Afro-Asians can present
themselves as powerful supporters of the Organisation, since what the

UN wants usually means what they want. But in both cases their opponents have for that very reason feared an increase in the Organisation's power. Where UN demands conflict with those of individual nations, they are still often resisted. Yet there is little the UN can do to enforce conformity. Most nations, rich north as much as poor south, are not yet ready to surrender any significant part of their independence of action to an international organisation; and especially not on the basic questions of peace and war where this surrender is most necessary if the Organisation is to perform the task the world has called it to undertake.

Having glanced at this broad picture of the environment in which the UN must operate, we can go on to look in greater detail at the individual elements of the UN system, the way in which they function today, and the way in which they need to be adapted to this changing world if the UN's effectiveness is to be increased.

FURTHER READING

J. Kaufmann, *United Nations Decision Making* (Rockville, MD, 1980).
A. Roberts and B. Kingsbury (eds), *United Nations, Divided World* (Oxford, 1988).
UN Department of Public Information, *Basic Facts about the United Nations* (New York, published annually).

1 The Security Council: Keeping the Peace

The chief body responsible for keeping the peace is the Security Council. If we wish to consider how the UN's role in maintaining peace can be improved, therefore, we must first examine the Council, how it has developed and the way it operates today.

When the UN was formed there was a general desire to learn the lessons of the League of Nations' failure. The League had failed, it was felt, for four main reasons. First, it had no teeth: no armed force of its own it could call on to withstand aggression. Second, it had lacked authority, above all the authority to impose collective decisions to defend a member that was attacked. Third, it had been paralysed during crises by the rule of unanimity, inherited from nineteenth-century conferences, by which all members had to agree (except the parties to a dispute) for any decision to be reached. Fourth, the absence of several major powers – the US throughout its life, the Soviet Union, Germany, Italy and Japan for much of it, had made it unrepresentative and impotent.

All these failings would be rectified in the UN. It would have armed forces permanently at its disposal for use against aggressors. Its Council would be given authority over every member in calling for collective action. The veto would be abolished for all except the five most powerful states of all. And it would be made more universal by making it as freely open as possible to all states. First, to provide the teeth required, all members were to negotiate with the Security Council for the allocation of armed forces, which the Council might use to keep the peace. Though held by the home state, they would be available for use by the UN immediately when needed. Armed with this weapon, the new Council might show itself more effective than its predecessor in dealing with threats to the peace.

Second, the Council was equipped with powers to make 'decisions' which the League Council lacked: that is, powers to command the obedience of all UN members. Under Article 25 of the new Charter every member of the Organisation was under an obligation to 'accept and carry out the decisions of the Security Council in accordance with

10

the present Charter'. When a threat to the peace took place, the Council could first call on all members in certain circumstances either to apply economic sanctions, the severing of communications or of diplomatic relations (Article 41) or, if necessary, to take such action 'by air, sea or land forces as may be necessary to maintain or restore international security' (Article 42). In this way the organisation should this time possess the power to act decisively which the League had conspicuously lacked.

Third, the unanimity rule was largely abandoned. In the Assembly it was given up altogether. In the Council it was confined to the Big Five, who were enabled to protect themselves through the exercise of a veto: a contrary vote by any of them would cause a resolution to fail. Otherwise a decision could be reached by majority vote (seven votes out of eleven). The granting of the veto power to the largest states of all could be said to represent merely a recognition of reality. Whether or not such a veto had been explicitly accorded, in practice the Organisation could not have been used wholly against the will of any one of the major powers without disaster, for example provoking it to leave the Organisation altogether. The veto could thus be regarded as an essential safety-valve, which served to prevent dissension among its leading members from exploding the whole machine. Without it, the Organisation, if urged to take action against one of those powers, could have been destroyed.

The ideal of universal membership was also upheld, at least in theory. The Organisation was to be made open to all 'peace-loving' states, which at this time was expected to include all countries except ex-enemies – and even these, it was assumed, would be admitted as soon as they had purged their guilt and been reborn under democratic governments. But at the same time it was laid down that admission to the Organisation was to be recommended by the Security Council, which meant that in practice the veto applied to this too.

All four of these hopes were to be disappointed. The UN never had the armed forces at its disposal that had been hoped for. Discussion on the establishment of the force took place in 1946–7 in the Military Staffs Committee, consisting of the military staffs of the five permanent members accredited to the United Nations. Differences soon arose on the scope and character of the force. The Soviet Union wished the forces to be stationed only on the territory of those countries which provided them and objected to the use of foreign bases for this purpose (perhaps fearing some new type of capitalist encirclement): most of the others thought bases should be made available for the permanent stationing of the force. The Soviet Union wanted a limited force of not more than twelve divisions altogether and 600 bombers; the US wanted a large force with twenty ground divisions, three battleships, and fifteen cruisers. The Soviet Union wanted an assurance that such forces would be withdrawn after use within 90 days of the termination of any operation (apparently fearing that they might be used to influence the political situation after such an emergency); the others wanted greater flexibility on this question. The Soviet Union thought that exactly equal forces should be provided from all the permanent members, while the USA wanted it to be possible for variable contributions to be made. But even if agreement could have been reached on the size and character of the force, it seems unlikely there would have been agreement on the circumstances in which it was to be used, and on how it should be controlled. Both of these issues – circumstances of use and method of control – have been important and difficult issues, which arose in acute form later over peace-keeping forces. (For recent suggestions, see p.187.)

This in turn meant that the second hope was disappointed: the authority of the Council was greatly weakened. Without a special force, it was held, it could no longer call on the use of force to resist aggression. Moreover, it was fatally divided by cold war disputes. These were reflected in the constant use of the veto by the minority power, the Soviet Union. All this made it clear that the Council was not going to be the dominant peace-preserving agency in the post-war world which had been originally conceived. It could recommend but not enforce. The hope that the UN would establish a wholly new 'enforcement system' for preserving peace was frustrated.

Thirdly, the voting system, though there was no universal veto, worked little better than before. The veto, even in its limited form, brought constant paralysis. All over the world East and West were in conflict. Almost at the Council's first meeting the Soviet Union registered its first veto on an issue (foreign forces in Syria and Lebanon) in which no vital interest was involved for her. This foreshadowed a whole series of similar occasions in the next few years when the Soviet Union exercised her veto on similar questions. Because the Western powers were at that time in a majority in the Council, these resolutions inevitably often reflected the Western viewpoint, but it could not be said that the Soviet Union's essential interests would have been threatened by any of them. She used the veto, in other words, not to protect vital concerns but to prevent the passage of any resolution with which she happened to disagree: a purpose for which it was certainly not intended (later, by the 1970s, Western powers, then themselves in a minority, vetoed more than the Soviet Union[1]). In consequence, over innumerable issues decisions were frustrated. By good fortune this did not affect the Council's response to the Korean War in 1950. Because she had not won her demand for the transfer of the China seat to the Chinese People's Republic, the Soviet Union had walked out of the Council altogether at the beginning of 1950: as a result, when the Korean War broke out in June of that year, the Council was able to take prompt and effective action the day hostilities began, solely because the Soviet delegate was not present to cast the veto he would surely otherwise have used. Even then the Council wisely only 'recommended' action by member-states to support South Korea, rather than 'deciding' on enforcement action under Article 25.

Finally, even universal membership was not secured. Because recommendations for membership had to be made to the Security Council, the veto applied. Each side in the cold war therefore used the veto to keep out its opponents. The West blackballed the East European states (except Poland and Yugoslavia which were in from the beginning). The Soviet Union vetoed Jordan, Portugal and many others. Only a few that were mutually acceptable (such as Israel) escaped this blockage. Eventually in 1955, under a 'package deal' (which both had previously accepted and refused at different times) most of the applicants were let in together. But even then for another sixteen years, because of ideological antagonism, the government controlling the mainland of China and 98 per cent of her population was not admitted to represent that country.

The effect of all these problems was that the Council was far weaker than many had hoped. Because it had no enforcement powers it had to rely on negotiation. But this too was inhibited because the cold war conflicts soon enveloped the new Organisation. The Security Council was particularly affected by these because they stimulated the use of the veto. It could no longer take the leading role planned for it. As a result to meet the changed situation some changes began to be made in the UN system by the then ruling majority.

Various measures were introduced to give a bigger role to the Assembly, where the veto did not apply (see Chapter 2 below). Some steps were also taken to improve the working of the Council. It came to be accepted that an abstention did not represent a veto: in other words the 'concurring' vote of all the permanent members required under Article 27(3) did not have to be an affirmative vote by each. Later the tradition of the 'consensus' emerged, by which a proposal or statement of the Chairman (comparable to the summing-up by the prime minister or the chairman of a cabinet committee in Britain) was taken to represent the sense of the meeting, and avoided the necessity of taking a vote. More important, with the passing of the Uniting for Peace resolution in the autumn of 1950, it was laid down that even a question of peace and security for which the Council was supposed to have primary responsibility could be taken out of the Council's hands and placed in that of the Assembly in a situation of crisis (despite the terms of the Charter) if there was deadlock in the Council, and that the Assembly itself could call for the use of force if necessary – a still greater liberty with the apparent division of labour laid down in the Charter.

During the early 1950s, therefore, the Council played a more muted role. The number of its meetings declined.[2] Its resolute response to the Korean crisis was the last effective peace-keeping move it was to undertake for a considerable period. Many of the major problems of this period were not dealt with in the UN at all. A whole series of questions was tackled, and in some cases resolved, outside it altogether: in the Berlin talks on Germany (1954), the Geneva conference on Korea and Indo-China (1954), the Vienna discussions on Trieste (1954–5), the signing of the Austrian State Treaty (1955), the Geneva Summit Conference (1955) and other meetings. Some of the questions which did come up in the UN were not resolved: Kashmir, Guatemala, Tunisia, Algeria, Yugoslav complaints against threats from East European countries, similar complaints against the US by the Soviet Union and Czechoslovakia, not to speak of endless complaints of violation of the cease-fire in the Middle East. Some began to despair of the Council as a peace-keeping body; even of the UN as a whole.

In 1956, with the simultaneous eruption of conflict over Suez and Hungary, the UN began to be used once again as the chief instrument for tackling major issues in dispute. Even then, discussion and decision was in both cases primarily in the Assembly. Similarly, when disputes emerged over the Lebanon, and subsequently Jordan, in 1958, though the Council discussed them in the first place, and though the Council set up the UN observer force in the Lebanon (UNOGIL), the decisions which finally resolved both issues were reached by the Special Assembly called to consider them in August of that year.

Only from about 1960 onwards did the Security Council come into its own again as the UN body primarily responsible for peace and security. Over the Congo crisis, which began in that year, most of the important decisions, including the dispatch of a force to assist the

Congolese government (ONUC), were decisions of the Council. Though there was a Special Assembly in 1960, and the Assembly continued to consider the situation in subsequent years, the important decisions throughout were those reached by the Security Council – for example, on the degree of force to be used by the UN contingent, the manner in which it should be used, the policy to be adopted on the secession of Katanga, the call for a reconvening of the Congolese parliament, the recognition of President Kasavubu and the Adoula government, and the Stanleyville operation in November 1964, all these questions were determined by the Security Council.[3] Similarly, it was the Security Council which met to discuss the Cuba crisis in October 1962, and considered the replies received by the Secretary-General from President Kennedy and Mr Khrushchev to the requests which he had sent to the two leaders. It was the Security Council which dealt with the question of Cyprus in the early part of 1964 when fighting broke out between the two communities: and finally decided to send a peace-keeping force to take over responsibility from British forces in the area. It was the Security Council which considered the problem that arose in the Dominican Republic during 1965, when authority was being contested between right-wing and left-wing forces there and US troops were despatched to intervene. It was the Security Council which dealt with successive African questions, including arms for South Africa, Rhodesia on a series of occasions, Namibia, and a series of complaints against Portugal over her African territories. It was also the Security Council which considered, briefly and ineffectively, the war in Vietnam in January 1966 (after a long and angry debate, it was finally decided to place the question on the agenda but it was never effectively pursued), the June Arab–Israel war and its aftermath in 1967, the India–Pakistan war in 1971 and yet another Middle East conflict in 1973.

By the 1980s the Council was providing valuable assistance for the resolution of conflict and tension in the Gulf, Afghanistan, Angola and Namibia, though other questions (such as the Palestinian problem, Cyprus, Cambodia and Western Sahara) remained unanswered.

Meanwhile the composition of the Council had changed. From the beginning of the 1960s, with the big increase in the membership of the UN, there had been proposals for an increase in the size of the Council. This was designed partly to give more members the opportunity of serving on it; and partly to reflect more accurately the composition of the Organisation's membership, particularly to provide more seats for Africans and Asians. The proposal was resisted for some time by the

Soviet Union, probably because of her objection to any amendments to the Charter at all, which could in her eyes only be to her detriment. Eventually, in 1963, she relented. From the beginning of 1965 total membership was increased from eleven to fifteen; and at the same time the number of affirmative votes required to pass a resolution was raised from seven to nine (so marginally reducing the proportion needed).

This involved a change in the representation of geographical groups in the Council. Nothing had been laid down in the Charter on this. Under Article 23 it is provided that in electing non-permanent members due regard should be specially paid 'in the first instance to the contribution of members of the United Nations to the maintenance of international peace and security and to the other purposes of the Organisation, and also to equitable geographical distribution'. Under a 'gentleman's agreement' reached shortly after the Organisation was founded, a system of geographical distribution was in practice adopted: two seats went to Latin America, one to West Europe, one to East Europe, one to the Commonwealth, and one to the other Afro-Asian countries. When the Council was enlarged, the Commonwealth seat was abandoned. In the new Council there were to be two Latin American seats, two West European and others (that is, including old Commonwealth countries), one East European, and five Afro-Asian (usually held by two Africans, two Asians and one Arab[4]) in addition to the permanent members. This time the arrangement was clearly laid down in the resolution of the Assembly. In effect, therefore, of the two criteria laid down in Article 23, that of geographical distribution was now to predominate. This was symbolic of the huge importance that has come to be attached to geographical distribution throughout the Organisation. Whilst there must always be some regard to that principle, it can be argued that if the Council is to be accorded greater respect more account should be taken in electing members of the size and potential contribution of the country elected.

PROCEDURE: HOW DOES THE COUNCIL OPERATE?

The Security Council has often been regarded as a public spectacle. It frequently performs before the eyes of the world. This is perhaps one of its gravest weaknesses. In a way it resembles an elaborate war game, played out in a brightly-lit studio, in which the players compete with each other before the glare of intensive public scrutiny. The spectators, whether in the gallery or beyond the television screen, urge on and cheer their own protagonists, dealing imaginary death-blows to the enemy. The object of the game, not unnaturally, appears above all to win victories: not to reach effective decisions, still less arrive at accommodations, but to score points off opponents, and so win the match.

To the audience the players are tiny figures, seated at a long horseshoe table, on a spotlit stage where every movement, gesture and sign is intently watched by those without. Above them, on either side, are the rows of glass windows, from which the television cameras, the press and the interpreters minutely record every move of the game. The mural at the back of the Council Chamber depicts, in gaudy colours, a particularly bloodthirsty scene of violence and slaughter.

The umpire, the President for the month, sits at the back, with the Secretary-General at his right, and the Under-Secretary for Security Council affairs to his left. (The habit of appointing a Russian to this latter position was continued even after the 1992 restructuring of the Secretariat (see p.176).) Round the table, behind the little boards marking their countries, sit the other fourteen delegates, usually with three or four advisers sitting behind each one, eyeing each other suspiciously and waiting for the next move. Though the atmosphere is often tense, the moves proceed at a leisurely pace. There is no sharp cut and thrust of debate, interjection and interrogation. For the most part each delegate makes a set speech in turn, anything from ten minutes to an hour long, usually read and carefully prepared well in advance. According to the strict letter of the rules, each speech must be delivered twice, once in the original language, then again by the interpreter in consecutive translation in English or French (even though there have already been simultaneous interpretations), so slowing the tempo still further: fortunately, this curious procedure is now nearly always dispensed with. None the less, the stately exchange of measured altercation moves only very slowly. Sometimes this serves to heighten the drama and intensity. From time to time it is the President's turn to play; he rules on a point of procedure, or he calls for an adjournment for further consultations.

This stylised drama emphasises the element of confrontation. It is, moreover, a confrontation that is carefully and deliberately staged in the full glare of the public gaze. Nobody ever forgets for a moment the billion watching eyes at the other end of the television cameras. The Council operates as a brightly lit and expensive cabaret show, not a syllable or gesture of which escapes the hawk-eyed audience. If one delegate appears unshaven, half New York will ring up that same evening offering to lend him a razor. When one Latin American delegate rashly admitted to being unmarried, he received 327 proposals of marriage in the first post next morning. For this show Security Council delegates must be actors. And just as actors pitch their voices so that they can be heard always at the back of the gallery, so the Council delegates pitch their speeches so that they will always have maximum effect at the back of their gallery: among the reporters and television cameramen peering down from their vantage points above, above all among the vast audience at home glued to their sets.

Thus, as with other shows, the posturings on the stage are closely influenced by the demands of the spectators. Not all the effects are bad. The Council has influence mainly by being able to speak direct to a world audience. Like the Pope the UN has no divisions: only the television cameras. It is only the fact that the world's eyes are focused on its debates that gives it power. The points at the end of the game are won, not according to the votes that are cast, but according to the hearts and minds that are influenced. If the speakers often play to the gallery, they are at least playing to quite a large gallery.

Other effects are less desirable. For the part of the audience most in the mind of each delegate is that in his own home country. Often he will win honour and glory, not for his conciliatory manner and ingenious compromises, but for his verbal victories and debating points: not for turning the other cheek but for a resounding left and right to the jaw. Even where there exists a genuine desire to shake hands and settle for a draw, it will only be so long as this does not involve the least concession which could be derided and denounced at home.

An arrangement has, however, been devised, and increasingly used especially since the late 1970s, to circumvent these distortions of publicity. This device is recourse to informal consultations – in effect, closed sessions. So useful are these meetings that a special room is now available in which to hold them. Furthermore, since the late 1980s representatives of the five permanent members have been in the habit of holding private meetings.

How does a question come before the Security Council in the first place? Any member of the UN can call for a meeting to consider any issue. The member need not be a member of the Council itself. And the question need not be one that affects particularly that country: under Article 35 'any member of the UN may bring any dispute or any situation which might lead to international friction or give rise to a dispute to the attention of the Security Council'. But in practice members almost never ask for meetings except to consider situations that concern themselves. There is no good reason for this. And it means that many situations which may be serious threats to the peace – Berlin, Laos, Cambodia, Vietnam for most of the time, Angola, Ethiopia–Somalia, Lebanon (1976) for example – have not been brought before the Organisation, because the powers mainly concerned do not choose to do so. The Secretary-General may call for a meeting to consider any matter which may 'threaten the maintenance of international peace and security' under Article 99. But he too has only once used this power (when Hammarskjöld called a meeting on the Congo).[5]

When a request has been made, the President will call for a meeting of the Council, usually within twenty-four hours. He will normally do this as a matter of course, though difficulties sometimes occur: once, when the Malian delegate was President, he hid himself away for a week when a meeting was requested, and the Council was not able to function till his government suggested it might be a good thing for him to emerge. When the meeting takes place, extra places are found for all the states concerned in the dispute at the end of the horseshoe table. The delegate who has called for it will usually speak first, often denouncing in violent terms some onslaught on his country's territory, a threat, the shooting down of an aircraft or a similar outrage. If he makes charges against another state, that other state will be given the opportunity to reply. After the parties have had their say, other members of the Council who wish will speak. When all have spoken who desire to do so (and on this first occasion very few may speak), the President may suggest an adjournment until another day.

Then intensive consultations will take place between the delegations. This is where the genuine negotiation takes place. A resolution, sometimes two or three resolutions, may be drafted and several times amended to meet the views of different delegations without a word being spoken in the Council itself. Support will be mobilised for each of them. Each may then be amended further to meet the views of other groups whose support is required. A permanent member may threaten to veto, and this will be a particularly powerful inducement to amendment. Sometimes consultations take place within an entire group, even those not members of the Council: African members of the Council often represent the African group as a whole in dealings with other members.

If the matter is an urgent one, a further meeting of the Council may take place within a day, or even a few hours. Then votes may take place on the resolutions. Sometimes the negotiations may take weeks: when mandatory sanctions against Rhodesia were first introduced – one of

the few occasions where a 'decision' under Article 25 has been reached
– there were six weeks of intensive negotiations before a mutally
acceptable resolution could be agreed on. On the other hand, if a war
has broken out, it will usually be possible to reach agreement on a
simple cease-fire resolution within a matter of hours. By the time the
resolutions come to a vote, it is usually known by all how much
support there will be for each. Often all except one will be withdrawn.
Sometimes, there is no attempt to pass a resolution at all, and all are
content with a consensus pronounced by the president to avoid the
difficulties of a vote which would demonstrate the weakness of a
divided Council.[6] Even on resolutions hostile votes are usually
minimised – through the way the resolution is drafted and the need
to avoid a veto. Over the Congo, though there existed acute dissension
on the actions taken, on the five Council resolutions passed in 1960 and
1961 not a single hostile vote was cast. In a sense the Council here does
the job it is intended to do: through the process of negotiation it secures
a consensus.

The resolution passed will be in the time-honoured form, universally
used in the UN, with a preamble, containing a series of phrases
recording varying degrees of concern and agitation: from 'recalling',
'bearing in mind that', 'conscious of', to 'concerned over', 'determined
to' and 'deploring' (the strongest word in the UN vocabulary is
'condemn': this was once only sparingly used but the currency is now
increasingly debased). These preambular paragraphs are followed by
what are termed the operative paragraphs, which usually call for
particular types of action, whether by the parties concerned, by the
Secretariat, or by the UN membership as a whole. Such a resolution
may merely call for restraint by all parties. It may call for a cease-fire,
or a withdrawal of forces. It may, like the series of resolutions on
Rhodesia, call for sanctions of various kinds, voluntary or 'mandatory'
(that is, reached under Chapter VII of the Charter, and recording a
'decision' which every member must obey under Article 25). It may,
like the famous Resolution 242 on the Middle East, even seek to lay
down the general outlines of a settlement of some particular conflict.
The Security Council showed especial determination in its reaction to
Iraq's seizure of Kuwait in 1990. It at first imposed tough economic
sanctions and subsequently (with twelve positive votes) authorised the
use of force (see pp.179–80).

Sometimes the meeting will be preceded by a long procedural
wrangle: on whether such and such a delegation will be heard, on which
resolution will be voted on first, on whether a particular issue is or is

not procedural (there is no veto on procedural matters). Such wrangles seem petty and pointless but invariably mask a difference in the substance. Procedural arguments are used, often with great skill and persistence, to make it easier or more difficult for a particular resolution to be passed on a particular subject, or to influence the form which discussion may take.

This is an inevitably simplified account of the procedure of the Council. It gives little idea of the complexity of the negotiations which are often necessary if a resolution is to be passed. The resulting resolution is thus in a sense an act of diplomacy, nearly always a compromise representing the highest common factor of the attitudes of a number of different delegations: occasionally all of them. The weeks of negotiation on Resolution 242 produced a resolution that was eventually passed unanimously, though until the Russian delegate raised his hand nobody knew how he would vote.

All this intensive activity of course will not necessarily bring a settlement itself, though it may set procedures in motion. Often further resolutions will be needed in subsequent months or years. On some questions, such as Cyprus or southern Africa, there have been many resolutions over many years. On the Middle East over a hundred resolutions have been passed in the Council over the years (seven in 1990 alone). Sometimes the substantive negotiations will take place elsewhere than in the UN: over the Cuba crisis, over the India–Pakistan war of 1965, over Vietnam, the real negotiations took place on the hot line, in Tashkent, and in Paris (though all were discussed also in New York). But the resolutions of the Security Council may provide a kind of framework within which such negotiations take place. And on a number of issues – the Berlin blockade, the Suez Canal, the Middle East, Cyprus, the Iran–Iraq war, Afghanistan, Angola/Namibia – negotiations have taken place directly under the auspices of the UN.

Apart from discussing threats to international peace and security, the Security Council has a constitutional place in the UN system. It makes recommendations concerning the election of new members. It recommends the appointment of a Secretary-General (to be approved by the Assembly). It elects the judges of the International Court of Justice. Although in some cases it shares this role in theory with the General Assembly, in practice the Council has the more powerful voice. No new member can be elected without the recommendation of the Council. Only one name is given to the Assembly for Secretary-General. In this, as on many other matters, it is the Council which calls the tune.

How does this procedure affect the Council's capacity to decide and to act? We shall consider some aspects of this at the end of the chapter. For the moment the main point to be made is that the system of public confrontation which we have described is scarcely a procedure calculated to assist effective decision making. Indeed it is difficult to think of a decision-making body in any other system, from national cabinet to a board of directors, which makes decisions in public. The main condition of effective decision making, especially within a political body joining representatives of many radically different viewpoints (say the cabinet of a coalition government), is to use a procedure which maximises consensus. Yet the procedure of public confrontation as practised in the Security Council is one which maximises dissent. It must maximise dissent because, to impress the vast audience watching without, to win hearts and minds and deny them to the antagonist, each participant must promote the maximum distinctiveness of appeal for his own brand-product, and the maximum denigration of all rival brands. It is of course true that these public meetings are, in a sense, only the tip of the iceberg: the part visible to the naked eye. The other six-sevenths beneath the surface, the confidential discussions in the corridors and the informal consultations represent the heart of the matter. However, if it is known that a public encounter in open session is to follow confidential discussions, this knowledge can colour even the negotiations behind the scenes. Positions must be protected which will enable the desired image to be projected with the maximum effectiveness at the public showing. The message is the medium: and the message which this medium promotes is the loudest and clearest indignation, abuse or righteous self-justification. This may not matter so much in the Assembly (which may be expected to reflect the political battle as clamorously as a national parliament does). But it matters very much in the Council, which is expected to be a body that can reach collective decisions rather than discursively debate.

FUNCTIONS

If this is *how* the Security Council operates, let us next consider *what it can do* in exercising its decision-making function. One could try to answer this question by reference to the terms of the Charter. Chapter VI sets out a series of procedures that may be used by the Council in seeking to secure the 'peaceful settlement of disputes'. Under Article 34 it may 'investigate' a dispute or situation to see whether it is likely to endanger international peace and security: it did this, for example, in sending commissions to the Balkans to investigate disturbances on the Greek border, and more recently to investigate tension in the Israeli-occupied Arab territories (1979, 1980). Under Article 35, it may consider any dispute or situation brought 'to its attention' by any member: this is the procedure normally employed by the Council. Under Article 36, it may 'recommend appropriate procedures or methods of adjustment' on any dispute or situation: this was requested, for example, by Britain in the Corfu Channel case (see p.91). Under Article 37, it may consider a dispute which it thinks likely to endanger international peace and security and determine whether to 'recommend . . . terms of a settlement': in effect, though not in name, this is what the Council did in setting out the general principles of a Middle East settlement in Resolution 242. And it may, under Article 38, make such a recommendation at the request of the parties (but no such request has ever been made to the Council).

Chapter VII sets out the procedures that may be used when a situation has gone past the stage of being a 'dispute' and has become a 'threat to the peace', a 'breach of the peace' or an 'act of aggression' (terms that are never clearly defined). Under Article 39, the Council is to 'determine the existence' of such a state of affairs and decide what recommendations to make. It can decide to call, under Article 40, for certain 'provisional measures' by the parties, without prejudice to their rights, claims or position: a cease-fire or mutual withdrawal from a border might be a measure of this kind and the Council used this Article in ordering a cease-fire in Palestine in July 1948. If this has no effect, the Council can decide to use sanctions of various kinds, including the interruption of economic relations or communications (Article 41): this is what it did over Rhodesia. Finally, if these are inadequate, it can decide to take action by air, sea or land forces 'as may be necessary to maintain or restore international peace and security'. It is sometimes claimed that this last provision for the use of force by the Council cannot now be fulfilled because of the failure of the negotiations to establish a Security Council force in 1947–8. In fact there is no good ground for this conclusion. Article 42 speaks only of 'air, sea or land forces', and does not specify that they must be a pre-existing UN force. The reason the provision has never been used is not because of the non-availabilty of the forces required, which every member has in only too great abundance. It is because of the political difficulties and dangers of making such a call on member-states which hold widely varying opinions on the merits of every dispute, and which in any case are not usually filled with wild enthusiasm to commit themselves to armed action in conflicts in which they may have no overriding national interest. This, the long-recognised difficulty facing any collective security system, has not in practice yet been overcome by the words of the Charter binding members to obey Security Council 'decisions'. Even the campaign to oust Iraqi forces from Kuwait was not conducted strictly under the provisions of Article 42.[7]

But a description of the types of action possible to the Council under the Charter is in any case misleading. The Council has over the years been less and less inclined to be tied to any particular formula laid down in the Charter. It has shown considerable flexibility in the methods it has used. Although Article 33 lays down that bilateral procedures of settlement should be exhausted before the UN becomes involved, in recent years disputes and threats have been brought to the Council from the beginning, even if no attempt at bilateral settlement has been made. The procedure for 'investigation' has rarely been used explicitly. The Council practically never lays down in any detail the 'terms of a settlement' as empowered to do under Article 37. Most often the Council's resolution nowadays mentions no specific Article of the Charter. It calls for some procedure: the appointment of a representative of the Secretary-General to pacify a conflict, of observers or even a peace force to quieten a border (none of which are mentioned in the Charter at all). The most common message of a Security Council resolution is a general call for restraint to both sides to a dispute.

There are, however, particular *techniques* which have been used a good many times by the Council. They can perhaps best be described by reference to particular examples. The commonest of all is the *appeal*, for the observance of a cease-fire, say, or for a withdrawal of forces. In some cases, as over the Suez war in 1956 and the India–Pakistan war of 1965, this has in fact been followed fairly rapidly by a cessation of hostilities, though the two have not necessarily been cause and effect.

In other cases the Council attempts a form of *conciliation*: the appointment of a mediator, a committee of investigation, or (increasingly) a representative of the Secretary-General. Over the dispute between the Netherlands and Indonesian forces in 1948, a Good Offices Committee, and later a Commission for Indonesia, was set up to search for a settlement. Over Palestine (1948), Kashmir (1950) and Cyprus (1964) individual mediators were appointed to promote agreement. Over Korean reunification (1947), Palestine (1947), Kashmir (1948), the Congo (1960) and apartheid in South Africa (1962), committees were appointed designed to explore possible solutions (though it cannot be said that any of them were particularly successful in their results). A representative of the Secretary-General was appointed over the Middle East (1967), Bahrein (1970) and other questions. In some cases the Secretary-General himself has instituted negotiations between the parties; this occurred over the Berlin blockade (1949), Chinese intervention in Korea (1950), and the nationalisation of the Suez Canal (1956). Occasionally discussions are inaugurated under UN auspices among the big powers, even though they are not themselves directly involved, on the assumption that if they can reach agreement they may in turn help to secure its acceptance by the parties: this is what happened over the Middle East in 1969–71. The Secretary-General or his representative played active roles on behalf of the Security Council in the various crises involving Iraq and Iran from 1984 to 1991.

Next, there are the procedures which may be called *fact-finding*. In some cases, a committee is sent simply to verify the facts on the ground: the United Nations Special Committee on the Balkans did this in the case of the infiltrations into Greece from Bulgaria in 1948–51; a sub-committee was sent to investigate complaints by Laos of invasion from North Vietnam in 1959; a five-man Committee was sent to investigate Guinea's complaint of a raid from Portuguese Guinea in 1970 and a similar complaint from Senegal in 1971. Observers may be sent for the same purpose: the United Nations Observer Group in the Lebanon was set up to check whether there had been infitration from Syria and other countries in 1958. Over the Cambodia–Thailand dispute (1958), Buraimi (1963), Muscat (1965) and Bahrein (1970), a representative of the Secretary-General undertook a general investigation of the facts and reported, with or without recommendations for a settlement, to the Secretary-General. Between 1984 and 1988, seven investigatory missions were dispatched to report on the use in the Iran–Iraq war of poison gas, a weapon forbidden by international law. Technical commissions may serve to establish the essential facts and propose solutions: the World Bank was used successfully to resolve the dispute over compensation for the Suez Canal nationalisation and over the Indus Waters. The Secretariat itself issues background papers, particularly to the committees of the Assembly, which serve as useful assemblages of the essential facts where issues are being considered within the Organisation.

In some cases the object is not merely fact-finding but *interposition*; the placing of some kind of barrier or presence between the two conflicting parties. The UN Truce Supervision Organisation (UNTSO) was sent to Palestine to maintain the cease-fire from 1949 to the present day, and mixed armistice commissions were established to hear complaints of violation. Observers patrolled the Kashmir cease-fire line between India and Pakistan forces for nearly twenty years. An observer team was sent to seek to prevent the dispatch of arms and men from Saudi Arabia and the UAR in the Yemen. In more acute cases, this function of interposition is performed by UN peace-keeping forces. This has essentially been the role of the UN forces in Cyprus since 1964 and in Sinai and Syria from 1974. In 1989–90 a UN group helped materially in the peaceful transition of Namibia to independence.

In a few cases, the Security Council has agreed to undertake a more positive stand in the *determination* of solutions in conflicts. Over Palestine in 1947, the General Assembly asked the Council to implement the solution of the problem it had adopted and, though the Council declined to do this, it did in subsequent resolutions effectively endorse partition; and again later, in Resolution 242 of November 1967, the Council committed itself to a particular *type* of settlement after the June War of that year. In the Congo, the Council sought to decide certain internal Congo questions; which government should be recognised, that the Congolese parliament should be recalled, and that the secession of Katanga should be prevented. In Cyprus, though the Security Council action was primarily designed to keep the peace, in practice here too its decisions at first served to reaffirm the unity of that country. In West Irian, though the UN presence was only transitional, the UN endorsed the transfer of the territory to Indonesia, only qualifying this by a theoretical commitment to a subsequent 'act of choice' (which it never effectively controlled). On Bahrein, the Council endorsed and legitimised the territory's independence from Iran when a representative of the Secretary-General reported this to be the wish of the people. On Namibia, it consistently maintained that South Africa's occupation was unlawful. And in 1990 the Security Council categorically condemned the illegality of Iraq's seizure of Kuwait.

The most extreme measure open to the UN, when security has totally broken down, is to institute an act of *collective security*, calling on members to take up arms to defend a country under attack. Only twice, over the Korean War and Iraq's seizure of Kuwait, has the UN adopted this course. And in neither case was the support for the use of force unanimous. Enforcement action of other kinds has been used, however, on several occasions: in a resolution ordering a cease-fire in Palestine in July 1948; in demanding mandatory sanctions against Rhodesia in May 1968; in extending these mandatory sanctions in March 1970; in 'deciding' that South Africa had no further rights in Namibia in January 1970 (though this was not strictly taken under Chapter VII and no sanctions were then employed); in placing an arms embargo against South Africa in 1977, and a general embargo on Iraq in 1990. Economic sanctions may be derided as falling far short of the kind of pressure necessary to implement a genuine collective security system. Yet at least the UN received a far more universal response to its call for sanctions against Rhodesia than the half-hearted sanctions measures once instituted by the League.

Among the available procedures for extending the UN's authority, the greatest hope has been placed in *peace-keeping*. When the negotiations for a Security Council force failed, various alternatives were suggested. Trygve Lie, the first Secretary-General, called for the establishment of a UN ground force to maintain security in disputed areas, such as Trieste and Jerusalem. Observer and truce supervision forces were set up in Palestine, Kashmir and elsewhere. But it was not until the Suez affair of 1956 that a fully-fledged peace-keeping force was established, drawn from a dozen countries and set up for peaceful patrolling, with the consent of the host government. A still larger force was sent to the Congo in 1960 (by the Security Council) and was for a time engaged in actual fighting, though this was not originally anticipated, to maintain order, put down factional fighting and end the secession of Katanga. A smaller force was set up in 1962 (by the Assembly) to supervise the transfer of authority in West Irian from the Netherlands to Indonesia. In 1964, a force was sent by the Security Council to Cyprus to keep the peace between Greeks and Turks, and has remained there since, though at a continually declining level. In 1973–4 two UN forces were sent to separate Israeli from Egyptian and Syrian forces. The region remained unsettled and in 1978 a force was sent to southern Lebanon to act as a buffer between that state and Israel. In 1989–90 a UN group briefly supervised the transition of Namibia to independence. Most recently UN peace-keeping forces have been despatched to Cambodia and the former Yugoslavia; in the case of Cambodia, the biggest force ever deployed by the UN. Table 1.1 shows how many new forces were organised from the late 1980s onwards. Such forces, though their power is limited (since they are not expected to fight), can often maintain the peace effectively in a troubled

Table 1.1 UN Peace-keeping and observer operations

Duration	Name of force	Place	Maximum strength
1948–	UN Truce Supervision Organisation (UNTSO)	Palestine	572
1948–	UN Military Observer Group in India and Pakistan (UNMOGIP)	Kashmir	35
1956–67	UN Emergency Force I (UNEF I)	Egypt	6 073
1960–64	Organisation des Nations Unies au Congo (ONUC)	Congo	19 828
1963–64	UN Yemen Observation Mission (UNYOM)	Yemen	150
1964–	UN Force in Cyprus (UNFICYP)	Cyprus	6 411
1973–9	UN Emergency Force II (UNEF II)	Suez Canal & Sinai	6 973
1974–	UN Disengagement Observer Force (UNDOF)	Syria	1 317
1978–	UN Interim Force in Lebanon (UNIFIL)	Lebanon	5 827
1988–91	UN Angola Verification Mission (UNAVEM)	Angola	60
1988–90	UN Iraq–Kuwait Observation Mission (UNIKOM)	Iraq & Kuwait	1 440
1988–	UN Iran–Iraq Military Observer Group (UNIIMOG)	Iran & Iraq	400
1989–90	UN Transition Assistance Group (UNTAG)	Namibia	4 650
1989–	UN Observer Group in Central America (ONUCA)	El Salvador, Honduras & Nicaragua	1 100
1991–	UN Mission for the Referendum in Western Sahara (MINURSO)	Western Sahara	2 000
1991–	UN Iraq–Kuwait Observation Mission (UNIKOM)	Iraq & Kuwait	1 440
1991–	UN Observer Mission in El Salvador (UNUSAL)	El Salvador	113
1991–	UN Advanced Mission in Cambodia (UNAMIC)	Cambodia	460
1992	UN Transitional Authority in Cambodia (UNTAC)	Cambodia	15 500+
1992	UN Protective Forces (UNPROFOR)	Croatia	9 000
1992	UN Military Liaison Officers' force (UNMLO)	Yugoslavia	14 000

area by exploiting the moral authority they can invoke: the only
sustained period of peace in the Middle East from 1948 to 1982 was the
decade between 1957 and 1967 when UN forces patrolled the frontier
between Egypt and Israel. They are a measure, if not of increased
power at the disposal of the UN, at least of the increased authority it
enjoys in the contemporary international society.

These initiatives have led, however, to acute friction over the
responsibility of Assembly and Council (and Secretary-General) for the
authorisation and control of the forces, and especially over their
financing.[8] The Soviet Union claimed that only the 'aggressors' should
pay the costs of such operations (which are not provided for in the
Charter), whether the force was set up by the Assembly or by the
Council. France denied the constitutionality of an Assembly force; yet,
somewhat illogically, she was prepared to pay for UNEF I, established
by the Assembly, but not for ONUC, established by the Council
(perhaps because de Gaulle was not in power when the first was set up).
A number of countries have paid voluntary contributions to help
overcome the financial problem, but the question has not been
resolved. The Organisation remains in debt over peace-keeping
expenses. For this reason many recent peace-keeping forces have
been paid for entirely by voluntary contributions. But there was a
major advance in October 1973: the peace-keeping force then set up to
police the Middle East cease-fire was financed by all members from the
regular budget, even if on a special scale of assessment. Also, three of
the 'Big Five' members of the Council agreed to pay substantial
amounts of their arrears in 1986.

Peace-keeping forces have thus been an important means of
extending UN authority over recent years. To enable them to play a
continuing role, however, there is need for clearer guidelines about the
ways such a force may be used, and for some acceptable procedure for
keeping such a force under political control.

CONCLUSIONS

This, roughly, is how the Council operates today. Why has it not been
more successful in preventing wars?

It is undeniable that the achievement of the Security Council in
keeping the peace over the past half-century is considerably less
impressive than had been hoped at the time of the UN's foundation.
Yet one should not exaggerate the failure. As we saw in the

Introduction, one reason for the disappointment often felt at the UN's performance lies in the unrealistic expectations placed on it. The chief factor contributing to these has been the Charter itself. The machinery proposed in Article 43 of the Charter for a Security Council force raised many hopes, but was probably always unworkable. Even if it had been possible to reach agreement on the composition of the force, it would almost never have been possible to use it. For one permanent member or another would almost always have been fearful that this might have been to the disadvantage of its own side or interests, and so have used its veto. If there had still been, as occasionally occurred in the inter-war period, 'disputes' or 'situations' that were wholly local, distinct and unrelated to the global ideological conflict, there might occasionally have been a possibility of 'great-power unanimity': joint action by the five permanent members acting in concert. But in the post-1945 world, there were virtually no such conflicts. A proposal for UN action in any dispute in whatever part of the world – over Greece, Berlin, Indonesia, Guatemala, Laos, Lebanon, the Dominican Republic, Vietnam or Angola – must have inevitably affected the interest of great powers and so invited a veto. Only with the ending of the cold war did the effective use of Article 43 become remotely feasible. Yet it was not even then invoked precisely against Iraq in 1990–91.

But the fact that the Security Council has not been able to undertake its enforcement role does not mean that it has not had any part to play. It has at least, unlike the League, continued to hold the centre of the stage. The immediate instinct when conflict breaks out, still remains normally to turn towards the Council, and to call for its judgement. Even if it is not expected that it can *solve* a dispute, or immediately halt fighting that has already broken out, it may at least be able to bring to bear the weight of outside opinion. This in itself represents a contribution and certainly an advance on previous ages.

The trouble is the Council has never adjusted to its changed role: to the fact that it has no force to call upon. The Council is in a sense in the position of an umpire among burly and unruly football players. It may be called upon for judgement in certain types of situation, even where it cannot by its own strength enforce that judgement. It can lay down the general terms of a settlement, as over the Middle East in 1967. If both parties are willing it can even *resolve* an issue, as over Bahrein. In other cases it can indicate the procedures that may in turn lead to a settlement, as over Berlin in 1948. It can call for a cease-fire: five times it has called for cease-fires in the Arab–Israeli conflict and five times they have been accepted. At the very lowest it can censure and condemn: and even such judgements, however impotent, do represent, especially if unanimous, some influence on action. The injunctions expressed – stop bickering, talk it over, make it up, go home again – crude though they are, often reflect the general feeling of the outside world, and because this is recognised exert some pressure (Israelis' and the Arabs' eventual reluctant acceptance of Resolution 242, at least as a basis of negotiation, at the expense of previous positions, is one example of this). In this respect they may be compared to the judgement of village elders on some complaint brought before them by contending rustics. The judgements cannot be enforced but they carry considerable weight. To have reached even this stage of authority is something.

The Council could capitalise further on this authority. In a world as small as today's, no government is wholly indifferent to outside opinion. None is quite oblivious of its good name. None cares to be thought completely defiant of the outside world. In some cases, if a government believes that its vital interests are at stake, the Council's influence may only be weak, at least in its immediate effect: such a government may indeed feel 'to hell with world opinion', as with South Africa's reaction to resolutions on apartheid, or the Soviet Union's over Hungary and Czechoslovakia. But in most cases, governments may be influenced, slowly and almost unconsciously, by international pressures to modify their policies to avoid the odium of public condemnation. Public opinion, in a word, can be a powerful influence on conduct, in the international community as in smaller societies, and can, by the same almost imperceptible processes, gradually build up a code of acceptable international conduct.

The Council can in this way expand its general authority. It need not, however, as at present, always seek to pronounce on the details of individual disputes. Because of its size, because of its political differences, because it meets often only in public, the Council is not at present well equipped to formulate *detailed* settlements of particular disputes. Even over the Middle East war it set out, in Resolution 242, only the general outline of a settlement, and left the details to be worked out through the mediation of the Secretary-General's Special Representative, or in negotiations among the parties. Over the Cuba crisis, the India–Pakistan war of 1965, and Cyprus, the Council was able to agree on relatively neutral pleas for peace and a cease-fire, while the details of a settlement were worked out elsewhere. This is not necessarily wrong: it does not mean the UN is being 'by-passed', or that secret diplomacy is coming in by the back door. The two are not exclusive. There is a role both for international organisations, to provide the general guidelines and judgements of principle, and for private diplomacy, to provide the detailed settlements. The Security Council should not seek to replace diplomacy. But it may supplement it, by shaping the general principles which the world community expects to see observed in detailed settlements, and by providing the framework for the negotiations that are anyway essential.[9]

The Security Council should therefore perhaps be seen above all as a bargaining mechanism, permanently available, for negotiating agreed courses of action over crisis situations among individual powers and groups of nations, or at least promoting negotiations elsewhere. Every decision will therefore be a compromise. The Council is not, like cabinets in national states, a unified and single-minded decision-making body, joining ministers who are already close colleagues and committed to a common policy. It is rather like an *ad hoc* committee formed among mutually distrustful parties, in which every decision has to be negotiated among the adherents of different points of view. Where interests are not too divergent it may be possible to achieve consensus on some matters at least[10] (as over Cyprus, Congo, the Middle East and Iraq). Over other issues, where there is direct conflict affecting permanent members (Hungary, Vietnam), this may be impossible, though even here negotiation may sometimes be promoted.

There are some institutional changes that could be made to improve the Council's effectiveness. There have been suggestions for establishing sub-committees to look into particular disputes and recommend settlements: this was done in 1971 over Guinea's complaints against Portugal and Senegal. A panel of mediators, or conciliators, may be established for use in such cases: such a panel was set up in 1950 but has virtually never been used. Fact-finding machinery could be set up: this exists in theory in the Peace Observation Commission, set up in 1950 and still re-elected every year, but only once used, and in the Secretary-General's personal representatives; but the real difficulty is in securing political consent for such missions, not finding the personnel. Agreements under Article 43 could be reached by which members made forces available to the Council (as an Assembly resolution of 1970 urged): but again this could not solve the political problems of using such forces. The Council could seek to investigate situations (under Article 34) *before* they reached the stage of open conflict, when they might be more amenable to influence; but it is not sure many countries in dispute would agree to such investigation unless there was danger of imminent war.

Some of these changes might have marginal value. But the fact is that it is not new procedures that are lacking to the UN: these are always available if required. It is the willingness to use them. It is not so much new institutional arrangements as new attitudes that are most needed. If the Council is to maximise its influence, there are six essential conditions which must be met.

First, the Council needs to be made more *representative* and so more authoritative. By 1990 the obsolescence of Article 23 had led to the framing of new proposals for permanent membership of the Security Council. Three schemes have been mooted. The Soviet Union suggested that Germany should be a sixth member. Brazil suggested that three or four Third World countries (including Brazil) should be given seats but without veto powers. Italy has made the most plausible proposal: the UK and France should surrender their seats for one EC seat and the spare seat be allotted to Japan. A more significant change would be for non-permanent members to become explicitly the representatives of their continent, so that they must consult with their own group and express group views in the discussions of the Council: this would both ensure that widely held views were represented and give greater substance to the membership of very small states. These would be obliged to behave responsibly and be known to represent the views of a large number of members. If the Council were made more clearly representative in this way its authority would be enhanced.

Second, the Council should get away from the tradition that its main purpose in life is to pass resolutions. For much of its history it has devoted hours, days and occasionally weeks to negotiating the terms of resolutions that are sometimes almost immediately forgotten thereafter. Resolutions should be regarded as merely one available means to an end: the securing of a settlement. The main aim should be to promote substantive *negotiations*. Sometimes these can be held at the UN itself (as over Suez in 1956); or under its auspices (like the Vietnam settlement and the Middle East negotiations of 1973–4); or under a UN mediator (as with the Bahrein settlement). Time could be given for private discussions, within or outside the Council, to examine the causes of a dispute, or to negotiate a settlement, before the drafting of a resolution is even begun. In some cases a simple resolution calling on the Secretary-General to promote negotiations is all that is required. In others a small group of three or five members could be appointed as a conciliation team between the parties (as was done two or three times in the UN's early years): Article 29 provides that the Council 'may establish such subsidiary organs as it deems necessary for the performance of its functions'. When a resolution is needed, instead of waiting for highly partisan texts, which are either amended out of recognition or vetoed, a drafting group could be appointed to find a mutually acceptable form of words. On this basis, the Security Council might finally (as Article 38 of the Charter provides) 'make recommendations to the parties with a view to a specific settlement of the dispute'. The Council did in fact use more flexible methods, not least 'secret diplomacy', in the late 1980s to good effect. It thus facilitated the end of the Iran–Iraq war, the withdrawal of Soviet forces from Afghanistan, the withdrawal of Cuban troops from Angola and the independence of Namibia.

Third, the Council must take under discussion *every* major conflict that arises, even if it cannot always discover a satisfactory solution. If it cannot be foreseen in advance whether or not the Council will consider a particular problem, potential disputants are not deterred or influenced. Though there have been understandable reasons for some conflicts in recent years having gone by almost unobserved by the Council – Berlin and the German question, Vietnam, Laos, the China–India and China–Soviet disputes, the situation in East Pakistan during most of 1971, Angola (1974–5), Ethiopia–Somalia (1977) and many others – the result of UN inattention is that the general public ceases to look on it as the world authority that will automatically take action in time of crisis. It becomes marginal, an occasional resource, to be used when convenient. Similarly, the failure of the Council to take account of many civil wars, though understandable in the light of UN constitutional doctrine, ignores the realities of the modern world, in which most wars are civil wars, and most civil wars are international wars in some sense. The wars in Nigeria, Chad, Indo-China and Angola, which the UN ignored, have been as international as those in Greece, Lebanon, Congo and the Yemen, which have been discussed. If the Council is to retain its central role, it will need to discuss all conflict situations everywhere.

Fourth, the Council's authority needs to be publicly recognised by governments. It would receive greater world attention and respect if its meetings were more often attended by foreign ministers, or even prime ministers, rather than permanent delegates. In the League, even though travel was so much more difficult than today, foreign ministers habitually attended meetings of the Council. Today, though they will often speak in the Assembly, they rarely speak in the Council, even though its meetings are usually far more important.[11] Moreover, its meetings, where they remain public, should secure greater coverage, on press, radio and television. At present it secures this in the United States, where long debates are sometimes relayed live for days on end, but in other countries there is almost a conspiracy of silence over its activities, by press and television alike.

Fifth, if the Council needs far more publicity, it also needs more secrecy. Many of its meetings must inevitably be public meetings, because they are designed for the public eye and ear. The changed circumstances of the post-cold war period have made private meetings increasingly possible and fruitful. It is no coincidence that this new style of deliberations has led to greater practical activity both in the exercise of diplomacy and in the deployment of peace-keeping and observer forces. The continuation and development of UN 'secret diplomacy' should therefore be encouraged.

Finally, what is needed, above all, if the Council is to maximise its authority, is for it to develop a *policy*. This means a conscious attempt to build up a body of consistent principles of international behaviour in the judgements which it reaches. Only the development and consistent application of such a code of conduct could exert any firm and predictable influence on national behaviour. Only the conditioning which repeated affirmation of clear principles might bring about, both in statesmen and in their publics, could, in the absence of enforcement powers, fundamentally influence the action of states. At present there are large areas of national conduct for which no recognised norms exist: intervention in civil conflict, support for revolutionary governments, rights over international waterways, the rights of intervention to protect nationals – on these and many other questions, there are no generally recognised rules. By its actions in dealing with particular cases the Council could begin to establish those norms. In short, the society of nations is no different from many other societies. It requires the rules, the principles of interaction, which are the condition of a stable coexistence in any society. The Assembly at its 25th Anniversary promulgated some Principles of Friendly Relations among States[12] relating to some of these points. Though inadequate and sometimes ambiguous, these are a beginning. It remains for the Council to apply them consistently in its judgements. (Some observers blamed the UN for failing to make its position clear on the disintegration of Yugoslavia in 1992. If firmer and earlier action had been signalled perhaps the appalling slaughter, destruction and displacement of people, especially in Bosnia, would have been averted.)

The fact that the Security Council is above all a political body, mirroring the political differences and conflicts of states, is both a liabilty and an asset for it. On some questions, at the height of the cold war, almost all discussion degenerated into accusation and counter-accusation, competition to outdo, outwit and outvote an opponent. Even here it merely reflected the reality of the age. The problems the Council deals with are political problems (international politics is necessarily political); and it therefore requires political techniques to resolve them. Just as a parliament or cabinet, or a committee, or a board of directors, must find the political means to resolve, through adjustment and compromise, the disputes and differences that emerge within them, so must the Security Council. This is an alternative method of politics from those of traditional international conflict. But it is still politics. And it is a political game that needs to be played more subtly and more skilfully than it was so often in the Council in the past: to promote negotiation not gesticulation, compromise not confrontation. Often it may need to be content not to *settle* a dispute. But at least it should provide the forum and impetus for negotiation among the parties *towards* a solution.

During the nearly half-century of its existence the Security Council has worked with varying degrees of success. For the first two decades it was generally hamstrung by the ideological intensity of the cold war rivalry. From the mid-1960s to late 1970s it began to reassert itself. It imposed sanctions on Rhodesia; set up three peace-keeping forces; claimed the right to lay down the general terms of a settlement in the Middle East, something rarely before attempted by an international organisation after an armed conflict. It was also for many years the basic focus for pressures for change in South Africa. Then, for another decade, marked by the 'new cold war', the Council's influence again declined. Finally, since the mid-to-late 1980s it has played a central role in the general revivification of the UN (see Chapter 8).

Whether the recent successful activity of the Security Council can be sustained will depend on two major conditions. One is the harmonious working relationship between the Council and the Secretary-General. The other is the willingness of the members, particularly the permanent members, to use the mechanisms available for peace-keeping rather than ignoring them in pursuit of self-interest.

FURTHER READING

S. Bailey, *Voting in the Security Council* (Bloomington, 1969).
S. Bailey, *The Procedure of the UN Security Council* (Oxford, 2nd edn, 1988).

G. R. Berridge, *Return to the UN: UN Diplomacy in Regional Conflicts* (Basingstoke, 1991).

A. Boyd, *Fifteen Men on a Powder Keg* (London, 1971).

I. Claude, 'The Security Council', in E. Luard (ed.), *The Evolution of International Organisations* (London, 1965).

I. Claude, *Swords into Ploughshares* (New York, 4th ed., 1970).

R. N. Gardner, *UN Procedure and Power Realities* (Washington, 1965).

R. Hiscocks, *The Security Council: A Study in Adolescence* (New York, 1973).

E. de A. Jimenez, *Voting and the Handling of Disputes in the Security Council* (New York, 1960).

T. J. Kahng, *Law, Politics and the Security Council* (The Hague, 1964).

A. Verrier, *International Peacekeeping: United Nations Forces in a Troubled World* (Harmondsworth, 1981).

2 The General Assembly: Discussion of World Issues

If the contemporary international society were compared with a national state, the UN General Assembly could, with a little poetic licence, be held to represent the parliament in which the affairs of the world are debated and discussed by representatives of every region and resolutions passed to decision-making bodies.

The comparison is not completely far-fetched. The Assembly is a meeting-place where the representatives of different regions gather to discuss common problems, like parliaments within states. It is called together at certain intervals, as parliaments were in earlier days. It allows the views which are widely held within the whole political society to be ventilated, as in a parliament. Its power of decision is small, like that of most parliaments until recently, but its voice carries, as theirs did, considerable moral authority.

But the Assembly is not, not yet at least, a world parliament in any real sense. It has no government. The ministries, the UN agencies, do not come directly under the General Assembly: they have their own assemblies and decide their own policies, and the UN General Assembly has only the most fragmentary power or influence over each. Still less are member-states committed to obeying the Assembly's injunctions. So the Assembly can discuss or recommend, but rarely decide.

Again, the General Assembly is not representative of *peoples* in the way that an elected parliament is today supposed to be. It is representative of governments, and these may or may not themselves represent accurately the views of their own populations. Governments are represented on a highly uneven basis, with a nation of 50 000 people having the same representation as one of 500 million. At most, therefore, the Assembly might be compared with a parliament of several centuries ago, composed of representatives of pocket and rotten boroughs, often varying grotesquely in populations, making occasional pleas to the powers that be, but exerting a decision-making authority which is at best extremely marginal.

The ancestry of the General Assembly can be traced back to the periodic conferences and congresses of the Concert of Europe in the nineteenth century. The thirty or forty conferences of this kind between 1815 and 1914 among the 'powers' met on average every two or three years (instead of every year like the Assembly). But they none the less discussed most of the great issues of the day. In many cases they reached effective decisions on them: for example on the division of the Low Countries, the 'autonomy', and subsequent independence, of Serbia, Greece, Romania and Bulgaria; the neutralisation of Belgium and Luxemburg; the disposition of Crete and Cyprus. Those conferences reached effective decisions that were then implemented, in a way the Assembly virtually never does. They were also limited in membership, confined to the great powers which could often do deals with each other. The Assembly is dominated by smaller powers and the deals concern only the terms of resolutions.

What can the Assembly do? In theory, it can discuss any question within the scope of the UN Charter: and this means almost anything under the sun which is of international significance, ranging from the world protein shortage to the definition of aggression. As the world becomes smaller and more closely interrelated, there is of course an increasing number of these questions which need to be discussed and decided internationally, from questions of peace and security to those in the field of trade, development, raw materials, human rights, disaster relief, decolonisation and questions of international law. Most of these subjects the Assembly has regularly under its scrutiny. The only exception is the area of peace and security, where the Security Council has the 'primary' responsibility, but the Assembly nonetheless has a supplementatary role (and increasingly seeks to make recommendations to the Council).

Some of these are somewhat specialised questions and the Assembly has therefore a number of separate committees (originally six but now seven) where different types of issue are discussed. These are 'committees of the whole', that is to say every member-state is represented in each.

The First Committee is concerned with major political questions, especially disarmament. But it was soon found that one committee could not cover these subjects adequately, and an additional one, a sort of one-and-a-half committee, was established. This is called the Special Political Committee, and it deals with major current political problems: for example the Korean question, apartheid, the Palestinian problem, or the work of peace-keeping forces. The Second Committee deals with world economic and financial questions. The Third Committee is concerned with social, humanitarian and cultural matters: above all human rights, reflecting the concern of the founders of the UN with this latter question. The Fourth Committee was originally concerned with Trust Territories but later increasingly moved into the field of the remnants and aftermaths of colonialism, for example, Rhodesia and East Timor. The Fifth Committee is concerned with the Organisation's budget and the secretariat. And the Sixth is concerned with questions of international law (and is attended largely by international lawyers).

As in the League, most of the discussion takes place within these seven committees. All the items proposed for the agenda (that is everything apart from the 'general debate') are discussed and first voted on there. Most of the cut-and-thrust, the passionate eloquence, the loud-mouthed accusations and the angry responses in 'right of reply', which receive such publicity outside, take place in the committees rather than in the Assembly itself. And it is in the committees, too, that the difficult, prolonged, and intensely frustrating work of negotiating the terms of resolutions (see pp. 43–51 below) takes place. Since the composition of the committees is the same as that of the Assembly, the subsequent vote in plenary is something of a formality. It often takes place without discussion, and naturally varies scarcely at all from that in the Committee (the main difference is that some delegations from very small countries cannot keep all the committees manned throughout, but will usually come in to record their votes in the Assembly).

So much for the structure of the Assembly (Table 2.1). Before considering how effective it is as a mechanism for debating world issues, let us examine in rather greater detail the procedure at present employed.

PROCEDURE

Normally the Assembly meets once a year for about three months, from the third week of September to just before Christmas. Occasionally, though now very rarely, it spills over into the post-Christmas period. From time to time extra meetings are called to discuss critical matters. By 1991, eighteen special sessions had been held and nine emergency special sessions. These latter, dealing with matters over which the Security Council was deadlocked, covered the Middle East (1958 and 1967), Hungary (1956), Suez (1956), the Congo

Table 2.1 General Assembly

Procedural Committees	Main Committees	Standing Committees and Boards	Various bodies reporting to General Assembly
General Committee 29 members: President of GA, 21 Vice-Presidents, 7 Main Committee Chairmen Credentials Committee (9 members)	First (Disarmament & security) Special Political Second (Economic & financial) Third (Social, humanitarian & cultural) Fourth (Decolonisation) Fifth (Administrative & budgetary) Sixth (Legal)	Over 30, dealing with political and security matters; development; legal questions; administrative and financial questions	IAEA UNRWA Disarmament Conference (Geneva) ECOSOC

(1960), Afghanistan (1980), Palestine (1980), Namibia (1981) and the occupied Arab territories (1982).

The Assembly meets in a large, almost circular hall. It is a little like an arena, for slow and rather ponderous gladiators. At one end, on the raised platform, sits the President for the session, flanked usually by the Secretary-General on his right, and the Under-Secretary for General Assembly affairs on his left. In front of them, at a somewhat lower level, is the speakers' podium with desk and microphone, to which the rival orators ascend in turn. Opposite, and still lower, is the vast hall where the assembled delegations sit, arranged in alphabetical order (to avoid any possible advantage in the placing system, each year lots are drawn to decide who will sit at the front left-hand corner, after which everybody follows on accordingly). There are six places provided for each delegation, but for most of the time only one or two are there: sometimes no delegates at all. Some will be chatting among themselves, or doing a crossword, or preparing a speech for the next day, as the speaker's voice drones on. Behind the delegations, sloping more steeply, come the seats of the spectators, usually only scantily filled – not surprisingly, since the proceedings of the Assembly are not wildly exciting as a rule.

On one side are glass boxes within which sit the representatives of the press and television, peering down at the gesticulating gladiators in the hall before them. At the back, behind the President, is a vast illuminated score-board, with the names of every country. When the contest is over and the voting takes place, it will flicker into animated activity as each delegate presses his own button, with a sudden clatter and rattle and flickering of lights: green for yes, red for no, orange for abstain. And when it comes to a halt, the spectators scan it with eager eyes to see if their side has 'won'. For the most important votes, voting takes place by 'roll call', that is, one by one, so everybody present will watch attentively to see how each other delegation votes: they even, it is said, sometimes change their minds at the last minute to ensure they are on the winning side.

The Assembly begins each year with the 'general debate', in plenary session. This is addressed mainly by foreign ministers, occasionally even by prime ministers or heads of state. Debate is scarcely the word, for there is no argument involved nor any continuous thread of discussion at all: simply a leisurely succession of dignified statesmen, reading in measured tones carefully prepared statements of their governments' views on the great issues of the day. Only when one is rash enough to utter some sentiment offensive to another, perhaps a claim to a disputed territory, or an accusation of subversive activity, will the assembled delegates begin to sit up in their chairs in a sudden flutter of attention. The representative of the offended country, demanding his 'right of reply', may then stride to the platform to rebut the charge; and probably respond with new accusations and insinuations of his own. There may be a whole series of replies to replies to replies. So that eventually each of the pair – India and Pakistan, say, Morocco and Mauretania, Israel and Egypt – will have made three or four speeches each against the other. But for the most part the stately parade of somnolent platitudes proceeds on its amiable way, with perhaps three or four speeches a morning (and sometimes an afternoon as well as a morning), and occasional breaks when nobody wants to speak, for the first month of the Assembly. This performance is scarcely thrilling to listen to, but it has its uses. Views are exchanged on the issues that preoccupy the world's attention; and even the smallest nation can feel it has the chance to make its voice heard. Eventually the foreign ministers pack their bags and fly home again, leaving the field to permanent representatives of each country and the rest of their delegations. The Assembly hall is left empty for a while, even sometimes used by one of the committees, until the resolutions begin to come back from the committees to be endorsed in plenary.

Let us consider the course of a particular item, from the moment it is proposed by a government. First, the item must be inscribed on the agenda. Any nation may propose a matter for discussion however obscure the subject matter. This proposal will then be considered by the General Committee. That Committee must decide, first, whether to accept the item; and then to which committee to send it.

Most of the items proposed will be accepted in some form, unless they can be shown to be totally out of order. During the 1950s some of the colonial powers used to resist the inscription of items dealing with their colonial territories: they claimed these were within their own domestic jurisdiction and so, under Article 2(7) of the Charter, beyond the competence of the UN. Nearly always they lost in such battles and the items were inscribed. In some cases different items are put together under one heading. Sometimes the title is altered to make it more innocuous. Some items appear each year automatically: the reports of other UN bodies or of committees, and of conferences which have met during the year. In other cases an item may appear regularly, year after year, because the question has not been resolved: this has been true, for example, of some of the items on remaining colonial territories, or on such questions as the policy of apartheid in South Africa or 'the

Korean question'. Occasionally items are resisted because they appear too late; or because the title of an item is disputed (there have been bitter disputes over the title of the issue on the Korean question, East and West each wishing for different aspects of the problem to be debated): or because they are held out of order (such as Cuba's proposed item on 'the colonial system in Puerto Rico').

Thus the General Committee vets the *items*. The *delegations* are vetted by a Credentials Committee. This has nine members, who are elected *ad hoc* each Session: though no delegations are automatically members of the Committees, in practice the USA, Russia and China have recently always been on it. To a large extent its activity is a formality, for, except in the case of South Africa recently,[1] there is little disposition to challenge the credentials of delegates. After civil wars and coups d'état, delegations from successor regimes have usually been accepted without demur or even debate. Even after the Hungarian and Czech invasions, there was no serious attempt to challenge the credentials of the successor regime. And when there is a major dispute about representation (as for years over the Chinese delegation), this is usually fought out in the Assembly itself rather than in the Committee.

A complex difficulty arose over Cambodia. Because of the vicious brutality of the Khmer Rouge regime, the Vietnamese army invaded in 1979 to install a more humane government. However, the Khmer Rouge retained the Cambodian UN seat because of the hostility of the USA and China in particular to Vietnam. In 1982 the Khmer Rouge entered into coalition with two other groups, whereupon the coalition was recognised as the legitimate holder of the UN seat.

Soon after the general debate has begun, usually about the second or third week of the Assembly, the main committees begin to meet. The chairman of each committee, usually very much assisted and advised by the Secretariat, prepares a provisional agenda including all the items allocated to that committee. It must be provisional because the General Committee may continue to allocate items even after the Assembly is well under way. This is put to the committees and usually adopted without much dispute. Often the chairman will also propose a timetable for the discussion of items, which is accepted with acclamation, in the vain hope that delegates will actually abide by it. This 'work programme' is, however, a wholly theoretical document, because no committee has even been known to keep to it. It is an ideal vision, the optimum conceivable programme of work, which the chairman vainly dangles, with increasing desperation, before his committee to goad it into more rapid activity.

The difficulty of keeping to it occurs partly because of the prolixity of speakers, and the determination of all to make themselves heard on almost every subject, even if they have nothing new to say. But it is also because many meetings and days are wasted, especially at the beginning of the session, because nobody is prepared to speak at all at the appointed time. Then suddenly, just when the debate is about to be closed, they all rush forward, so that the list of speakers which was almost empty suddenly has thirty names on it.

The character of the proceedings naturally varies considerably from one committee to another. The First Committee is concerned with wide issues of disarmament, nuclear testing, non-proliferation, bacteriological warfare and other 'security' issues; and it has long debates on each one. Often some delegates arrive from the Disarmament Conference in Geneva to speak for their countries on these subjects. The Special Political Committee has equally long, and even more bitter disputes, on some of the most contentious political issues of the day: most notably the Palestinian problem. The Second Committee, dealing with economic and social affairs, often has to deal with twenty-five or thirty items, so that it has time for only two or three days on each; none is discussed adequately and there is much hectic drafting and redrafting of resolutions. The Third Committee deals with 'social, humanitarian and cultural' affairs (quite an agenda) and is more colourful than most; it has more women delegates than any other main committee (since it deals with women's rights among other things) and delectable scarlet saris and yellow head-dresses put the men's sober suits to shame. It spends a considerable amount of its time on the difficult and tedious task of drafting conventions and covenants; though it is hard to think of a body less well fitted for drafting complicated legal documents than a UN committee (masculine or feminine). From the late 1960s its proceedings have tended to be increasingly dominated by what are really political issues: human rights in the territories occupied by Israel, application of the Geneva Conventions to freedom-fighters in Southern Africa, and other questions raised by delegations with a special interest.

The Fourth Committee was very important in the 1960s at the height of the decolonisation process. Since then the volume and contentiousness of its work has declined considerably.

The Fifth and Sixth Committees meanwhile are occupied with matters of quite a different kind. The Fifth Committee is concerned not only with the budget of the UN and related financial questions, but with the organisation of the Secretariat as a whole. In many cases those who attend are the representatives of finance ministries rather than foreign offices (just as those who attend the Second committee are sometimes economists and development experts rather than diplomats). These representatives are all in theory concerned to secure the maximum economy in the UN's operations, but in practice some are much more so than others. Certain countries, though they may want value for money, want larger budgets, while others want to cut them down. This is therefore one of the many bodies in which the basic political conflict of international government today is fought out: the demand of poorer countries for a higher volume of international redistribution through larger budgets against the attempt of most richer ones to resist this. The Communist countries were particularly fervent budget-cutters. We shall consider the work of the Fifth committee in greater detail when we discuss the financing of the system later. It is enough at present to note that controversies over wastage and shortage of funds still impede the smooth running of the Organisation.

The Sixth Committee is concerned with international law. It is mainly peopled by international lawyers, usually those who work for foreign offices. These are engaged partly in drafting conventions and 'declarations', or debating such documents drafted elsewhere, usually in the International Law Commission (ILC) (see pp.82–8) and partly in discussing general problems of international law, some of which, such as the 'question of aggression', persisted year after year, in this case, being resolved only after twenty-two years of discussion! Though the drafting of conventions within a UN committee in this way is a somewhat less hazardous procedure when undertaken by international lawyers than when attempted in the non-expert Third Committee, the general atmosphere of the Assembly undoubtedly heightens the political overtones of the debate. And it is almost certainly a less satisfactory method of proceeding than the more normal way of leaving all the preliminary work to the ILC, and following this with a full-scale international conference.

This is only a sketch of the type of issues which the Assembly is mainly engaged in debating. Enough has been said to show that the agenda covers a wide, expanding and increasingly specialised range of topics. Recent agendas have covered subjects varying from the situation in the Middle East to the 'question of the elderly and aged', from a comprehensive review of peace-keeping operations to the establishment of an international university, from the brain drain from developing countries to the question of the human environment, from the sea-bed to outer space, from the punishment of war criminals to international trade law, from 'criminality and social change' to the world trade in narcotics.[2] It is undoubtedly of value that there exists in the Assembly a meeting-place where it is possible to discuss international issues of this kind which might not become the subject of a full-scale international conference. On the other hand discussion of such an array of often technical subjects places a considerable strain on the resources of delegations, especially of the smaller ones (the increasing complexity and technical character for the issues discussed, and the difficulty for delegates in keeping abreast of them mirrors an exactly similar problem confronting national parliaments). Inevitably debates can only scratch the surface of each one. It is arguable that there would sometimes be more point in calling separate international conferences, among acknowledged experts, on particular subjects than to undertake this type of fleeting, diffuse and disorganised altercation, in practice almost immediately forgotten once completed. The purpose, in the eyes of the delegates, is probably to focus attention on urgent needs or pressing preoccupations (and sometimes they are indeed followed by a more expert conference, to plan more concrete results). Even for this purpose it may be doubted if most of the discussions appreciably extend public knowledge or interest in the subject, for few are even reported in the press.

Unfortunately, moreover, there is very little likelihood of a general reform of the Assembly's proceedings, of the type that seems to be needed if a more compact and relevant agenda is to be substituted. The agenda emerges, in practice, by default. If a single delegation wants a subject to be discussed, normally it will be, and many hundreds of man-hours will then be expended in the process. Unless some new procedure is implemented, by which a more searching examination of proposed agenda items can be undertaken, either by the General Committee, or by each individual committee after an item is remitted to it, so that only the most important are retained, the present proliferation will continue, and even increase, and the attention that can be devoted to any one item will become more cursory.

Let us now look at the way our resolution passes through a committee. On each item, a committee will usually first hold a general discussion in which every delegation may join: this may last a day or two weeks. When this is almost exhausted, the delegation that proposed the item will put forward a resolution, either alone or, more often, with others: it will find 'co-sponsors' to give a broad representative look to the sponsorship. Rival resolutions may be put forward. In some committees, or on some subjects, the African and/or

Asian, or on economic questions the 'Group of 77' (G77) developing countries (now about 133) will be expected to propose the resolution (since they alone will have more than enough votes to carry it). A particular group[3] sometimes itself sets up a drafting committee to prepare the resolution: the composition and chairmanship of the drafting committee will then be of great importance, because it will determine the character of the original form of each resolution.

The draft will be discussed then in the group as a whole. The moderates are often better represented in the whole group than in the drafting committee, so it is sometimes somewhat toned down. Next, representatives of the African group, if it comes from them, may discuss it with other groups. The Latin American group, the closest ally, will be consulted first, but may request certain modifications (usually to moderate its tone), some of which will be made. There may then be further consultations with the West European group, or some members of it, or the East European group, each of whom may make further suggestions. The purpose of these consultations is not to ensure passage of the resolution: the African group alone could probably do this. But since the effect of the resolution is primarily as a demonstration of opinion, there is a desire to maximise the vote in favour: by consultation and a slight moderation of wording it may be possible to raise the number of favourable votes. If the support, or at least the abstention, of most of the Western group for example, especially the larger powers, can be secured on a vote on Southern Africa, then South Africa, with perhaps one or two others may be left in total isolation. This will then demonstrate far more strongly the force of world opinion on the subject, and may be thought, even by radicals, more valuable than passing a more extreme resolution, for which a smaller majority will be obtained (much of the tactical debate in the UN indeed concerns the relative advantage of a larger vote, or a stronger resolution).

This *formal* consultation between groups on resolutions became far more important than that which is often talked about: the informal consultation between individual delegations in the corridors. Sometimes that too is significant. On some types of issue for example, human rights questions or issues of international law, the preparation of resolutions is not by the geographical groups at all. It may be done by a chance assemblage of delegations (the 'co-sponsors'), put together to give a broadly representative appearance, proposing the resolution. They may lobby hard, in New York and even in the capitals, to win the support of others. On some issues, such as the sea-bed, and some disarmament items, there are new groupings of those sharing similar viewpoints, which do not correspond at all with the regional groups: 'landlocked and geographically disadvantaged' and the potentially nuclear. On economic questions there are divisions not only between rich and poor but between less and least developed. In all these cases, though corridor consultations remain important, the groupings involved are quite different from the normal geographical groups.[4] In consequence of these discussions amendments will be made, either voluntarily accepted by the co-sponsors, or more rarely, formally proposed in the committee and voted through.

The regional groups are much less cohesive than usually believed. There have been many studies of their voting patterns.[5] The most monolithic for much of the history of the General Assembly was the East European; though even before the end of the cold war their discipline sometimes slipped. The Latin Americans (this now includes the Caribbeans) have been the next most uniform, seeking to reach agreed positions on many issues, and quite often bringing significant influence to bear on other groups. The Afro-Asians, though often thought of as powerful blocs, are powerful only in numbers: it is only on a relatively small number of issues, such as colonies and Southern Africa, that they have consistently voted together; and on many issues they are completely divided, even after the process of consultation described. This is true not only on political issues, such as the East–West and Arab–Israel disputes, but even on many questions of development and human rights. The West European and Others (that is West Europe, the USA, Canada, Australia and New Zealand) is the least organised group: indeed, it is hardly a group at all, since some members refuse even the principle of joint consultations. But they do meet together sometimes to compare notes on voting intentions and lobby each other for support; and the EC now seeks more actively to take a common position.

Thus there is some mutual consultation and the common idea that resolutions are blindly forced through by the majority is mistaken. Resolutions are normally amended to please other delegations. Conversely, however, UN conformism accentuates majorities. UN delegations mostly have a marked disinclination to finding themselves in small minorities. This is especially so when the minorities include such international outcasts as South Africa, Iraq and (formerly) Portugal. The result is that some whose real inclination is to vote against a certain resolution instead abstain. Abstainers similarly vote yes, to show they are one of the boys. The effect is that an abstention is utterly ambiguous; and the important comparison is the number of noes against the number of votes in favour[6].

So, eventually, our resolution has been discussed, amended and voted on in the committee, and is finally passed on to the plenary for endorsement. Towards the end of the Assembly, as pressure increases, there emerges a sudden realisation that only half the agenda of each committee is completed, with only three weeks remaining. There is a scurry of extra committee meetings, night sessions, and even more intensive consultation. Usually the last few items have to be rushed through at break-neck speed, and with little discussion: it is only the absence of time which now at last induces delegations to tame their eloquence. Then the final day or two is spent in the Assembly itself, in voting resolution after resolution, with each unfortunate delegation trying to find its way through a maze of amendments, and amendments to amendments, and new clauses and paragraphs, and hoping desperately that they are voting on the right one (sometimes they do not, and have to announce their real intention later: though they cannot amend the votes, this change of mind is recorded). But somehow or other, almost always, the delegations eventually manage to get away in time for Christmas.

With the need to keep fully abreast of each committee's work the life of a mission during the session is a hectic one. Delegates will have to be in the office of their mission in the morning at eight-thirty or earlier, to begin to prepare for the day's proceedings. They will probably have a large pile of communications from home to read, giving detailed instructions on the various resolutions and issues arising.[7] They may have speeches to prepare for the day's meetings. There will be research to do on the background of the different items. They may have to do a great deal of consultation by telephone with other delegations. Many missions have a morning meeting, at which they discuss the items coming up in the various committees and decide on tactics. At about ten-thirty most of them will proceed towards the UN building on the East River. Each committee is supposed in theory to begin its meeting at ten-thirty, but the UN has a time of its own and none ever starts until half an hour later (every chairman of a committee begins the session pleading piteously for punctuality, but none has ever yet succeeded in securing it). Delegates may then stay in the UN building throughout the day. At lunchtime they perhaps visit the bar in the large delegates' lounge for a drink, over which they may sound out other delegates concerning their voting intentions, or learn the latest news of proposed resolutions. They may have lunch in the delegates' dining-room, or at a nearby restaurant, with a delegate of another country, or take part in a formal lunch, of which many are given during the session, usually by one delegation for others within the same committee. In the evening, when the committee finishes work, he will have to go back to the mission to send off a report about the day's proceedings, and perhaps to ask for voting instructions.[8] Then there may be receptions at two or three of the missions, and a dinner-party after that. No wonder the head of one mission said he could just survive the hectic activity of the Assembly, and even the other delegates' speeches: what finally finished him was all the eating and drinking.

EVOLUTION

We do not need to consider here the history of the Assembly's actions on specific issues.[9] What we are concerned with is the part the Assembly has played, within international politics and especially in the UN system. In a simplified form, the history of the UN General Assembly might be described in three fifteen-year periods. In the first (1945–60) it managed to increase its authority and influence, especially in relation to the Security Council. The second (1960–75) was a period of decline. The third (since 1975) has witnessed a revival of the Assembly's importance in economic and environmental issues.

The first moves to increase the role of the Assembly were made at the founding conference in San Francisco. Here the mass of the membership, meeting for the first time to consider the new organisation, found themselves faced with a complete blueprint already worked out privately by the USA, the Soviet Union, Britain and China. This reserved the 'primary' authority on all security matters for the Security Council (in which they themselves possessed permanent membership as well as a veto power). The smaller countries therefore exerted maximum pressure at San Francisco to redress this balance. They succeeded in winning some increased powers for the Assembly. Article 10 of the Charter empowered it to discuss any matter within the scope of the Charter, including security questions, and to make recommendations on them to member-states or the Security Council, unless the Security Council was 'exercising its functions' on that question. Under Article 11 it could specifically draw the attention of the Security Council to situations likely to endanger international peace and security: a power it has rarely used. And under Article 14 it could recommend measures for the peaceful adjustment of any situation likely to impair friendly relations among nations: which again it has rarely done. As a result, though the Security Council was to have the primary responsibility for considering threats to the peace, and all powers of decision in dealing with such threats, the Assembly was now at least able to make *recommendations* on almost anything it liked, so long as that matter was not actually under consideration by the Council (and even that limitation was increasingly ignored).

In the first few years of its life, the Assembly's role was increased further. Because the Security Council was perpetually frustrated by the free use of the veto, mainly by the Soviet Union, ways were sought, especially by the US and other Western powers, to by-pass the Council altogether. Special Assembly sessions were called to consider particular problems: for example, the problem of Palestine in April 1947. Later in the same year, an Interim Committee, sometimes known as the Little Assembly, was established, which was to be available to be called at any time between sessions if the need arose: this might serve as a substitute for the Security Council on occasion. It was, however, in practice rarely used. Finally, and more important still, in 1950, after the outbreak of the Korean War had demonstrated what might then have happened if the Soviet delegation had not then been absent from the Council (in protest at its refusal to seat Communist China), a further and more decisive step was taken. A resolution, known as the Uniting for Peace Resolution, was passed enabling a special Assembly to be called at any time when the Security Council found itself frustrated by a veto from taking effective action, on the affirmative vote of seven members of the Council (later increased to nine) or a simple majority of the Assembly; and this was moreover to be able to recommend if necessary the use of force (this was the real extension of the Assembly's powers). The resolution also created a Peace Observation Commission, and a Collective Measures Committee, under the Assembly, to help that body protect international peace and security, though after the first two or three years neither was used.

In the late 1950s, this Uniting for Peace procedure was used two or three times. It led to the zenith of the Assembly's powers. A special Assembly was called by this means at the time of the Suez and Hungarian crises in 1956. Over Suez it led to the creation of the United Nations Emergency Force by the Assembly, and that force was thus also controlled by the Assembly (in practice through a committee advising the Secretary-General). Over Hungary, the special Assembly was able to achieve little, though it perhaps served to focus public attention on the crisis and to express the verdict of the majority of world opinion on Soviet action. The Uniting for Peace procedure was used again over the crisis concerning Jordan and the Lebanon in 1958, when a force of observers (the UN Observation Group in the Lebanon) was sent to cool down the situation and to deter foreign infiltration. Finally, over the crisis in the Congo in the early sixties, though the UN force was authorised and controlled by the Security Council, the Assembly also kept the situation under close consideration, and played a dominant role in the next two or three years in influencing UN action in the area.

During the 1950s, therefore, the Assembly had come to play a major part in determining the UN's response to a number of world crisis situations. From 1960 onwards, however, the role of the Assembly on war and peace questions began to decline. There were a number of reasons for this. First, the outright opposition of the Soviet Union and France to the use previously made of the Assembly, their refusal to contribute to the costs of peace-keeping operations the Assembly had authorised, and the prolonged financial crisis which resulted from this constitutional difference of view, all served to induce some caution among other major powers in mobilising the Assembly. Second, the increasing size of the Assembly, as well as the change in its composition (in which Afro-Asian members came to hold more than two-thirds of the votes) meant that it came to be thought a less suitable instrument for use in such situations, by the US as much as by the Soviet Union. Third, the far less frequent use of the Soviet veto in the Council reduced the need for an alternative agency. Finally, the desire of the other permanent members to retain the special influence which they held in the Security Council also encouraged the restoration of the Council's supremacy in security questions. There were still occasional Special Assemblies: on Rhodesia (1965), South-West Africa (1967), on the June War (1967) and on North–South issues in 1974–5. But later peace-keeping operations, in the Congo and Cyprus, were discussed and authorised by the Security Council and not the Assembly. The prolonged discussions on the settlement of the Middle East crisis from the autumn of 1967 onwards were undertaken in the Security Council. So was the main debate on Southern Africa in the late seventies. In times of crisis, it became once more the Council rather than the Assembly to which injured parties looked for redress.

On other questions, however, the Assembly extended its role. This resulted partly from the change in its membership, both in numbers and in composition. From a membership of 51 in 1945, it grew to 127 in 1970. This transformed the regional balance. On the UN's foundation, the largest single group was the Latin American, with 20 members. There were only fifteen West European and others (including the USA, Canada, Czechoslovakia, Greece and Turkey); five East European; nine Asians; and two Africans. By 1970 the order had been almost reversed. There were over forty African, over thirty Asian (again including the Arab countries), while the West Europeans and others had only increased to about twenty, the East Europeans to ten (including Albania and Mongolia), and the Latin Americans had been only marginally increased through the addition of four Caribbean countries. Developing countries now represented well over two-thirds of the total membership and that proportion continued to grow. In mid-1992 total membership stood at 175. Only nine sovereign states had not joined. These were six micro-states and three others (Taiwan, Switzerland and the Holy See) for which there were special reasons for non-membership.

This inflow of new members inevitably meant an increasing focusing of attention on the problems of concern to them. The primarily European problems, the division of Germany, Berlin, human rights in East Europe, air incidents and similar issues, which had dominated the early years, were now rarely discussed. For a period in the 1950s and early 1960s, colonial issues dominated, beginning with discussions of Morocco, Tunisia, and Algeria in the early 1950s, and culminating in debates, often of great intensity, mainly on African questions in the mid-1960s. From the mid-1960s to the mid-1970s the questions of Southern Africa had more time devoted to them than any other single problem. This was partly the result of African voting-power; but it was mainly that these issues – apartheid, Namibia and Rhodesia – were at that time perhaps the most important issues the world confronted.

The most visible effect of the influx of new countries has been the growing emphasis on development problems in the work of the Assembly. Today no single issue receives so much attention. There is an almost uninterrupted series of meetings of innumerable committees on innumerable subjects associated with ECOSOC – the regional commissions, the UNDP or other development agencies – either in New York or Geneva or elsewhere over the year. This has brought about a significant change in the organisation of missions in New York. Because a number of the bodies concerned with development meet in New York at intervals throughout the year, even countries which are not represented on the Security Council and which at one time kept no permanent missions in New York, now nearly always keep a mission of some kind there throughout the year or at least cover the UN from Washington. And some of their members have to be competent to discuss economic and other technical matters.

The shift in the balance of membership has brought many other changes. The discussion of human rights questions has been affected. In the early years this involved a great deal of drafting of Declarations, Conventions and other documents, affirming great ideals and impeccably good intentions in many areas of human rights, above all on the classical human rights questions covered in early Bills of Rights and reproduced in the Universal Declaration of Human Rights (civil and political rights, rather then economic and social).[10] The hideous experience of the Second World War encouraged the drafting of a Convention on Genocide, on refugees and stateless persons, on prisoners of war, on forced labour and similar questions. But gradually the emphasis shifted. There was increasing emphasis on political rights and on racial discrimination. Many years were spent by the Third Committee in drafting two Covenants, on Civil and Political Rights and on Economic, Cultural and Social Rights. A system of periodic reporting on performance in the field of human rights by all members which ratify has been established, and a committee has been appointed to evaluate and comment on each report. With the change in membership of the Organisation, however, discussions in this field, even on apparently remote subjects, tend to be heavily influenced by political attitudes and so diverted to discussion, for example, of apartheid or the Arab–Israel conflict.[11] Most controversially, the Assembly approved a resolution in 1975 defining Zionism as a form of racism. Nevertheless, further work has been undertaken in the field of human rights in recent years, for example, the Convention against Torture entered into force in 1987 and the Convention on the Rights of the Child in 1989.

In the First Committee the character of disarmament discussions has also changed over the years. During the early years concern was concentrated on the development of nuclear weapons and the possible ways of abolishing these altogether. Two Commissions were established, on atomic energy and on conventional armaments, to consider developments in both these fields. When these were dissolved, a whole series of other bodies was appointed in their place: a Disarmament Commission of fourteen members, a Sub-Committee of five from this, consisting of the USA, Canada, Soviet Union, Britain and France (1952–7), a new enlarged Commission, later enlarged again to embody the whole membership (1957–8) and finally from 1962 a group has met in Geneva. Since 1984 it has been called the Conference on Disarmament and consists of forty members. For a long time discussion was concentrated on very ambitious measures, designed to bring about 'general and complete disarmament'; or the total abolition of nuclear weapons; or to institute 'measures to prevent surprise attack' by the observation of frontiers. During the 1960s more modest efforts at arms control were discussed and submitted to the conference. On a number agreement was reached: the Nuclear Test Ban Treaty, the Outer Space Treaty, the Non-Proliferation Treaty, the Sea-bed Treaty and the Treaty on Biological Weapons have resulted. Here the role of the Assembly is in issuing guidelines to the Geneva Conference. There are too many delegations for serious debate and negotiation on the terms of a treaty. As on other questions the Assembly represents a form of pressure by the small on the great, sometimes for more attention to a particular subject, sometimes for a particular concession on a particular treaty: several modifications were made to the sea-bed treaty (banning weapons of mass destruction placed on the sea-bed), for example, to meet objections widely raised in the Assembly.

The most significant change in the work of the Assembly in recent years has been the introduction of a new kind of item, scarcely considered in early Assemblies: technological in character but political in implication. Prominent examples of this are the discussions of outer space, of the exploitation of the sea-bed, and of the environment. Others of this kind are satellite broadcasts, natural resource surveys, population, the application of science to development, sovereignty over natural resources, trafficking in narcotics and so on. The problems of the global environment have become worrying matters for the Assembly. It took the initiative in convening the Conference on the Human Environment in 1972; establishing the United Nations Environment Programme (UNEP) later that year; passing the resolution in 1983 which led to the creation of the World Commission on Environment and Development; and convening the UN Conference on Environment and Development in 1992. UNCED was, in fact, the first time that the General Assembly had organised a world summit conference.

With the increasing technical interdependence of the world there will undoubtedly be increasing discussion of issues of this kind in the UN, where alone all members are permanently represented.

THE FUTURE

The Assembly symbolises all the strengths and weaknesses of the UN system. On the one hand, the glass-fronted UN building often seems nothing but a factory of words, spoken or written, declamatory, self-righteous, angry, accusing and vainglorious: in an almost literal sense a tower of Babel, in which every delegation babbles interminably in its own way on its own preoccupations, even in its own language (in the Assembly any language is permitted if translation is provided), scarcely listened to or understood by any other delegation. It was on these grounds that one cynical ambassador, anxious to save time, called for the replacement of the system of simultaneous translation by one of 'simultaneous oration': under this, all the speeches would be delivered simultaneously into the different microphones – since no delegate ever listened to any speech other than his own, nothing would be fundamentally altered and a great deal of time and money would be saved. The production of written words even rivals that of spoken words. For example, the documentation in preparation for the 1992 Conference on the Environment and Development covered 24 million sheets of paper!

It is this aspect of its activities, the torrent of unproductive and unheeded words for which the UN is perhaps best known to the public, and which perhaps has most discredited it in the eyes of the world. This criticism, though sometimes exaggerated, has undoubted substance. Yet it reveals also one of the Organisation's potential sources of strength. The very multiplicity of languages and words symbolises at least the coming together of many peoples: the extent to which the variety of humankind is represented in New York. It may be better that 150 languages are being spoken, however stridently, all in the same building, than that they should be mouthed and muttered in isolation from each other, in 150 separate corners of the earth. The hubbub of voices may not be much listened to, but that they speak to each other at all shows that they are aware of others and concerned about their response. The barrage of words, the verbal duals and battles of paper may be wearisome and fruitless; but they are less dangerous and costly than a barrage of bullets, duels of tanks, or aircraft battles; and occasionally may help to make the latter less likely.

The fundamental function the Assembly performs is indeed to make all more conscious of the attitudes and interests of others and so more inclined to take account of them. The Assembly is above all what its name implies: a meeting-place, where the nations can assemble and talk and discuss their problems with each other, instead of each pursuing their own private destinies in total isolation as once they did. Its effectiveness is maximised if it can be made a forum for dialogue rather than dialectic; for serious negotiation rather than angry posturings. But to perform this function effectively, there is need for considerable reform in procedures and structure.

The general debate is most often criticised, but is not in fact without its uses. It does allow every foreign minister, even from the most Lilliputian state, to enjoy his little hour before the floodlights, to declaim to the world the views and aspirations of its people, however parochial. It can on immediate issues give expression to widely felt opinions and attitudes which are not always without influence: as when, after the invasion of Czechoslovakia in 1968, a very large proportion of the speeches expressed the almost universal condemnation of that action, a healthy reminder to the Soviet Union of its heavy political costs. But the debate could be given far greater focus and effect than at present. One way of achieving this would be if every year some particular subject were set down, perhaps by the President, as the topic for the year. This might be either an international issue of the day, say the Middle East or the environment, or, more usefully, some UN activity or topic, peace-keeping, UN human rights activities or the work of the Assembly itself. Alternatively, discussion could be focused on the Secretary-General's report, or a particular part of it. Though speeches could scarcely be confined exclusively to those topics, each foreign minister might be expected to devote part of his speech to it. In this way the general debate would become a debate in the real sense of the word, with some theme and relevance, rather than a disjointed succession of pious platitudes and devout declarations.[12]

Changes in the Assembly's committees could also help. At present some agendas are so crowded that each item is rushed through with little debate or thought, while others have not enough to do. The Fourth Committee has now virtually to run out of colonial territories to discuss;[13] others, especially the First, the Second, and the Third, are overloaded with items. There is need for a new structure. A totally new committee may be required to take over discussion of the increasing number of scientific and technological items now emerging: outer space, telecommunications, the sea-bed, the environment and so on (and there will be more and more of such items in the future). A committee devoted to these topics might be manned by delegates who were technically qualified for the type of issue to be discussed.[14] Some changes in the Councils might also be necessary. ECOSOC, for instance, needs some drastic remodelling of its procedure if it is to become a more effective co-ordinating body; and this should become a standing body, meeting throughout the year.

But if the Assembly is to be made a more effective, and more widely respected body, structural changes of the sort suggested alone are not enough. Difficult though it is to achieve, some effort will need to be made to cut down on the proliferation of committees, meetings, paper and staff which so damages the reputation, and depletes the resources, of the UN at present. This has been proposed many times before. Innumerable good resolutions have been passed on the subject. The Assembly has itself been conscious of the problem and made various efforts at reform. In 1963 a Committee was set up to consider the matter, and made some minor proposals for limiting the length and number of interventions in debate, and on other questions, but mainly contented itself with looking for greater restraint by member-states themselves. In practice no significant change resulted. In 1970, the Assembly set up a thirty-one-member Special Committee 'to study ways and means for improving the procedures and organisation of the Assembly', including the allocation of agenda items, the organisation of work, documentation, rules of procedures and related questions. The next Assembly, however, on the basis of its report, proposed only marginal changes. Finally, in 1971, the Joint Inspection Unit proposed more radical changes,[15] but few were implemented.

Among the main requirements seem to be: limitation of the length of speeches, either generally or for particular debates; much firmer control of the agenda by the General Committee and the bureau of each committee; the selection by these means of only a few items for each committee each year; early establishment of drafting groups to negotiate resolutions; a strict timetable for each item; earlier deadlines for submission of resolutions and for closing the speakers' list; and the starting of meetings on time by abandoning the quorum rule.

With the ending of the cold war and the exacerbation of North–South tensions the five geographically defined electoral groups (see p.49) have become less relevant. Any revision of the system inevitably raises the whole question of voting and representational procedures. These problems have been magnified by the number of very small states which, having acquired independence, now attain UN membership. This not only devalues UN votes, by making them less representative of population but lessens respect for the UN as a whole. A considerable number of very small states can control the

Organisation; and this in turn makes it easier for those countries so inclined to ignore UN resolutions. The first step is to limit membership to states above a certain size. Some believe that a minimum population of about one hundred thousand should be laid down (though there are already several states with populations below that). Others think economic resources should be taken into account as well. The Security Council set up a committee to consider the question in 1967 but no firm conclusions were drawn. The best thing would be if some type of associate membership were devised for very small states. This could give them some of the privileges of membership and attendance, but would not accord full voting rights. If UN votes are going to retain any authority at all, the sooner this happens the better.

A more radical step would be to introduce weighted voting in the Assembly. This has been often discussed.[16] It can well be argued that, so long as the Maldive Islands, Malta and Madagascar have more voting-power together than the USA and China between them, so long as Africa has over forty times the voting strength of the USA, with only about twice the population, there will be little respect for the resolutions passed, since they will not enjoy the representative character which is their chief claim to authority.

There is undoubted substance to these criticisms. Designed to be representative, the Assembly becomes less and less so as time goes on. Unfortunately it is improbable that the small powers will obligingly vote away their own voting power: some have declared flatly that they will not. A small step forward would not necessarily be too difficult. States having over a hundred million population could be given three seats, or at least three votes; those between twenty million and a hundred million two; and the rest one. This would still be a long way from an equitable system, giving weight to population, but it is probably as much as would be acceptable to many states at present, and would at least be a beginning.

In the long-term future, consideration might be given to the creation of an assembly of parliamentarians as an addition to the existing assembly of *government* representatives only (just as in the EEC before 1979 there was a parliamentary assembly as well as representation in the Council of Ministers). As in the Community, this would no doubt at first be formed of existing members of parliament, not directly elected, and would have no powers of its own. Even so, it might be useful in representing the feelings of populations as a whole, in addition to those of governments. Already today many countries send parliamentary delegations to the Assembly, and it would need little change in organisation for it to be arranged that all these were present at the same time, perhaps in the first two or three weeks of each Assembly, and met together. Alternatively, the Inter-Parliamentary Union, which holds annual conferences of members of parliament from every country of the world, might hold their conferences at least every two or three years in New York, and arrange to discuss some of the same issues being considered in the General Assembly itself. This would provide a useful counterweight to the purely official views that are expressed in the Assembly. (For further discussion of the 'democratisation' of the UN, see p.185.)

Though at the centre of the UN system, the Assembly is not a decision-making body. It can make noises, fulminate or exhort; it cannot compel. Even so it could, if it conducted its proceedings appropriately, wield a considerable influence on world affairs. But the influence of the Assembly depends on its moral authority. If it is to retain this, it will need to make itself more representative and well organised than it is today.

FURTHER READING

H. R. Alker and B. M. Russett, *World Politics in the General Assembly* (New Haven, 1966).
S. Bailey, *The General Assembly of the UN* (New York, 1964).
I. Claude, *Swords into Ploughshares* (New York, 4th edn, 1970).
H. F. Haviland, *The Political Role of the General Assembly* (New York, 1951).
T. Hovet, *Bloc Politics in the UN* (London, 1960).
P. C. Jessup, *Parliamentary Diplomacy* (Leiden, 1956).
J. Kaufmann, *United Nations Decision Making* (Rockville, MD, 1980).
R. O. Keohane, *Political Influence in the General Assembly* (New York, 1966).
H.G. Nicholas, *The UN as a Political Institution* (Oxford, 5th edn, 1975).
J. P. Renninger (ed.), *The Future Role of the United Nations in an Interdependent World* (Dordrecht, 1989).
D. Steele, *The Reform of the United Nations* (Beckenham, 1987).
M. W. Zacher, *Dag Hammarskjöld's United Nations* (New York, 1970).

3 The Economic and Social Institutions: Securing a Fairer World

ECONOMIC ACTIVITIES

When the League of Nations seemed on the point of expiry in 1938 the Australian delegate, Stanley Bruce, had the bright idea that the best way of bringing it alive again might be to give it something else to do besides arguing ineffectually about the great-power conflicts of the day: in particular to provide it with new functions in the economic and social field. A commission was set up to consider how this might be done. In the late summer of 1939, only a few days before war broke out, this Bruce Commission delivered its report. It recommended the expansion of the existing economic and social activities of the organisation, and the establishment of a high-powered council within the League to organise this work. The coming of the war prevented the recommendations from being implemented. But when, at the conclusion of that conflict, a new organisation was established to keep the world's peace, the main features of the report were put into effect.

It was decided that a high-level council, the Economic and Social Council, should be established as one of the 'principal organs' of the new organisation. This was to supervise the economic and social activities of the UN system. It was to oversee the activities of the specialised agencies, some already in existence and others shortly to be created. It was to have more directly under its aegis a number of specialised commissions and bodies in the UN itself. And above all it was supposed generally to co-ordinate the activity of the entire UN family, including the specialised agencies (which were not part of the UN proper, but were members of 'the UN system').

Many people hoped that these non-political activities would be one of the most important features of the new organisation. Some subscribed to the notion of 'functionalism': the idea, that is, that cooperation among nations in various functional fields would encourage and promote cooperation in the more difficult political area. Eventually the process might lead to a more peaceful world generally. Responsibility for organising cooperation of this kind should be shared between the specialised agencies, each confronting particular areas – labour affairs, civil aviation, health, education, meteorology and so on – and subordinate bodies of the UN itself.[1]

It was provided in the Charter that the new Economic and Social Council should have eighteen members (subsequently increased to twenty-seven, and eventually to 54). It was to meet between sessions of the General Assembly to discuss world economic and social problems and to try to coordinate the fast-growing family of children which the organisation was spawning. Besides the specialised agencies, which were not directly subject either to ECOSOC or the General Assembly, but technically autonomous, there were an increasing number of committees and commissions within the UN itself. Directly under ECOSOC, for example, there were a number of specialised commissions, each meeting every year or sometimes every two years. There are now six. They deal with statistics, population, social development, human rights, status of women and narcotic drugs.

Each of these has considered the problems in their own field, passed recommendations, and sometimes put in hand studies of their own, or enquiries among members. Some have undoubtedly done very good work. The Statistical Commission, for example, has managed to standardise the preparation and presentation of statistics of many kinds as well as publishing important statistical documents of its own and supervising the statistical department of the UN. The Commission on Population has, similarly, done much to stimulate accurate and scientific demographic studies among governments and has also published important studies of its own, including a Demographic Yearbook. The Commission on Narcotic Drugs has become increasingly important in recent years. The most important of all, at least potentially, is the Human Rights Commission, which we shall consider shortly.

There were also established, but in this case only slowly over the years, a number of regional economic commissions. The first to come into existence was the Economic Commission for Europe (ECE), based in Geneva, which has studied problems affecting the whole of the European economy, East as well as West, and published many technical studies in specialised fields. Not long after, the Economic Commission for Latin America (ECLA) emerged, based in Santiago in Chile and performing similar functions for that area. A little later there appeared the Economic Commission for Asia and the Far East, subsequently renamed the Economic and Social Commission for Asia and the Pacific (ESCAP), based in Bangkok; the Economic Commission for Africa (ECA), based in Addis Ababa; and finally, the Economic and Social Commission for Western Asia (ESCWA), with its headquarters in Baghdad. All of these bodies undertake continuing studies of the economic problems in their own areas, organise conferences among governments of the region in specialised fields and commission a large number of reports by experts.

Most of this kind of work represents *study* of the problems, rather than an attempt to do much about them. But within the new organisation pressures began to build up for more active programmes in the economic field. Developing countries among the membership, especially new members such as India and Indonesia, began to demand programmes of assistance for poor countries. In 1948 the first very small step was taken in this direction: the establishment of a tiny programme of technical assistance, of only a few hundred dollars, financed out of the regular budget. The rich countries, however, were totally opposed to financing aid out of their compulsorily raised contributions to the Organisation. A year or two later, therefore, in the Extended Programme of Technical Assistance (EPTA), the principle was adopted of asking for *voluntary* contributions by government in this field. This battle between the advocates of voluntary and compulsory donations has been fought ever since. Throughout the 1950s, the developing countries demanded the establishment of a Special United Nation Fund for Economic Development (SUNFED). This was originally suggested in a report produced by 'experts', who proposed a fund that might finally rise to three billion dollars in size. The rich countries fought to the last ditch against any fund based on the principle of compulsory contributions. In 1958 they secured instead the establishment of a 'Special Fund', financed by voluntary contributions, which financed pre-investment programmes to survey and prepare for large-scale capital projects; a far more modest, and so, to the rich countries, more acceptable undertaking. The Special Fund was eventually merged with the UN Technical Assistance Programme in 1965 to establish the UN Development Programme (UNDP).

The UNDP has remained as a voluntary programme for development work, mainly of a technical assistance nature, often implemented by experts working for the specialised agencies. The funds are contributed to it in an annual pledging conference, during which governments announce what they can provide for the following year. Offers mounted fairly steadily to nearly 500 million dollars a year in the mid-1970s; 3.5 billion dollars were allocated during the quinquennium 1987–91. During the 1960s there also emerged another programme, only slightly smaller in size, the World Food Programme, designed to make use of agricultural surpluses or gifts in kind (such as shipping space) to send food to developing countries, particularly to help feed the labour forces for large-scale construction projects and for disaster relief.

In 1964 the UN was launched on another venture in the economic field. Pressures had built up among developing countries for an organ that would be concerned specifically with the development and trade problems of poor countries. Rather unwillingly, the rich countries committed themselves to a conference on the subject, which took place in Delhi in 1964. This in turn led to a regular series of conferences in this field, and to a board and permanent secretariat being established, which operate in Geneva between conferences. Thus though the organisation, the United Nations Conference on Trade and Development (UNCTAD), is still termed a Conference, in practice it is a permanent organisation. The conferences themselves take place every three or four years. They sometimes launch important new initiatives for changes in the world economic structure: as for supplementary financing, a generalised system of preferences, a 'common fund' to finance commodity schemes. But much of the important work is done in the constant negotiation and discussions which take place in committees of the Conference in Geneva. A whole series of these discusses such questions as shipping, commodities, insurance, preferences and similar matters. Probably UNCTAD's single most important achievement is the scheme for a generalised system of preferences for developing countries, under which these receive more favoured treatment than rich countries for trade purposes in most of the markets of the developed states, without having to give reciprocal privileges in return. Also UNCTAD has launched its scheme for an integrated series of commodity agreements designed to stabilise the price of commodities not already covered by such schemes, and for a 'common fund' to help finance these schemes. This fund was eventually set up in 1989.

In parallel with UNCTAD there has emerged the United Nations Industrial Development Organisation (UNIDO). This grew out of the Committee for Industrial Development which was set up by ECOSOC in 1960 to consider what the UN and its members could do to help industrial development in poor countries. This in turn established a Centre for Industrial Development as part of the Secretariat for New York. Eventually this was turned into an autonomous body rather similar to UNCTAD, established in Vienna in 1966. The administrative expenses of this were financed out of the UN's regular budget, while its assistance work was paid by voluntary contributions. In 1986, UNIDO was made into an autonomous specialised agency.

In addition to all these operational activities the UN of course undertook a great deal of discussion of economic and developmental matters in various forms. The Second Committee of the Assembly, as we saw in Chapter 2, regularly discusses such questions. A large number of *ad hoc* conferences are arranged. A huge army of commissions, committees and sub-committees meet in New York, Geneva and occasionally elsewhere to examine a particular topic, or negotiate particular agreements. Some of these have become more or less permanent. There is, for example, a Centre for Development Planning, Projections and Policies, composed of independent experts rather than government representatives, which gives advice on the development strategy of UN bodies and of poor countries generally. Six Standing Committees handle policy in their respective areas. The most important in many ways is the Committee for Programme and Coordination (CPC), which, in addition to the Secretary-General's Administrative Committee on Coordination (ACC), strives to promote the most effective use of the large number of UN bodies and specialised agencies involved in social and economic work.

Thus, even apart from the vast work of the specialised agencies, including the World Bank and the IMF, a large amount of economic discussion and some development assistance takes place within the framework of the UN itself. Some of this work may appear to be little more than talk. But even talk, especially if it arrives at concrete agreements among states or a new principle of economic relationships (such as the generalised system of preferences), has its value. Other programmes, such as those of the UNDP and the World Food Programme, are practical programmes of assistance which have grown steadily and today represent a significant part of the world's total development effort. The UN has built up a team of technical and economic experts of its own for this work. Thus, while it still may not match the aspirations of some, the UN, far more than is believed, does today organise a substantial programme of economic work to match its political activities.

SOCIAL AND ENVIRONMENTAL ACTIVITIES

Besides supervising these various activities in the economic field ECOSOC also took over responsibility for social questions. Some activity in this field had been begun by the League. In the field of drug abuse, for example, there had then existed two bodies, the Permanent Central Opium Board and the Drugs Supervisory Body (though their powers of control were in fact very weak). One of the Commissions set up under ECOSOC when the UN was founded was the Commission on Narcotic Drugs which took over the functions of both the earlier bodies. This kept the world situation in this field under review and re-examined the existing system of control. It eventually drafted and brought into force the 1961 Single Convention on Narcotic Drugs, which unified the previous separate instruments in this field and established a single system of control. An attempt was made to ensure that the production of addictive drugs did not exceed what was required for medical purposes all over the world. A new system to regulate poppy cultivation was introduced (since most hard drugs are produced from opium, derived from the poppy). This ran into difficulties because of the problems of enforcement, and because some populations had become dependent on the crop for their livelihood and could not easily readapt to other types of agriculture. A new Convention to cover so-called 'psychotropic' substances such as LSD, barbiturates, pep pills and others, was signed in 1971 to control the trade in these products too. A few years later the UN established its Programme for Control of Drug Abuse, which was financed by voluntary contributions. This grew to substantial proportions because of a large financial contribution made by the US, then becoming increasingly concerned about the problem of drug abuse among its own population. This undertook a far more active programme for controlling the production and trade in drugs. Finally, in 1987 the first International Conference on Drug Abuse and Illicit Trafficking was held in Vienna. This produced a comprehensive list of recommended actions to combat this scourge.

The UN, like the League, also established programmes to help the hundreds of thousands of refugees left stranded by the Second World War and subsequent events. At the end of the war there was founded an International Refugee Organisation (IRO) to seek to assist these people and to help to settle them elsewhere (usually for political or other reasons they could not return to their own country). This

1951

managed to settle about a million refugees by negotiating with governments to receive them, and by providing temporary accommodation and transport. In 1961 the Organisation was replaced by a High Commissioner for Refugees (UNHCR) based in Geneva, with a far smaller staff and more limited budget. The administrative budget of the High Commissioner was provided by the UN itself but relief funds came from voluntary contributions by governments: these steadily grew though they have never been fully adequate to the need. The High Commissioner has carried on with the work of negotiating with governments for resettlement, helping to make temporary arrangements in crisis situations (as with the six or seven million refugees from East Pakistan who went to India in 1971), and issuing travel documents to stateless persons where necessary. It has done invaluable work in looking after, and in many cases resettling, millions of refugees, not only from the Second World War in Europe but from disasters elsewhere, such as those in Vietnam, Sudan, Congo, Angola, Ethiopia and Afghanistan and many other areas. In addition to this the UN has established a separate agency to help Arab refugees from Israel and their descendants, the United Nations Relief and Works Agency (UNRWA), which looks after over a million refugees in Jordan, Syria and other countries. The scale of the problem has become horrendous. It was estimated in 1991 that there were 18 million refugees, and nearly a further 20 million displaced persons living in their own countries but unable to live in their own homes.

This work for refugees is one of the most essential and worthwhile of all UN activities, though it is not one which receives much publicity or recognition. Another 'charity' that is run by the UN is the organisation of programmes to help children in need, undertaken by the UN Children's Fund, usually known as UNICEF. This was originally designed to help children who had been made destitute by the Second World War, taking over this work from the UN Relief and Rehabilitation Administration (UNRRA), just as the IRO had in the case of refugees. The Children's Fund supplies assistance in kind in the form of clothing and food; runs clinics for mothers and children; supplies special children's and babies' foods; builds day centres and playgrounds; and even provides education, in association with UNESCO. Nowadays it gives particular help to children of developing countries, especially those living in deprived areas such as slums and shanty towns.

Yet another world charity run by the UN is the Disaster Relief Organisation (UNDRO) based in Geneva. This seeks to co-ordinate relief work whenever there is a disaster, such as an earthquake, a flood or a cyclone. It does this in co-operation with UN bodies such as the UNHCR, UNICEF and the World Food Programme, all of which are equipped to help with particular aspects of the work, as well as with charities such as the Red Cross, Oxfam and so on. It seeks to help governments prepare themselves in advance for disaster situations by making contingency plans and stock-piling supplies; it helps to organise communications required in such situations; and has limited funds of its own which it can call on in providing supplies in an emergency. Since the 1970s increasing attention has been given to continuous disasters such as the drought and advancing desert conditions in various parts of Africa.

Another activity which has grown steadily during the UN's life is its programme for population control. This is a subject which the UN in its early years had to approach with kid gloves because of the strong religious objections which certain governments, especially in Latin America, felt to birth control measures. At first, therefore, activity was confined to the publication of demographic studies, and general research on the effect of population growth on development. But, increasingly, such studies brought out the effect of a rapid rate of population growth in impeding economic progress. In 1964 the Secretary-General appointed an *ad hoc* committee of experts to examine the subject further. This reported that the UN should institute programmes for training experts in population studies and population control where these were desired by governments. The most important step was the establishment in 1967 of the UN Fund for Population Activities (UNFPA, now called the UN Population Fund). Like other controversial programmes this was financed by voluntary contributions. None the less the funds provided rapidly increased and within little more than five years had reached more than fifty million dollars a year. By 1990 it was thirty times that amount. The resistance of governments to such programmes has gradually declined, though the Papacy is still opposed. UNFPA has thus done a good deal all over the world to spread knowledge of contraceptive techniques and to help organise family planning facilities.

Another area in which the UN has become increasingly involved is the protection of the world environment. Some work in this area had been done for some time by a number of specialised agencies: for example, WHO, which for long has had an interest in atmospheric pollution, and IMCO, concerned with marine pollution. In 1968, at the instigation of Sweden, it was decided to hold a major UN conference on the environment. This took place in Stockholm in 1972. It covered a huge range of subjects, ranging from the protection of certain wild life species, the preservation of archaeological treasures, to the conservation of the earth's resources, the protection of arid areas such as the Sahara, the problems of human settlements, and especially the establishment of some effective monitoring system to record the changes in the world's environment. Eventually it was decided to establish a large-scale UN environmental programme, UNEP, with its headquarters in Nairobi, once again to be voluntarily financed, but assured of 100 million dollars over the first five years. By 1990 its annual budget was about 40 million dollars.

Pollution and degradation of the environment have become increasingly worrying problems. The General Assembly and the Secretariat as well as UNEP have given closer attention to the mounting crisis in recent years. UNEP has been responsible for setting up the Global Environmental Monitoring System (GEMS) and the International Register of Potentially Toxic Chemicals (IRPTC) to provide essential data. Its Convention on International Trade in Endangered Species (CITES) has had some success. The Montreal Protocol of 1987 to protect the ozone layer was the product of a UNEP initiative. By that time, however, attention was being drawn to the interrelationships between environmental strains, on the one hand and the economic issues of heavy industrialisation in the northern hemisphere and poverty in the southern, on the other. The biggest international conference ever was called in Rio de Janeiro in 1992 to face up to these complex dangers. This was the UN Conference on Environment and Development (UNCED). Its principal tasks were to retard the depletion of the world's species and the pace of global warming and to agree a comprehensive list of urgent measures for the foreseeable future. The practical outcome, however, was not very impressive.

This represents only a small sample of the activities of the UN in the social field. The UN has had a long-standing interest in housing matters, which have been discussed endlessly in a Committee on Housing, Building and Planning, and there is a permanent Centre with the same interest within the Secretariat. These build few houses but organise many discussions. This programme of talking reached a climax in the enormous and expensive habitat conference in Vancouver in 1975, where 100 million dollars were said to have been spent, which many felt could have been better expended on actual housing.

The UN also takes an interest in the problems of women. The Commission on the Status of Women has prepared Conventions relating to women's rights; for example, one on the political rights of women and on marriage, minimum age for marriage, and registration of marriages. It has generally sought to secure more equal employment opportunities for women and to remedy some of the legal disabilities which women suffer in many countries.

All of these subjects and many others are discussed annually in the Third Committee of the General Assembly. The agenda is inevitably something of a hotchpotch of diverse matters, none of which can ever be treated in more than a rather superficial way. Discussion is dispersed in many organisations and committees and activity is often too small-scale. But it does none the less provide an international dimension to a type of discussion which is normally conducted only within a narrow national framework. At least social problems are now looked at sometimes in an international as well as a national perspective; and so seem sometimes to demand international as well as national remedies.

HUMAN RIGHTS

There was one particular area in which, at the time when it was founded, the UN had great ambitions. It was everywhere hoped that the Organisation might be the means of preventing a recurrence of the enormities which had occurred in some countries, especially in Germany, in the preceding decade, by establishing an effective system for the protection of human rights.

Unfortunately the states which founded the UN did not recognise that this could only be done if a system was established for effective examination of the human rights situation within individual states, rather than talking in general terms and issuing pious declarations. This required a sacrifice of sovereignty which few of them were willing to contemplate. They created therefore a system in which the UN was responsible mainly for enunciating general principles in this field, rather than securing any assurance that those principles would be actually fulfilled. This was to prove, at least for the first twenty-five years, a fatal weakness of the system.

The principal body made responsible was the Human Rights Commission, established as one of the commissions with special responsibilities set up under ECOSOC. Under it was placed a sub-commission, the Sub-Commission on the Prevention of Discrimination and the Protection of Minorities, supposed to be composed of 'experts'. Both met for only a few weeks in the year, and considered the main proposals made to them in their own area. It was taken for granted for a long time that it was not the purpose of either body to look at the situation in individual countries, nor to investigate the complaints of individuals. They thus devoted themselves almost exclusively to drafting high-sounding documents, laying down general principles in various fields.

The first, and still perhaps the most important, of these was the Universal Declaration of Human Rights of 1948. This was an admirably well-balanced, though occasionally vague and general, statement of the individual rights which it was felt signatory states should see protected within their own countries. The very fact that it was signed, however, by many states which were renowned for their disregard of human rights, and manifestly failed to fulfil its provisions, was an indication that the mere drafting and signing of such documents did not in itself serve to protect human rights in any way. But the document did none the less represent a norm, a generally recognised standard of governmental behaviour, that could be quoted on occasions to secure an improvement in state practice.

The attempt was then made to draw up particular instruments in more specialised fields. A Convention on Genocide was drafted (this time by the Assembly rather than the Commission) which proscribed the crime of genocide: this was defined as actions intended to destroy, 'in whole or in part', a national, ethnic, racial or religious group as such. A new Convention on Slavery, the Slave Trade and Institutions and Practices similar to Slavery, as a supplement to the old Slavery Convention of 1926, was adopted and came into force in 1957. A Declaration on the Right of Asylum was prepared by the Commission in 1960, laying down the duty of states to accept people demanding asylum at their frontiers, except for 'overriding reasons of national security or safeguarding population'; but this was never adopted by the Assembly. The Sub-Commission made specialised studies on discrimination in education, in employment, in religious rights and practices, in the administration of justice and other fields: on education they drafted a Convention which was adopted by UNESCO in 1960. A number of Declarations, of varying degrees of vagueness were passed, such as the Declaration of the Rights of the Child of 1959 (though this was followed by a specific Covenant in 1988). Studies on particular topics, such as the right of everyone to be free from arbitrary arrest, detention and exile, or freedom of information, were undertaken; but these remained in general terms and studiously refrained from the criticism of individual states in either respect.

But increasingly, from the mid-1950s onwards, it began to be felt that it was not sufficient simply to draft Conventions and Declarations without making any effective attempt to see if they were observed. Attention therefore began to be focused on the subject of 'implementation' and the machinery to ensure this. At first this was not very rigorous. In 1956, ECOSOC asked all delegations to submit every three years reports describing developments and progress achieved in their own country in the field of human rights. Most member states submitted such reports. They were however usually highly uninformative. Nor was any specific action taken on any of them. A small breakthrough was made with the conclusion in 1966 of the International Convention on the Elimination of all Forms of Racial Discrimination. In this case it was provided that when the Convention came into force a Committee should be established to supervise the fulfilment of the obligations it contained by the various ratifying states. Each state had to submit a report on what it had done in this field, and it was subsequently subjected to cross-examination on its record. For the first time therefore (outside the ILO where such procedures had been used for many years) a procedure was established for testing whether commitments were really being fulfilled.

A similar, though perhaps more ambitious, attempt was undertaken in the drawing up of the two Covenants: on civil and political rights, and on economic, social and cultural rights. Drafting these was a long and laborious process which took well over ten years, being undertaken mainly in sessions of the Third Committee of the Assembly. Finally texts were arrived at which were acceptable to the majority of the states participating. Here too, it was provided that Committees should be established to examine the implementation of the Covenants by those governments which had accepted them. When the Covenant on Civil and Political Rights came into force in 1976, such a committee was set up. This now looks at the record of each government that has ratified in implementing the obligations set out in the Covenants and passes judgement. An Optional Protocol is also available for states to sign, allowing for individuals to file complaints against the ratifying states. The Declaration, the two Covenants and the Protocol are collectively known as the International Bill of Human Rights.

None of this, however, represents machinery for examining complaints, even of the grossest violations, by countries which have not ratified the Covenant (the majority), nor of violations in fields not specified in them. For this reason it has for long been felt that there is need for some procedure by which the complaints of individuals (or groups) can be looked at and seriously examined. Such complaints had been sent to the Organisation, usually to the Human Rights Commission, from the UN's foundation. For years however, they were simply pigeon-holed, and nothing ever done about them. From around 1970 there were demands that these communications should be considered in some more substantive way. Many governments resisted the demand, either because they felt that it would give leverage to small and unrepresentative groups trying to cause difficulties for them, or because they had skeletons in their own cupboard which they feared to reveal. Even so it was eventually agreed that the complaints should be looked at by a special working group which would consider how far they revealed evidence of a 'systematic pattern of gross violations' of human rights. This so-called 1503 procedure (named after the resolution in which it was established) came into effect from 1973 onwards. However, the procedure was long and cumbersome. Even if the working group received many complaints that were particularly well documented, it could not itself take action, but merely issue a report to the Sub-Commission. The Sub-Commission sometimes itself decided to take no action. Even if it did it could only send the complaints on to the Commission of Human Rights itself. The Commission in turn passed them to yet another Working Group. And even then, after further sifting, when left with the very worst cases of all for the first two or three years it decided to take no action. Thus the body whose main function was to secure protection of human rights resolutely turned its eyes away when actually confronted with violations. The only occasion when detailed investigations of the situation within individual states did take place was when ad hoc enquiries were set up concerning one or two widely popular targets, such as Chile and South Africa.

Thus the main weakness of the UN's work in this field is that it rarely looks into concrete cases. One proposal that has been made for many years for remedying this situation is for the appointment of a UN Commissioner for Human Rights, who might be empowered to look at individual cases that were sent for his attention, and issue reports to the Commission. This would certainly make for a more efficient system than exists today. The proposal, however, has always been blocked when discussed in the Third Committee of the Assembly because of the objections of certain governments (including the communist states), presumably because they feel they themselves might have reason to fear any more far-reaching scrutiny of their internal affairs than is possible at present. If such objections are maintained, it would, however, still be possible for a system of this kind to be established, and to operate among those governments which accepted. The hope would be that more and more would eventually be shamed into joining the system as time went on. Even so, one of the major inhibiting factors is the Organisation's adherence to the principle of state sovereignty as enshrined in Article 27 of the Charter.

If this side of the UN's work is to be made more effective than it is now, therefore, there is need for much greater resolution among the bodies responsible. If they continue to turn their eyes away from specific examples of gross violations, there will cease to be any respect for the work the UN does in this field. Either the Organisation will need to be more resolute in applying the existing 1503 procedure when the circumstances really justify it; or new measures, such as a UN High Commissioner (even on a voluntary basis), must be attempted. The UN may also need to pursue new aspects of the problem: for example the treatment of prisoners (the ideal would be some new world inspection system for prisons all over the world – again this could begin on a voluntary basis); adequate redress in cases of torture or other brutalities by the police; examination of the use of incarceration in mental asylums or other devices to restrict liberty; protection of the right to communicate by letter free of censorship; freedom to listen to foreign broadcasts and receive information; assurance of the right of emigration; and so on. There might be need for special conventions or special machinery to cover each specialised field of this kind. Since, moreover, some of the most effective bodies acting in this field have been regional ones, most notably the European Commission and Court on Human Rights, there might be value also if the UN were to take steps to promote the establishment of similar bodies in other regions of the world to promote these ends.

Extended and strengthened in this way, activity in the field of human rights might begin to be a central part of the UN's work and a more effective safeguard for human liberties all over the world than it has proved to be so far.

CONCLUSIONS

We have described only those activities undertaken by, or under, the UN proper. Within the 'UN System' there is a very large range of other operations that are undertaken by the specialised agencies, the autonomous bodies that belong to the UN family or 'system' but are not part of the UN itself.

Three of them are older than the UN itself. Two indeed, go back more than a century: the Universal Postal Union (UPU), concerned with organising the world's posts and the system of charging for them, and the International Telecommunication Union (ITU), which performs a somewhat similar function in relation to the world's telegraph and telephone network and supervises international radio frequencies. These operate to a large extent through large-scale conferences among all their members every three or four years; the conferences decide on any major changes in the existing system, and lay down guidelines for the future, while an executive council and many subsidiary committees run the system between whiles. The International Labour Organisation (ILO) was established after the First World War, as part of the League system. Its original concern was with conditions of labour all over the world, which it influences by negotiating Conventions on many different subjects: but it has now become increasingly involved in wider problems affecting the world's labour force, including unemployment, training, automation, incomes policy, labour legislation and much else besides. All three of these bodies, when the UN was founded, entered into 'relationship agreements', converting them into specialised agencies within the UN system. This meant that they submitted reports regularly to the UN, were represented at various meetings, and submitted in a rather theoretical way to the co-ordination of ECOSOC (though not to its control).

When the UN was founded two major bodies were established in the economic field. The International Monetary Fund (IMF) was set up in an attempt to avoid the restrictive and autarchic policies used in the pre-war period by many governments to maintain employment and protect their balance of payments situation. The Fund was established by the contributions member-states made in their own currencies, and to a smaller extent in gold: these were to be used to give support to the governments having payments difficulties, so that they could maintain generally liberal and expansionary policies while tackling the underlying problems causing the deficit – usually this meant overcoming inflationary pressures at home. In return for securing support from the Fund, the government being assisted would submit to certain disciplines and oversight from the Fund itself. This basic system was later supplemented by other devices and especially by the introduction of special drawing rights (SDRs), a form of credit or artificial currency, which could be used to increase the reserves available to all member countries, and again make it easier for them to cope with balance of payments problems without undue deflation. The World Bank, or International Bank for Reconstruction and Development (IBRD), to give it its proper name, was exactly what its name implied: a development bank, which secured funds from an initial subscription by members and by borrowing on the market, and used them for lending, primarily to developing countries – at first for basic infrastructure (roads, dams and hydroelectric schemes), later also for projects in the field of education, agriculture, small-scale industry and family planning. Both the Fund and the Bank differ from most other agencies in that voting power was related to the initial subscriptions made, so giving a greater influence to richer and larger countries, as against the one-nation-one-vote system used elsewhere. (This was not always less democratic, since because many rich countries were also large and most poor countries small, votes were probably more closely related to population under this system than any other.) The work of the World Bank is supplemented by the International Development Association (IDA) to help particularly poor countries.

There were two agencies concerned with transport. For civil aviation there had been an organisation even before the Second World War, but this had been small and unrepresentative and a new body, with a wider membership, was constituted after that war, the International Civil Aviation Organisation (ICAO). This was concerned above all with establishing uniform and safe systems of navigation all over the world and putting into effect a whole range of standardised procedures for this purpose, with a system of inspection for ensuring that the prescribed standards were met. (It was not concerned with the negotiation of routes between countries, which was undertaken bilaterally, nor with fares, which are considered by an organisation of operators, the International Air Transport Association.) The International Maritime Consultative Organisation, now IMO, concerned with shipping matters, which was established in 1959, is also primarily concerned with establishing safe systems of operation all over the world, standards of ship construction, navigational methods, signals, crew qualifications, traffic separation schemes and similar questions, but it has also become increasingly involved with the pollution of the seas by oil and other substances.

Other agencies look after specialised technical questions. The World Meteorological Organisation (WMO) concerns itself with establishing a world-wide meteorological system (the World Weather Watch), using standardised systems for better communication, and with research into a number of areas in this field, often organised on a world-wide basis. The International Atomic Energy Agency (IAEA) is concerned with the peaceful uses of atomic energy, including some derived uses such as the use of isotopes for agricultural and medical purposes; and in recent years it has become increasingly involved with inspection of atomic reactors and the transfer of fuels, to ensure that fuel is not diverted for non-peaceful purposes.

Finally, there are the social service agencies, concerned with similar subjects to the social service departments of national and local governments, such as health and education. The World Health Organisation (WHO) is the largest of all the organisations in terms of staff and budget. It coordinates research in a very large number of areas; it runs a system for the notification of various especially infectious diseases such as cholera, and for preventing their transmission, once notified; it helps developing countries organise their own health services and to train doctors and nurses and especially to improve their public health facilities; it launches world-wide campaigns against particular diseases, such as smallpox (now almost eliminated) and malaria (successful in some areas but often recurring unless public health standards have been sufficiently raised first). Since 1981 WHO has undertaken vital work to try to combat the spread of AIDS.

The United Nations Educational Scientific and Cultural Organisation (UNESCO) is concerned with education, science and cultural exchange: it helps train teachers for developing countries, organises exchange of culture and ideas, runs scientific conferences, oversees specialised bodies concerned with particular areas of science (such as the International Oceanographic Commission and several similar bodies), and helps to recover threatened architectural treasures (such as the Nubian Temples in Egypt threatened by the Aswan Dam, which were rescued by removing them bodily elsewhere). The Food and Agriculture Organisation (FAO) is concerned with the development of agriculture all over the world, with devising effective commodity schemes for some agricultural products, and with providing technical advice in agriculture for many developing countries. It also helps to operate the World Food Programme (WFP) for poor countries and the alleviation of famine.

The structure of all these agencies is roughly the same. There is always an Assembly (occasionally called a Conference) to which all members belong, and meeting anything between every one and every five years. This makes the basic policy decisions and elects the Council and the Director-General. There is a Council which meets regularly between whiles, often about four times a year for two to four weeks each, and runs the organisation meanwhile. Sometimes this has acquired an increasing degree of authority of its own, and has to take decisions in many fields without waiting for authority from the Assembly. There is a Secretariat, headed by a Director-General (though again the name used varies considerably from one agency to another), which performs the executive tasks, services meetings, and provides the basic administration.

In this chapter we have sketched only very briefly operations that cover every aspect of human activity. Except in times of dire famine the economic and social activities of the UN family receive far less publicity than do those of the political bodies, whose disputes the media tend to find so fascinating. Though much of their work is unglamorous and unnewsworthy, it is by no means unimportant. Some are more efficiently run and some are more valuable than others. All the work is deserving of publicity: operations to find homes for millions of refugees, to bring rapid emergency relief after grave natural disasters in any part of the globe, to wipe out smallpox from the earth, to stamp out the drug trade all over the world, to help organise family planning activities among much of the world's population, to organise the world's meteorological services, or abolish pollution in the oceans, to mention only a few. They are probably politically as significant as the speeches in the Security Council; and they are certainly far more lasting in effect.

The present structure for running and controlling these operations is far from perfect. It has not been possible (as was once hoped) to insulate them from political dispute (as we shall see in Chapter 7 below). Nor has any adequate system for the co-ordination of these multifarious activities been established.[2] The UN family has been allowed simply to proliferate with sometimes alarming abundance. But it has been enabled in this way to meet many basic needs that can only be adequately provided for by international action.

FURTHER READING

M. Hill, *The United Nations System: Co-ordinating its Economic and Social Work* (Cambridge, 1978).
L. Levin, *Human Rights: Questions and Answers* (UNESCO, Paris, 1981).
D. Williams, *The Specialised Agencies and the United Nations: The System in Crisis* (London, 1987).

4 The Legal Institutions: Laying Down the International Law

International society, like other societies, has needed to develop rules to govern behaviour among its members, and judicial machinery for interpreting and developing these rules. In international society both legal and political systems are much less developed than those which operate domestically. There is no direct relationship between the two: international law is not made by the political bodies of the UN, as domestic law is made by domestic parliaments. On the contrary, law comes first. International law of a kind existed, in the custom of nations, long before the UN or any other international organisation. Today such bodies often ask the *courts* to lay down the law, for example requesting advisory opinions from the International Court, even asking it for a ruling on a highly political issue such as Namibia or the law of the sea or American mining of Nicaraguan harbours, on the basis of the law already laid down. The Assembly's own resolutions on the other hand are not accepted as representing law. Thus law, as in primitive societies (and the international system is still a primitive society) is at present largely independent of political decision.

But the question still remains: how should the law be made? Governments of new countries sometimes regard international law, as it exists today, as an invention of the older nations, partly to protect their own established interests; and they often attach a greater importance to the direct decisions and pronouncements of UN bodies (where they are in a majority). But even they will accept that there exists, at least in theory, a body of principles which can be described as 'international law' and to which they would claim they seek to conform.

There is far less agreement on exactly what that law is: what are its substantive principles. What is the law, for example, on the supremely important question of the use of force by states; on the right to spread revolution or wars of liberation; on the use of the seas; or on 'sovereignty over natural resources'? Still less is there agreement on the precise interpretation of the law even where general principles are agreed. For this reason there has been generally felt to be an important need for procedures for making law, or at the least for 'codification', so that the existing law may be more accurately defined.

At present international law is incomplete, disputed and uncertain. It is *incomplete*, because there are large and important areas of national conduct, on which it lays down few if any rules at all: this includes the greater part of economic relations among states, as well as such questions as support for émigré governments, the broadcasting of propaganda and other questions. It is *disputed* because on some of the most crucial questions of international law – the criteria for recognising a new government, the degree and type of intervention that is permissible in civil wars, rights over territorial waters and the continental shelf – on these and many other questions international lawyers themselves are not in agreement (it is no chance that most of the major international disputes of the post-war world – the nationalisation of the Suez Canal, the blockade imposed at the time of the Suez crisis, Western rights in Berlin, East Timor and Western Sahara, US intervention in Vietnam and Cuban intevention in Angola – are questions on which international lawyers, even within the same country, let alone in different countries, have not been in agreement). Finally, international law has been *uncertain* because there are many essential elements of it, such as the right of 'anticipatory self-defence' – that is, the right to launch a war because it is believed another is about to attack – or of 'hot pursuit' or of 'innocent passage' and other important questions, on which the law itself, even if agreed, is so vague or open to such wide interpretation that it provides no clear guide to conduct.

Because of these inadequacies and uncertainties, members of the UN, from its foundation, regarded the codification of international law as an important part of its tasks. This process had begun earlier. During the period of the League, a Committee of Experts for the Progressive Codification of International Law was appointed, including members of the Permanent International Court and other eminent international lawyers. And in 1930 a special conference was held in The Hague. But neither made much progress. And eventually the effort to achieve codification was to all intents and purposes abandoned.)

When the new international system was being prepared after the Second World War, it was decided to resume the effort. Article 13 of the Charter laid down that the Assembly would 'initiate studies and make recommendations' for the purpose of 'encouraging the progressive development of international law and its codification'. And in 1947 the Assembly decided to establish a new Commission which would have this as its main task.

The International Law Commission (ILC) originally had fifteen members: it now has thirty-four. Its members are supposed to sit in their personal capacity, and not as representatives of governments. This condition has generally been fulfilled: for the most part, members of the Commission have not necessarily put forward the views of their governments on the points discussed, though they inevitably *reflected* the view prevalent among international lawyers in their own countries.

The Commission meets in Geneva once a year for a session of several weeks. Since its members are mainly busy practising international lawyers, its sessions are necessarily restricted in time-scale, usually to a few weeks, but a certain amount of preparatory work is done between sessions. The Commission seeks to prepare draft Conventions and other legal agreements, which it later submits to the Assembly. These are then considered in the Sixth Committee of the Assembly, which is attended mainly by international lawyers but in this case representing governments. Finally, when the Convention has been largely agreed in these bodies, a special conference is usually called to draw it up in its final form and open it for signature.

The Committee's normal method of work is to appoint a rapporteur to prepare the draft of a particular Convention, or at least some articles of it. After research and consultation, the rapporteur will produce draft articles, together with a commentary on them. The Commission considers these, revises them if necessary, and then provisionally adopts a particular set of articles. These are then sent to governments for their comments. Governments will either send written comments, or will give them orally at the next session of the Sixth Committee at the Assembly. The Commission then reviews the articles in the light of these comments. Eventually, when the whole, or most, of a Convention has been covered in this way, the Assembly will call a special conference to finalise its terms.

The first activities of the International Law Commission reflected the preoccupations of the immediate post-war period: those stemming immediately from the previous conflict. In 1947 the Assembly requested the Commission to seek to formulate more explicitly the principles of international law which had been provisionally established in the Charter of the Nuremberg Tribunal and in the judgments of the Tribunal: these related especially to the planning of aggressive war. The Commission formulated seven principles deriving from the trials and published them with its commentaries. The Assembly then sent these to member-governments for their comments. Some governments submitted their views, but because of disagreements no attempt was made to draft a Convention. Instead, the Assembly asked that the principles should be taken into account in another related task on which the Commission was then engaged.

This was the formulation of a 'draft code of offences against the peace and security of mankind'. The draft code listed a series of offences described as 'crimes under international law for which the responsible individuals should be punishable'. The important point about this was that, like the Nuremberg trials, the code was concerned with offences by *individuals*. And the Commission went on to consider the establishment of an international criminal court to try individuals charged with such crimes, including genocide. This reflected the desire, widely shared by some international lawyers for many years, to establish the principle that the individual as well as the state could be subject to international law. But it was sovereign states that considered the matter; and these were somewhat less enamoured of that principle and the erosion of sovereignty that it implied. A draft statute for an international criminal court of this sort was prepared by a special committee, and sent to governments for their comments. But there were many and substantial reservations. Governments finally decided to postpone consideration until progress had been made on yet another thorny problem, the vexed question of the definition of aggression.

Here was another type of codification: an act of definition.[1] It is a task which was discussed with little interruption in the Assembly for twenty years from 1951. Everybody knew 'aggression' was a crime: but what was it? Since the term is one that is widely and imprecisely used, and since it may be held, if proved, to provide justification for a response by force, this clearly had considerable importance in international law. There had been attempts between the wars to arrive at a comprehensive definition, but they had come to nothing.[2] In 1952, the Assembly set up a special Committee charged with defining aggression. Various texts were suggested, and comments from governments were received. In 1954 a new Committee submitted a report to the Assembly, with a number of suggested definitions. In 1957 the Assembly forwarded these to governments for their comments, but there was little agreement on the proposed texts. The main point at issue was whether the definition should be in general terms, or should specify examples of the types of action covered: and this dispute in turn concealed political differences, for example, whether such acts as anti-colonial revolutions or freedom-fighting constituted 'aggression'. The Committee was adjourned for a period in 1959, met again briefly in 1962 and 1965 and from 1967 took up its task again on a continuous basis. After several more years it finally produced a text most could accept; but this was so vague it did not advance things much.

Another subject of obvious importance to the international community is that of nationality and statelessness. This acquired a special importance immediately after the war, because of the number of refugees who had left their own countries. Thus a Convention on the status of refugees was adopted in 1951. The Commission later studied the whole question of married women, but later decided to devote itself to the specific question of statelessness. Two draft Conventions were prepared and a conference was held in 1959. This failed to reach agreement. A Convention on the Reduction of Statelessness was eventually adopted in 1961; but it has received little support, and only a handful of states have even signed the Convention, let alone ratified it. So here too there was little progress.

But the Commission has had some successes. Another field where a viable international society needs agreed rules concerns the practice of diplomatic relations (a subject of bitter dispute in earlier centuries). During the 1960s the Commission drafted two important Conventions on Diplomatic Intercourse and Immunities, and on Consular Relations. Though there existed on these matters a large body of international custom, dating back to the seventeenth century and earlier, there was no firm agreement on the exact practices which governments were required to follow in according privileges and immunities to diplomats in their territory. The privileges accorded were often based on bilateral treaties, and even the same government often accorded different privileges to different governments. The Commission began work on the former question in 1952. Eventually, after long preparation an international conference in Vienna in 1961 adopted the Vienna Convention on Diplomatic Relations, as well as optional protocols on the acquisition of nationality and the compulsory settlement of disputes. The Convention has now been ratified by a large number of governments and entered into force in April 1964. It sets out *minimum* treatment to be accorded to diplomats concerning freedom from arrest, protection, customs, privileges and so on (since many governments already provide treatment above this minimum under bilateral agreements, there are still charges of discrimination, and the question is not finally exhausted). The Convention on

Consular Relations was signed in 1963 and entered into force three years later.

Another area on which there must be agreement in a stable international community concerns treaties. Since treaties are the main instruments by which governments order their relations with each other, it is obviously essential to a viable international society that the law by which they themselves are governed shall be clear. The question was chosen as the subject of a Convention during the first year the commission met in 1949. It is a vivid example of the amount of time required for such an undertaking: in this case nearly twenty years. Eventually, in 1961 the draft was ready. It was considered by a conference in 1968. This was attended by 110 governments and approved the text of the Convention. In 1986 this work was extended by another Vienna Convention relating to treaties involving international organisations.

The Commission has drafted Conventions on various other topics including Special Missions (UN and other international missions not covered by normal diplomatic conventions) and the protection of diplomats (from the dangers of terrorism for example), which have been adopted by the Assembly. And there is considerable ongoing work, for example, on the law of State responsibility and the status of the diplomatic courier.

Some of the other efforts at codification have been less successful. At its first session in 1949, the Commission began to consider the law of the sea. This is a matter of great importance in international law – what rights governments have over the waters around their coasts, for example concerning the fish stocks there, in the continental shelf and in the high seas. Governments claimed differing breadths of waters, varying between three and 200 miles, for the territorial sea, and had differing views on other issues. Again a special rapporteur was appointed, who issued reports on many aspects, including fishing zones, the continental shelf and other matters. In 1958 a full international conference was held in Geneva and was attended by representatives of 86 states. Though there was agreement on some points, there was much dissension on others. The Conference finally produced four draft Conventions: on the high seas, on the territorial sea and the contiguous zone, on the continental shelf, and on fishing and the conservation of the living resources of the high seas. These were signed, and later ratified, by a varying number of states. But much remained vague or not agreed. At the 1970 Assembly it was decided that the whole matter should be considered, together with a new regime for the sea-bed, at the Conference on the Law of the Sea (UNCLOS), which started meeting in 1974.

The new Convention was ready for signature in 1982. This is a most comprehensive document of 320 articles. Territorial waters were finally defined as twelve miles in breadth, while an area 200 miles from the coast was accepted as an exclusive economic zone for that coastal state. Of great importance and a source of controversy are the articles relating to the mining of the sea-bed in international waters. Arrangements were also put in hand to establish an International Sea-Bed Authority and an International Tribunal for the Law of the Sea. Unfortunately the usefulness of all this important work has been in some measure undermined by the refusal of many states, most notably the USA and the UK, to ratify the Convention.

The UN and the Commission also seek to make the decisions of the International Court, and the provisions of customary international law, more generally known. The UN has published a comprehensive 'Repertory of Practice of the UN', detailing the interpretation placed on every Article of the Charter in the various decisions reached by the Assembly, the Council and other bodies. It publishes a Treaty Series giving the texts of all treaties registered with the UN (as all treaties must be under the Charter). It publishes a legislative series, publishing national legislation on matters of an international character (for example, continental shelf legislation). There is a Yearbook of the ILC. And since 1963 a UN Juridical Yearbook has been brought out annually, recording the main decisions of the International Court and other developments in the field of international law over the year.

THE COMMISSION'S ROLE IN CONTEMPORARY WORLD SOCIETY

The ILC thus has an important role in defining and developing the recognised rules of the contemporary world community: that is, international law. It corresponds in some ways to national bodies such as the Law Commission in Britain, which are concerned with the codification of national law, as the ILC is with that of international law. But there is a difference. The British Law Commission is largely concerned with the *consolidation* of law which already exists, sometimes scattered among many different statutes, dating from different ages, or derived from the traditions of common law. The ILC, though it often performs this role – consolidating the traditions built up through international custom or treaties – sometimes drafts quite new laws, which do not pre-exist in any form (as for example on the continental shelf or the protection of diplomats). In this case its function is not consolidation, but preparing legislation. Its role is comparable then almost to that of a cabinet within states; proposing new laws, to be approved by a parliament (that is the diplomatic conference): with the difference that in the international case the Convention, even if agreed by the conference, has to pass another hurdle, that of ratification by individual states. The ILC *proposes* legislation but there is no body to *pass* it into binding law: not the Assembly, not even the diplomatic conference. Legislation in this strict sense does not yet exist at the international level; but a decision by the International Court, or an overwhelming majority for a new Convention at a conference at the UN, come fairly close to it (though the Convention does not come into force until a sufficient number of governments have ratified).

The International Law Commission is not of course the only body which is responsible for preparing international legislation. The General Assembly's Sixth Committee, as we saw, prepares Conventions. The Assembly passes 'Declarations' – such as those on outer space and on sea-bed exploitation (1970) – which possess a considerable degree of authority. Bodies such as the UN Commission on International Trade Law (UNCITRAL), or the Outer Space legal sub-committee, draw up international instruments in their own fields. The specialised agencies of the UN frequently prepare Conventions, introduce regulations or take other decisions which effectively represent binding obligations for their members. The International Court, in its own judgements, also adds to the body of international law. Finally, national governments continue to enter into treaties on a number of questions, including those of a multilateral character (such as the Non-Proliferation Treaty) which have the force of international law for all signatories. In all these ways the general body of international law is being perpetually extended. The special role of the International Law Commission is to identify areas where codification of the law is particularly necessary, and to take the preparatory steps required in drawing up draft Conventions or other instruments.

The subjects covered by the Conventions drawn up so far are perhaps not the most dramatic, or those about which wars might otherwise break out. This does not mean that they are not important. It is an advance that, even on relatively uncontroversial questions, there should be agreed international principles. More significant, perhaps, the Commission has established the tradition of a regular and consistent programme of codification, which is likely to proceed for the foreseeable future. Eventually, principles of international law on a whole range of questions where it is at present uncertain or disputed may come to be more clearly laid down. In this way the first condition for creating a clear legal framework for the conduct of international relations may come to be fulfilled. General consciousness that nations are governed by a system of law begins to be increased, and respect for principles that are widely accepted is encouraged, even in more controversial fields.

It is, however, a matter for consideration whether the ILC might not play a more valuable role if it (and the Assembly's Sixth Committee which instructs it) were prepared to venture more often into more controversial fields in choosing subjects for examination. As we saw earlier, there are large areas where international law is uncertain, disputed or incomplete; and it is often over such questions that conflict breaks out in the modern world. Conventions on some of those questions listed earlier (p.80 above) would certainly be harder to arrive at. But they would be much more valuable once agreed. It no doubt seems more worthwhile to the Assembly that the Commission should devote its efforts to drafting conventions and instruments which it can be fairly sure will ultimately be widely accepted than to waste time in devising forms of words which finally are rejected. Against this, if the ILC refuses to turn towards the disputed topics, either the task will be taken over by other bodies, perhaps less well equipped for the task (such as the Sixth Committee of the Assembly or ad hoc committees appointed by it); or alternatively large areas of international law which are most urgently in need of codification will be ignored altogether, while only those which are uncontroversial are ever tackled.

Thus the ILC might perform a more valuable function within the international system if the General Assembly were more ambitious than at present in the tasks it entrusts to it.

THE INTERNATIONAL COURT OF JUSTICE

Besides machinery for codifying the law, an effective legal system requires also the machinery to interpret and apply it. The idea of a supreme international law court to decide disputes among nations has been discussed for centuries. It was put forward in writings of medieval and later times as one means of creating order among conflicting and lawless nation-states. Its practical realisation had to wait until recently; and when it did emerge it took a form considerably less ambitious than these writings had foreseen.

The establishment of a court arose partly from the tradition of arbitration between nations. Especially from the beginning of the nineteenth century it became common for European governments in dispute about a frontier, for example, to ask a neighbouring monarch to mediate or arbitrate. The king of the Netherlands was asked to arbitrate between Britain and the US (1831); the Czar of Russia between France and the Netherlands (1891); the king of Italy between Britain and Brazil (1904); the king of Spain between Britain and Germany (1909): these are only few among many examples.[3] In some cases arbitration commissions were provided to perform a similar purpose: the US and Britain arranged at the end of the eighteenth century for mixed arbitration commissions, composed of nationals of the two states, to resolve differences on the immensely long frontier between the USA and Canada. As this practice developed, so did the rules applied become more clearly formulated. In 1873, an Institute of International Law, to study and evolve the rules of arbitration, was therefore set up. And at the end of the nineteenth century an increasing number of bilateral treaties were concluded providing for agreed procedures to settle disputes in this way.

At the Hague conferences of 1899 and 1907, there were new efforts to develop the system. A Permanent Court of Arbitration was established in 1899. A Convention for the peaceful settlement of international disputes, which provided for mediation, conciliation or arbitration, was set up. A permanent panel of arbitrators to hear such disputes was set up.

After the First World War, it was widely hoped that the use of these methods might become the principal means of preventing wars in the future. So law might be made a substitute for war. All agreed under the Covenant to settle 'disputes' by peaceful means. Three alternative methods were provided for this purpose. Those that were regarded as purely political would be submitted to the League Council. For disputes that were partly legal, provision was made for submission to arbitration, through one of the arbitral arrangements already established or, later, to a procedure known as 'conciliation', under less formal legal procedures. Finally, for those that were purely legal, a wholly new procedure was established, to be known as 'judicial settlement'. This would be undertaken by a new body established for the first time: the Permanent International Court of Justice, which was set up at The Hague.

Many doubted whether any such clear distinction could be drawn between 'legal' and 'political' disputes. But there were two opposite conclusions to be drawn from this. Some fervent believers in international law, mainly the international lawyers themselves, held that there was no dispute, however 'political', which could not be resolved according to the principles and procedures of international law. Even the admitted gaps in the law could be filled by case law. Politicians, on the other hand, less convinced that the law could never be an ass, tended to maintain that for many issues only the traditional methods of diplomacy or the newly established League of Nations could provide solutions. Others held that there were no purely legal questions at all. And it quickly came to be established that an 'important' issue was automatically political rather than legal, and so 'unfit for decision by the Court'.[4]

In consequence, the Court was excluded from hearing precisely those issues most likely to lead to war. Most of the cases brought and decided by the Court were not of the first importance. Certainly none of the issues which ultimately became the occasion for war, or at least its justification – the treatment of Japanese citizens in Manchuria, the frontier dispute over Wal-Wal between Italy and Ethiopia, the demilitarisation of the Rhineland, the treatment of German minorities in Czechoslovakia and Poland – were ever even considered as possible items for submission to the Permanent International Court of Justice.

But the general belief that law could be made a substitute for war led to further attempts to strengthen the legal machinery established. It was proposed that nations should give a solemn undertaking that, for all disputes of a legal character, they would accept the jursidiction of the Court if the issue was submitted to it by another nation which had given a similar undertaking. Because of the opposition of some nations, especially Britain and one or two Commonwealth countries, this proposal was changed so that both the nations concerned needed to have given their prior consent to the Court's 'compulsory' jurisdiction. This was the famous Optional Clause to which governments might voluntarily accede. Even then many nations did not accede. Or they attached to their acceptance so many reservations, excluding all disputes of a particular kind, that much of its value was lost.

Thus, though the Court heard a considerable number of cases during this period, none of them was of the first importance; and it certainly could not be said that the Court, as had been hoped, normally provided an attractive alternative to war for a country which was in dispute. None the less, its very existence perhaps did something to impress on the public mind the idea that nations were subject to an international law which was above and beyond themselves. Lip-service at least to the Court's importance was widely paid.

After the Second World War, it was agreed to reconstitute the Court, now as an integral element of the United Nations system. In April 1945, even before the end of the war, a Committee of Jurists was invited by the US government to meet in Washington and made recommendations concerning the new statute. At the San Francisco Conference, it was accepted that all members of the UN should automatically become parties to the statute of the new Court.[5] This was to be renamed; the rash adjective 'Permanent' was dropped. The Court was made an organ of the UN (its predecessor had been separate from the League). Its statute became annexed to the Charter.

The statute was redrafted, though it remained closely based on the old one. Every member of the UN had to undertake to comply with decisions of the Court. The Optional Clause was reproduced in Article 36 of the statute; parties were able to declare that they recognised 'as compulsory *ipso facto* and without special agreement, in relation to any other state accepting the same obligation', the Court's jurisdiction over certain types of legal dispute. And it was laid down in the Charter that the Security Council could, at the request of one party to a dispute, 'decide on measures to be undertaken to give effect to' a judgement of the Court.

An effort was made to encourage more governments to accept the so-called 'compulsory' jurisdiction of the Court. This attempt was not, however, very successful. Well under half the members of the UN accepted such jurisdiction: in 1992 only 53 out of 175 members. Together the number of cases and requests for advisory opinions submitted to the Court have averaged about two per year. From 1947 to 1990, 61 contentious cases and twenty advisory cases were heard. And many of the cases that were heard were not of great international significance.

One of the first cases heard was among the most important. This arose from the damage to British ships, and loss of life, occurring as a result of the mining of the Corfu Channel, apparently by Albania, in 1946. Britain brought the question in the first place to the Security Council. But this recommended that the question was a legal one which should be referred to the Court. Albania, however, challenged the jurisdiction of the Court. The Court overruled this plea (under the terms of Article 36 of the Statute), and examined the question. Though it did not find it proved that Albania was responsibe for laying the mines, it did find that it had responsibility for the Channel in general, and that the mines could only have been laid with Albania's knowledge. On these grounds it awarded nearly a million pounds damages to Britain against Albania. Albania had made certain counter-charges against Britain concerning the passage of warships through the straits, but the Court found that the ships were exercising the right of innocent passage. On the other hand, it also held that the British minesweepers had had no right to sweep the mines from the Channel without the authority of Albania. Albania has consistently refused to accept the judgement of the Court and pay the damages awarded against her, despite the undertaking of all UN members under Article 94 of the Charter to 'comply with the decisions' of the Court. No effective steps have been taken to enforce it. And this raised doubts as to the value of raising major international disputes before the Court.

Interestingly, another case involving the sowing of mines has more recently led to the culpable state refusing to recognise the Court's verdict. This was the case brought by Nicaragua against the USA in 1984. Since then the matter has been regularly raised at the General Assembly. It has been an especially important case as it involved blatant attacks by the CIA on a state with whom the USA was not at war. It also revealed the weakness of Article 36(2), the so-called Optional Protocol: the USA declared that it did not recognise the jurisdiction of the Court on matters relating to Central America.

The Court had other cases concerning territorial waters and fishing rights. In 1951 it ruled on a long-standing dispute between Britain and Norway concerning fishing rights. This centred on the method by which Norway had drawn the base-lines from which its territorial waters were calculated. Where a coastline is sharply indented by bays, it is possible, by drawing the lines from the most protruding parts of the coast, to extend the area of territorial waters and fishing rights substantially. The Court held that the method used in this way by Norway was valid in international law but laid down certain principles for the drawing of base-lines.[6]

Later, in 1969, the Court gave an important ruling on the method of dividing the continental shelf beneath the sea, though it did not define the exact area in dispute (between West Germany, Denmark and the Netherlands) it did lay down the principles for defining such a shelf, on the basis that the shelf should be regarded as the natural prolongation of the land-mass of the countries concerned; the shelf should be divided generally on the basis of the median line but making allowances for special geographical features, such as sharp indentation or concaveness. In the dispute between Britain and Iceland over fisheries in 1974–5 it found Iceland had not complied with the relevant treaty but by the time judgement was given the two countries had reached an interim settlement. In the 1980s three disputes about continental shelf boundaries were settled: between Libya and Tunisia, Libya and Malta and Canada and the USA.

The Court also resolved a few territorial disputes. All concerned very small areas, of little value to either party. It decided that a small group of uninhabited islands and islets in the Channel Islands, disputed between Britain and France on the basis of medieval treaties (the Minquier and Ecrehou Islands) were Britain's. It ruled on two small pieces of land disputed between Belgium and the Netherlands, on the basis of a boundary convention entered into in 1843, and found they belonged to Belgium. On a dispute between Nicaragua and Honduras about villages on their border, which had been disputed since 1906 (after an arbitration by the king of Spain had awarded them to Honduras) the Court found that Nicaragua, having agreed to arbitration, was under an obligation to honour the award made by the king of Spain. Over a dispute between Thailand and Cambodia, concerning sovereignty over the temple of Preah Vihear, the Court found that the temple was situated in Cambodian territory. More recently, in 1986, a boundary dispute between Burkina Faso and Mali was settled. Rulings in all these territorial cases were accepted and honoured by the countries concerned. This was in itself a significant achievement. But, as can be seen, they did not concern territory of much intrinsic value. And there are a number of frontier disputes between nations which remain unresolved, sometimes concerning far more valuable territory, and which have never been submitted to the Court, either because one party's claim is not based on purely legal grounds, or because one or both are not prepared to submit to the Court's jurisdiction on the matter.

The Court has been faced with a number of cases concerning political asylum. When Colombia granted asylum to the Peruvian political leader, Haya de la Torre, in its embassy in Peru, Peru claimed that he was guilty of a criminal and not a political offence, and that Colombia had no right unilaterally to determine that he was a political offender in granting him asylum. The Court decided that Colombia was not so entitled, and that Peru need not allow such a refugee to leave its borders from the embassy under Colombian protection; but it also did not find Colombia was responsible for delivering him to the Peruvian government (since Peru had not proved that Haya de la Torre was a criminal offender). In a somewhat similar case concerning wrongful arrest and expulsion raised by Liechtenstein against Guatemala on behalf of a Liechtenstein national, the Court found that the former's case could not be upheld since the individual concerned was not in any true sense a national of Liechtenstein.

There were some cases concerning aircraft incidents. In two cases, the United States brought claims against the Soviet Union and Hungary in respect of aircraft shot down off Japan and one forced to land in Hungary. In both cases, the two governments concerned refused to accept the jurisdiction of the Court. Another case was brought by Israel, the USA and the UK, in respect of the shooting down of an Israeli civil airliner over Bulgaria in 1955. Here too, Bulgaria refused to accept the jurisdiction of the Court, and the Court held that the acceptance of the compulsory jurisdiction of the Permanent Court in 1921 did not bind its successor government in relation to the new Court. During the Iran–Iraq war a US warship in the Gulf shot down an Iranian airliner: Iran demanded that the Court require the USA to pay compensation. There have also been a number of relatively unimportant claims cases: between Greece and the UK, by France against Norway, by the Swiss government against the USA, and by Belgium against Spain. In addition Britain put to the Court the issue of nationalisation by Iran of the Anglo-Iranian Oil Company but the Court found it had no jurisdiction.

This is not therefore a very exciting or momentous list. But, besides these 'contentious cases', the Court has given a number of advisory opinions, which have in some cases been far more important. A number related to the UN's own affairs. A particularly important one was that relating to the costs of peace-keeping forces (see p.138). The Court advised that peace-keeping costs could be properly reckoned as normal expenses of the Organisation for the purpose of Article 19. Though this was overwhelmingly accepted by the Assembly, the UN finally decided not to apply Article 19 as the advisory opinion allowed. The Court gave an opinion in the early years of the Organisation on disputes concerning admission into the UN, confirming that no admission could be made without a Security Council recommendation. On a case arising out of the death of Count Bernadotte, the UN Mediator in Palestine in 1948, the Court ruled that the UN had the capacity to bring a claim for reparation for damage caused to the Organisation as a whole. The Court also advised during the McCarthy period when US staff were being dismissed, that the UN was not entitled to refuse to honour awards of compensation made by the UN Administrative Tribunal to staff whose contracts had been prematurely terminated. It advised that members of UNESCO whose services had been terminated (because accused by the US of being subversive) had the right to appeal to the Administrative Tribunal of the ILO which was designated to hear questions of a similar kind. Also, it ruled that Liberia and Panama should be accepted by IMCO for the purposes of membership of its Council as among 'the largest ship-owning nations'.

Possibly the most famous and important opinion of the Court was that concerning South-West Africa. The Court has given advisory opinions on a number of questions affecting the territory. In 1950, the Court had advised that the Mandate awarded by the League to South Africa over South-West Africa still existed and that, though South Africa need not convert the territory into a Trust Territory, she must submit to supervision of the Mandate by the UN as the successor to the League (which she never did). In 1960, Ethiopia and Liberia, as former members of the League, brought a contentious case to the Court to the effect that South Africa had failed in its obligations under the Mandate, and asked the Court to rule that South Africa should cease from its present policies and fulfil its obligations. South Africa claimed that the Mandate had lapsed; and that it had fulfilled its duties under the Mandate. The Court, with one judge missing through death, and by the casting vote of the President, in 1966 ruled that Liberia and Ethiopia had no legal right or interest enabling them to bring such a contentious case. Thus the long years, and many hours of pleading on the merits of the case were wasted, and the matter was dismissed on a procedural point. The judgement was widely criticised and in some cases attributed to political prejudice on the part of the majority judges (since the judges of developed countries had showed themselves more in favour of dismissing the case than those from developing countries). It remained open to the UN as a whole, as the successors of the League, to revive the proceedings. The Security Council in 1970 invited the Court to give an advisory opinion on: 'What are the legal consequences for states of the presence of South Africa in Namibia?' in defiance of a Security Council 'decision'. On this occasion the Court did give an opinion: to the effect that South Africa's presence in the territory was illegal and that other states were under an obligation to take no action which recognised South Africa's legal authority there. Finally, in 1988, South Africa agreed to UN assistance in the transition of Namibia to sovereign independence.

The composition of the Court is designed to make it fully international. There are fifteen judges, and there may not be two judges of the same nationality. Judges are nominated by the national groups in the Permanent Court of Arbitration. They are elected for nine years, and five of them come up for re-election every three years. The judges of the Court are elected by the Assembly and the Security Council in a complicated procedure of separate elections. The successful candidate must receive an absolute majority of the votes both from the Assembly and the Council.

The judges are supposed to be independent judges elected 'regardless of their nationality, from among persons of a high moral character'. However high their moral character, they are certainly not elected regardless of nationality. Elections take place with geographical distribution very much in mind: U Thant had to defend the Court by showing that the distribution of judges was exactly the same as in the Security Council.[7] It is laid down in the Statute that 'the representation of the main forms of civilization and of the principal legal systems of the world shall be assured'. And this provision is used to justify the same type of 'equitable geographical distribution' as for most other UN elections. The developing countries in particular are anxious to ensure that a substantial proportion of the judges are from their countries. As we saw, these countries often have the feeling that international law was made by Westerners for Westerners, and it is important to them that, at least in its application, the judgements of other parts of the world should play their part. This tendency was particularly pronounced after the judgements on the South-West Africa case: the OAU subsequently passed a resolution demanding an additional African judge, and another African was in fact elected at the next election.

A case which is brought before the Court may take several years to hear. The case is brought usually by a written application addressed to the Registrar. This indicates the subject of the dispute and the parties. The Registrar communicates this to those concerned and to all members of the United Nations. Counsel appointed by the parties concerned then present material, including a great deal of written evidence. The Court may require certain provisional measures to be taken to protect the rights of either party before reaching a final judgement. When a case is considered by the Court, countries which have no judges on it may nominate an *ad hoc* or national judge of their own choice to sit on that particular case (this is some indication that it has always been accepted that judges might be influenced by their nationality).

The first part of the procedure is written; each party presents a 'memorial' and 'counter-memorial' and, if it wishes, replies to each, together with papers and documents in support. This is followed by the oral proceedings, consisting of the hearing of witnesses, experts, agents, counsel and advocates. The Court can decide the form in which each party concludes its arguments and the time in which evidence must be submitted. Finally, the Court may refuse to accept any further oral or written evidence unless the other side consents.

Eventually, the Court submits its judgement. Frequently, this may be in the form of majority and minority judgements by the judges concerned. The majority judgement is signed by the President and by the Registrar and is read in open court. Each judgement is final and without appeal, except that at the request of any party the Court may construe its meaning; or, on the discovery of some new fact of a decisive nature not previously known, the Court may in very rare cases issue a revision (but this is almost unknown).

The Court is often criticised for being slow and cumbersome, but many of the delays are requested by the parties, to give further time to prepare their case. Where advisory opinions have been asked for, they have almost always been given within a year. There is in fact a Chamber of Summary Procedure, with only five judges, for hearing urgent cases. But this has never been used. States could thus get quicker justice if they really needed it.

THE IMPROVEMENT OF THE SYSTEM

The record of the legal bodies of the UN is not, at first sight, perhaps, impressive. There is only a limited category of cases that are brought to the International Court at all. Jurisdiction is entirely voluntary: either a nation accepts it for the particular case concerned; or it has entered into a treaty providing for settlement of disputes by the Court; or it has given a general undertaking to accept the Court's jurisdiction for a particular category of case in relation to other nations who have accepted the same thing. In a considerable proportion of the cases, the Court has had to find that it has no jurisdiction. Over two of the most important (the Corfu Channel and the mining of Nicaragua's harbours) the parties found responsible refused to comply with the judgement. In another important case (the South-West Africa case) the Court originally refused to pass judgement in the form in which it had been presented. None of the types of case that have most frequently led

to war have been taken to the Court at all. On the issues where
international law can be most uncertain or most contested, and which
most often give rise to conflict – the limits of permissible external
intervention in civil war situations, political support for revolutionary
movements, the right of nationalisation of international waterways or
other resources, respective rights in such areas as Berlin and its access
routes, Formosa and its offshore islands, Vietnam and Rhodesia,
between Israel and the Arabs – here neither the rulings of the
International Court, nor the work of codification of the International
Law Commission have been brought into play at all.[8]

A still more fundamental problem concerns the lack of enforcement
power available to the Court to secure compliance when it does make
judgements. The Security Council can, under Article 94, 'decide upon
measures to be taken to give effect to the judgment' of the Court, but
has never done so. This leads to a situation where many deride the
usefulness of bringing disputes to the Court, doubting, with some
reason, not only whether the other government involved will accept
jurisdiction in the first place, but whether it will comply with any
judgement obtained. If Albania can defy the Court with impunity, who
cannot? It is arguable therefore that, if it is really desired to make the
Court a more effective influence within the world's political system, the
Security Council should be more willing to take action to enforce its
judgements.

This lack of enforcement power has led to demands for wider
acceptance of the Optional Protocol. But even if more governments
could be induced to accept this, or if those which have accepted it were
to drop their existing reservations (such as the US government's
Connally Reservation), the real situation would probably not be very
much changed. There is no evidence that, even if jurisdiction was
guaranteed, governments would be any more willing to invoke the
Court. Indeed, if the acceptance of automatic jurisdiction is so
wonderful a solution as is suggested, it is remarkable that so few
cases under it have been brought to the Court by those who accept it.
The failure to use the Court is not so much the result of inadequate
prior commitment. It is inadequate present confidence: a disillusion
among states concerning what the Court can achieve, and a belief that
political remedies may be the better way to pursue contentious causes.

All this leads some to doubt if the Court has any useful role to play
in regulating the relations of states. Judgements of this kind (like
corresponding judgements on the UN as a whole) are usually based on
unrealistic expectations. The International Court has not yet been the

means for establishing a totally new international system, based on law and justice. But it would have been foolish to expect this. Although the judgements of the Court, and the Conventions drawn up by the Commission, have been mainly on relatively non-controversial subjects, this does not mean that they have been of no significance. The gradual building up of a wide body of international judgements, even of this non-controversial kind, may serve gradually to change the international environment. The increasing acceptance by governments of a system of internationally established rules, even in uncontentious areas, serves slowly to encourage the expectation that such rules are necessary and that national sovereignty is not overriding. The increasing range of matters in which such international norms are laid down slowly strengthens the general assumption that they shall operate everywhere and that the will of national governments is no longer the ultimate authority. The slow accumulation of international judgements and international instruments thus eventually contributes to the establishment of a more orderly community among states; in which mutual obligations are recognised, and expectations increasingly brought into alignment.

But for this to happen certain conditions have to be fulfilled. The first concerns the substance of the law applied. At present a great deal of international law appears to many of the governments of the world to be a code made in Europe for Europeans, which the peoples and governments of other continents have played little part in moulding. It can be represented as the ideological buttress for the status quo, designed to legitimise the existing distribution of possessions and power among states (as indeed can most legal systems). Some effort has been made to counteract such attitudes.[9] But in the long run the only way respect for that law will be increased will be if experience of the law, in the judgements of the International Court and the drafting of new Conventions, convinces those from developing countries that the law applied provides for change as well as stability, reflects feelings of justice felt in the world as a whole, and does not always work manifestly against the interests of the have-nots. Like any other law, international law must thus take account of the changing needs of a developing society if it is to retain the confidence of the world community.

Secondly, this means that the Court in its judgements may require often *explicitly* to take account of considerations of equity, as well as of prescriptive rights. Admittedly this is complicated by the fact that the power of the Court to invoke the principle of equity under Article 38 of its Statute is susceptible of different interpretations.[10] It is arguable that if the Court is to retain an important role in an evolving world society, it must allow its judgements to give expression to considerations that are partly political as well as legal: to be concerned with equity as well as legal rights.

Thirdly, it needs to be recognised that new norms need not always take the form of a strict and formal 'law' like the laws that operate within national states. The international community does not yet dispose of means of coercion to enforce a strict legal system. It thus resembles far more a primitive society, governed by custom and public opinion, than a highly organised modern state, and may require a corresponding type of norm. In some cases, an Assembly 'declaration', having a less binding character than international law in the strict sense, may be more appropriate as an indication of emerging international consensus than a strictly binding Convention. The 1970 Declaration on the use of the deep sea-bed and the Declaration of principles on 'friendly relations among states' were of this kind: they could be said to establish generally accepted norms, even if they do not have the full force of international law.[11]

Through the evolution of new principles in this way it might be possible to cover other forms of national behaviour on which international law gives no clear guidance – assistance in civil war situations (as in Greece, Vietnam, Angola and Yugoslavia), intervention to defend regional or ideological blocs (as in Nicaragua and Afghanistan), intervention to promote national interests (as at Suez), intervention for decolonisation (as in Goa and East Timor), intervention to promote revolution (as in Bolivia and Vietnam) or to prevent it (as in Hungary and Vietnam again).

Next, greater use could be made of the existing facilities of the Court and the Commission. The Commission might be asked to prepare Conventions on more controversial and significant topics than those chosen in the past. So far as the Court is concerned, among its most useful activities has been the issuing of advisory opinions which have guided the UN and the specialised agencies on a number of difficult issues. Even if governments continue to ignore the Court, therefore, it would be open to the UN General Assembly and the other agencies to ask for such advisory opinions more frequently, not only on questions of UN organisation and constitutional structure, but on contentious issues of international law:[12] for example, the question of the rights of host countries over international waterways, such as the Suez and Panama Canals, or the right of intervention in civil wars, which is not only one of the most disputed aspects of international law today, but one of the most important (because civil war is the commonest form of conflict today): during the Vietnam war international lawyers in the US were totally divided on the legality of US intervention, each half protesting with equal force and conviction that its own view was justified. Governments too could sometimes make use of the Court in this way to test disputed points of international law or even to evolve new principles.

The General Assembly is responsible under Article 13 of the Charter for 'developing' international law. If that process is to be carried much further, it should perhaps be more energetic in securing opinions on some of these points from the UN's legal bodies. It seems unlikely that a stable political system among states will be established so long as the law governing relations within it is as uncertain as it is today, and the means of creating it so incoherent.

FURTHER READING

R. P. Anand, *Compulsory Jurisdiction in the International Court of Justice* (London, 1961).

R. P. Anand, *Studies in International Adjudication* (Delhi, 1969).

H. W. Briggs, *The International Law Commission* (New York, 1965).

I. Brownlie, *Principles of Public International Law* (Oxford, 4th edn, 1990) ch.xxxi.

R. P. Dokhalia, *The Codification of Public International Law* (Manchester, 1970).

L. C. Green, *International Law through the Cases* (New York, 3rd ed., 1970).

M. D. Hudson, *The Permanent International Court of Justice, 1920–1942* (New York, 1943).

H. Lauterpacht, *The Development of International Law by the International Court* (London, 1958).

O. J. Lissitzyn, *The International Court of Justice: Its Role in the Maintenance of International Peace and Security* (New York, 1951).

A. Nussbaum, *A Concise History of the Law of Nations* (New York, 1947).

S. Rosenne, *The World Court: What it is and How it Works* (Dordrecht, 4th edn, 1989).

J. Stone, *The International and World Crisis* (New York, 1962).

5 The Secretariat: Running the Organisation

The problem of selecting and establishing an international secretariat had scarcely arisen before the League of Nations was founded. There were a few bodies for which multinational staffs had to be found before that time (for example the Rhine and Danube Commissions and the Universal Postal Union), but the numbers involved in these cases were tiny, and usually it was only a question of seconding temporarily a limited number of people from existing government services.

When the League was established, a much more ambitious task had to be faced. The job of Secretary-General was originally offered to Sir Maurice Hankey, the Secretary of the British Cabinet, who was known to a number of those at the peace conference in Versailles, and whose administrative talents were highly respected. He refused the appointment, and it went instead to another British official, who had formerly worked in the Foreign Office, Sir Eric Drummond. He brought with him to the League the tradition of faceless reticence of the British Civil Service. He was essentially a back-room boy, who never sought to achieve personal prominence or appear in the limelight, yet gave a great deal of wise and valued advice to the diplomats and statesmen who attended League meetings. Indeed the very fact that he never sought publicity, and could be relied on to be totally discreet, probably meant that his advice was more sought after than it would otherwise have been.[1]

His supreme achievement was in setting up a truly international civil service in Geneva, drawn from thirty countries (it was inevitably in practice largely European, partly because much of the membership was European, and partly because few applicants from other members, for example in Latin America, presented themselves). Drummond was not allowed a large budget for his Secretariat, but on his slender resources he demanded and achieved the highest standard of efficiency. He insisted on making all recommendations for senior appointments himself (though they had to be approved by the Council) and refused to accept necessarily the candidates put forward even by powerful governments. Drummond introduced the system of writing an annual report about the work of the organisation, later adopted by the UN. This was discussed in the 'general' debate of the Assembly and acted as a focus of discussion on such controversial questions as minorities and mandates for example.

There were some battles, not unlike those of today, about the proper organisation and manning of the Secretariat. There were demands from some countries, especially Italy and Germany, for greater representation in the League's Secretariat. The same countries tried, without success, to establish a political committee of the principal members (including of course themselves) to take over some of the powers of the Secretariat: an idea that foreshadowed the famous troika proposal of the Soviet Union thirty years later. The smaller powers, also as today, wanted more of the top posts. Eventually in 1932 it was accepted that of the three senior posts (the Secretary-General and the two Deputy Secretaries-General), one was to go to a non-permanent member. Further posts became vacant when Japan, Germany and Italy withdrew from the League, for their governments then ensured that their nationals resigned from the Secretariat. This is an outcome which could scarcely follow the withdrawal of a member in the UN today: perhaps an indication that the international civil servant is at least rather more international now than then.

When the UN was started, a new staff had to be created, though some ex-League officials joined. The international civil service now consists of people working for specialised agencies and for the UN itself. International administration is larger than that of some national governments. This staff works in a variety of roles that are not dissimilar to those of a national civil service.[2] At the top, there are senior officials with duties which are partly administrative, but partly political appraisal and advice. There are the Under-Secretaries-General, who, in the UN, may run whole 'departments' (say legal affairs, peace-keeping operations or administration and budget and so on). They act as the right-hand men of the Secretary-General in their own particular field. There are those who prepare the wide variety of factual and background reports required in the many different committees and other bodies of the UN: the preparation of these reports not only requires a great deal of expertise and highly detailed research (on such diverse questions, for example, as political and economic developments in the Solomon islands, the world protein situation, compliance with the Declaration on the Elimination of Racial Discrimination in all member states, the mineral resources of the sea-bed or the traffic in narcotic drugs) but often the exercise of delicate and balanced political judgement. Then there are the very large numbers who are employed simply in servicing the meetings, not only of the Assembly and the Council, but of the many committees and conferences that meet all through the year all over the world on innumerable subjects. These include the clerks who take the record and service the meetings, secretaries, the translators needed to translate every document issued, amounting to hundreds of thousands a year, into several different languages, those who copy and distribute the documents, and the interpreters in several languages who provide their highly skilled services for all these meetings. There are the administrative officials who undertake the large volume of correspondence going in and out of the UN every day. And there are the many undertaking far more humdrum jobs: typists, guides, guards, messengers and others.

Then there are large numbers engaged on the economic side. Here, in addition to the same administrative services as for the political bodies, large numbers with special economic or statistical skills are required for the assessment of projects, for the formulation of programmes, for the negotiation with governments concerning those programmes, for studying world or regional economic problems, and many other functions. There are even more involved in similar capacities in the field: the UNDP resident representatives and their staffs in the capitals, those involved in the implementation of particular projects, the advisers who may be travelling round lecturing or talking to farmers, giving technical advice, or installing equipment, in every country covered. Here too there are those who have to prepare the large number of detailed factual reports that are issued every year in the economic field: for example the highly detailed statistical reports covering innumerable aspects of the activities of every government, the annual reports prepared on many individual subjects, the world economic surveys produced every year by the UN, and the surveys of individual industries and regions prepared either in New York or by the Regional Commissions.

Next, there are a large number involved in information work for the UN, seeking to create greater understanding for the UN's activities. There are nearly 70 information offices scattered all over the world. These hold UN records and reports available for reference and study, and seek to contact and service the mass media in the countries they cover, as well as the public. Much of this information work must be regarded as ineffective, if success is measured by the amount of coverage given to the UN in the newspapers and television services of the world (which is virtually none), or the degree of public interest in the UN. Many efforts have been made to remedy this situation. A committee, including public relations experts, was set up in Hammarskjöld's day and recommended changes which he then largely ignored. Such attempts at reform always come up against the difficulty that every piece of material which these offices prepare must be carefully sterilised against all political bias. For this reason they are usually totally insipid and colourless to read. The UN has a prose style of its own which is among the most graceless yet devised. Only if journalists, rather than UN officials, were more often used in information work to give its publications more kick, might they acquire greater impact. The supreme administrative division of the UN Secretariat is the office of the Secretary-General himself and the heads of department. This structure became very complex and drew complaints that the Organisation was top-heavy. When Boutros-Ghali became Secretary-General he initiated a slimming down restructuring (see p.176).

There are also a number of miscellaneous agencies run by the UN. One is the field service, established in 1949, and responsible for running services for UN missions of various kinds abroad. There are the observer teams which are sent to supervise various areas and cease-fire lines. There are the two refugee organisations; the Regional Economic Commissions; and the UN Institute for Training and Research. There is the posts and telegraph system which is organised by the UN for its own highly voluminous communications; the publishing service; the office of general services, with its own contracts section and purchase and transportation service; a large and expensive library which is scarcely ever used, and much else. There is even a school run in New York for the children of UN personnel there.

At the head of this whole pyramid is the Secretary-General himself. And it is to his role that we should now turn.

THE SECRETARY-GENERAL

When the UN was established, it was always intended that the Secretary-General should play a more prominent role than the Secretary-General of the League. Some wished him to be a kind of super-statesman, a world conciliator and arbitrator. President Roosevelt believed he should be called the 'World's Moderator', who would seek to mediate all the great conflicts that arose. And many others felt that he should at least be given greater powers of initiative than the somewhat anonymous League Secretary-General had had.

For this reason the Secretary-General of the new organisation was provided with a new authority: the power himself to raise matters which he thought should receive the attention of the Organisation. Under Article 99 of the Charter, the Secretary-General was enabled to 'bring to the attention of the Security Council any matter which in his opinion may threaten the maintenance of international peace and security'. He was to be a sort of watchdog, who would be on guard for situations that might *lead* to violence or war (as well as those which had already reached this stage), and wake his masters up to them, demanding what action was to be taken. Subsequently, under the Rules of Procedure of the Assembly, he was also given the right to put an item on to the agenda of the Assembly or to 'make either oral or written statements to the General Assembly concerning any question under consideration by it'. In this way he acquired the right of initiative, both in the Security Council and the Assembly. In addition to this, he was to perform 'such other functions as are entrusted to him' by the Assembly, the Security Council or other councils of the Organisation (Article 98): although in practice those organs have not conferred on him any new *general* powers not provided for in the Charter, they have entrusted innumerable particular tasks to him: the establishment of committees on particular topics, the preparation of reports, the despatching of missions, the organisation of peace-keeping forces, and so on. Finally, under Article 98, the Secretary-General 'shall make an annual report to the General Assembly on the work of the organisation'; and all Secretaries-General have used this authority to make constructive, and sometimes controversial, proposals to the Organisation on its future work.

The history of the office during the United Nations period is one of ever-increasing caution in its use: a caution that has been forced on the occupants, whatever their own views, by political factors within the Organisation. When the first Secretary-General was to be appointed, many thought that the best choice would be the Belgian statesman, P.-H. Spaak, who would certainly have interpreted the role in an active way.

But he was entirely unacceptable to the communist countries because of his forthright and well-known anti-communist views. Lester Pearson was another strong contender. Eventually, as a compromise between the Western powers and the Soviet Union, the Norwegian, Trygve Lie, was chosen.

He showed himself an active, courageous and imaginative Secretary-General, who played the role as many thought it should be played. But he did not always show the tact and discretion which is essential to anybody entrusted with this delicate appointment. As a former politician, he had strong views of his own on many subjects, which he did not hesitate to express. He was regarded by some as having shown a pro-Israeli attitude during the war of 1948, when he would have liked to see stronger UN action to assist the new state against the intervention of the Arab countries. He was a powerful and persuasive champion of the idea of a UN guard, which might have been used to garrison Jerusalem, Trieste, or other disputed areas. And he called strongly in 1950–51 for the transfer of the China seat to Communist China, and even travelled round the world's capitals seeking to achieve this. In these and other matters, he was generally pursuing a legitimate aim for a Secretary-General: that is, calling for a strong and broadly representative UN. But since all of these were contentious issues, inevitably he was accused of taking sides (indeed both sides). And while he won the praise of some for his outspokenness and firmness, he won the hostility of others for officiousness or wrong-headedness.

The action which won him the greatest hostility, and ultimately made his position untenable, was perhaps the one which had the greatest justification: his support for the decision of the Security Council, taken by an overwhelming majority, and so reasonably regarded as the considered view of the Organisation, to call for member-states to go to the defence of South Korea when she was attacked in June 1950. By his outspoken support for that decision, and his help in organising the UN effort in Korea, he won the undying hostility of the Soviet Union and her allies (which claimed the entire UN action there was unlawfully authorised). They accused the Secretary-General of acting on behalf of the US and her friends against the communist states. They also claimed, with more reason, that the Uniting for Peace resolution introduced immediately afterwards[3] was an illegal violation of the Charter, which the Secretary-General should have prevented from being passed. They accordingly vetoed his nomination for a further term in February 1951. This veto was evaded for a time by a device: the Assembly (without the normal recommendation from the Council) 'continuing him in office' for a period of three years rather than re-electing him (another move of dubious legality). But the Soviet Union and her allies refused to have anything to do with him. They insulted and ignored and boycotted him. By this time some in the US too were critical of him for allowing alleged 'pro-communist' Americans to work in the Secretariat, and for appearing to resist attempts by the US government to control his choice of staff. His failure in fact to resist US interference during the McCarthyite period of 'communist witch-hunting' led to a certain collapse of morale among the internationally-minded staff at head-quarters.[4] In consequence of his growing impotence, at the end of 1952 Lie resigned altogether, even though his extended term had not yet expired.

He was succeeded, after a considerable search for a suitable successor, again by a compromise candidate, Dag Hammarskjöld, previously Director-General of the Swedish Foreign Ministry. Though virtually unknown at the time, he became the preferred candidate of almost all groups. When he was finally elected, only one vote was cast against him.

Hammarskjöld from the beginning conducted himself with considerably greater discretion and tactical finesse than Lie had done. He avoided making outspoken statements on controversial subjects. Indeed he made few public statements at all. Those he did make were obscured in such calculated ambiguity of language that it was almost impossible for anyone to take offence (and indeed sometimes difficult to know exactly what he meant). He was skilful in finding the appropriate fig-leaf of constitutional respectability for actions which he had decided to take in any case. He sought when possible to obtain clear authority from the Security Council (or sometimes from the Assembly) for such actions, but reserved the right (based usually on Article 99) to take initiatives of his own: as in appointing personal representatives to visit particular countries, for example, in Laos and Guinea.

But the main reason why the Secretary-General came to fulfil a far more active role at this time was not any particular attributes which he himself possessed. It was that there was a deliberate effort among many members to make use of his good offices in a number of cases where the political bodies of the UN were deadlocked, or needed to delegate authority. At first the commissions given him were relatively uncontroversial. He was successful in securing the release from China of US airmen who were imprisoned there in 1955 (he was fortunate in that this was the moment when the Chinese government was more conciliatory to the outside world than at any other for the next fifteen years). He was asked to tour the Middle East early in 1956 and recommend measures to calm the situation. After the nationalisation of

the Suez Canal in 1956, he organised private meetings between the chief
parties to the dispute, and came near to securing agreement in them.
Finally, after three of the countries most involved in these discussions
launched their attack on Egypt at the end of October, 1956, he was
given a still wider role: when the Canadian proposal to set up a UN
peace-keeping force had been accepted, he was asked to make the
necessary arrangements for it. Accordingly, he assembled the force and
undertook the difficult negotiations with Egypt on the terms on which
it would be accepted and on its composition. He subsequently
negotiated a status of forces agreement with the Egyptian government, and made the corresponding arrangements with the governments
who provided the forces, including agreements on the way that they
would be used. Throughout this operation he was skilful in retaining
the goodwill of the membership of the Organisation as a whole, by
consulting closely with a committee of the Assembly set up to guide
him. This in fact had little power, but gave the membership an illusory
feeling that the Secretary-General was being kept under their
supervision.

From this time, for the next few years, 'leave it to Dag' became the
watchword for many members of the Council and the Assembly. In
1958, when a new crisis broke out in the Lebanon, and an observer
force had to be organised, it was natural to ask the Secretary-General
once again to take responsibility. Over Jordan later that year, he
appointed his own representative to remain in the area and keep an
eye on the situation. Over Laos in 1959, he personally acted, without
authority, after visiting the country, to appoint a representative,
nominally to advise on the economic situation in that country, but in
reality to keep him informed of all developments which might
threaten its integrity from without or within, so that he might, if
necessary, call for further UN action. Finally, over the Congo in 1960,
by explicitly involving Article 99, he secured the authority to organise
the despatch of a peace-keeping force; and once again he and his
representatives were involved in the difficult and delicate task of
negotiating with the host government on the terms on which the force
was to stay and the task which it was to undertake. In this case the
situation was even more difficult than in the Middle East, both
because it was not always easy to know what was the government of
the Congo at any particular time, and because the task for which the
force became finally responsible – restoring the authority of the
central government throughout the country – was one that was
politically highly controversial.

It was because of the difficulties of this particular task that Hammarskjöld finally found himself, like his predecessor, playing a more active and committed role than his exposed position would easily allow him to undertake. In fulfilling his duties he and his officers were obliged at one point or another to decide, among other things, which among the contending factions was the effective and legal government of the country; and this choice could never have pleased all members of the UN simultaneously. Although he tried to obtain authority from the Security Council for all important decisions, it was impossible to do it for all the innumerable administrative acts which had to be undertaken throughout the Congo operation. Especially where the political organs were themselves unable to reach agreement, some active choice by the Secretary-General became inevitable. Some of Hammarskjöld's choices, and in particular his eventual recognition (in practice if not in theory) of Kasavubu and Mobutu, rather than Lumumba, as the effective authorities within the Congo by closing an airport to Lumumba's forces, aroused the undying hostility of the communist countries. As a result, like his predecessor, he found his position becoming increasingly untenable. Even if he had not been killed in an air crash in September 1961, it is possible that his useful role in the UN was at an end, and he might have had to suffer the same fate as his predecessor.

Certainly when U Thant, his successor, was appointed, he recognised that he must see his role in considerably more modest terms. By now, the Soviet government was demanding the adoption of an entirely new concept. There were no neutral men, so Mr Khrushchev declared, and therefore even the appointment of a 'neutral' Secretary-General was inadequate to preserve the Organisation's impartiality. In place of a single Secretary-General, therefore, there should be a 'troika'; three Secretaries-General appointed simultaneously, one representing the West, one the East, and the other non-aligned. Quite apart from the fact that the proposed system would have given an inflated share of power to the communist representative, who could have spoken for only a tenth of the membership, it was obviously unworkable since, where no action could be taken without agreement among the three, often no action would have been taken at all. Whether or not this was the object, effective UN activity would have been impossible. U Thant did on election appoint a carefully balanced group of under-secretaries, including representatives of different geographical groupings, which perhaps went a small distance to meeting the understandable desire, not confined to the communists, that influence in the top levels of the

Secretariat should be as widely and as fairly distributed as possible. But the troika proposal as a whole was overwhelmingly turned down.

After his predecessor's experience, U Thant inevitably found it necessary to act with circumspection. He felt he could not afford initiatives which would antagonise important groups in the UN. Even so, on issues on which he felt strongly he spoke out in impassioned terms. On Vietnam on a number of occasions he made statements strongly critical of US actions, and called for the withdrawal of all foreign troops. He did not bring the question to the Security Council under Article 99, no doubt because he feared that little progress would be made at such a meeting (Vietnam was eventually brought to the Council by the United States government, but without effect). Indeed U Thant never made use of his powers under Article 99, and virtually never spoke at a Security Council meeting, as his predecessors occasionally did. But he was often active behind the scenes. He set up special committees to consider particular questions, for example the effects of nuclear warfare, which had a significant impact on world opinion. He sent missions to East Malaysia and to Bahrain (without reference to the Security Council) to assess the wishes of the people in the area, and so help resolve territorial disputes which could otherwise have been a source of contention for many years.

It is by these latter means, the sending of a mission or a special representative, an occasional speech or statement, the setting up of a committee, that the Secretary-General exerts most influence.[5] In his annual report he has a regular opportunity of expressing his own views on a large number of subjects, both those relating to international affairs, and to the internal organisation of the UN. At the same time he is engaged in continuous consultation with national delegations to the UN, especially those to the Security Council, and can make proposals to them which are sometimes of considerable importance. And, as we have seen, there have been monthly lunches for the Security Council and such private occasions give him the opportunity to make his own views well known to delegates on a variety of subjects.

Because of the nature of his responsibilities, the UN Secretary-General is bound to come in for considerable criticism from one quarter or another. U Thant was heavily criticised for his decision to remove the UN force from Sinai, when this was demanded by President Nasser in 1967. In fact his freedom of action at that time was extremely limited. It had always been laid down that the force was present only with the consent of the host government. Many of the governments supplying the troops were already calling for them to be withdrawn.

Though possibly some delay could have been brought about by deliberate procrastination, this could scarcely have affected the final outcome; the only result might have been to cause UN forces to be swamped by the war (as it was they were fired on by Israeli forces). But the hostile comments this action evoked demonstrate the vulnerability of the Secretary-General, whatever policy he may decide on in crisis situations.

The Austrian Dr Kurt Waldheim (1972–81), who succeeded U Thant, was in office when Third World and environmental issues forced themselves to the forefront of the Organisation's attention: the Stockholm Conference was held and the concept of a New International Economic Order was formulated at this time. In addition to such perennial problems as Cyprus and the Middle East, the issues of nuclear disarmament and Namibia became more critical and the USA quarrelled bitterly with Iran. On all these matters Waldheim made personal interventions. He appeared to many observers to be the typical, courteous diplomat. Indeed, he was so considerate to so many powers that he was the only Secretary-General to have been considered for a third term in office. However, behind the scenes a very different personality was evident: ambitious vanity laced with a violent temper. These traits led to corruption and demoralisation within the Secretariat. And when his wartime Nazi activites were later revealed, the UN seemed retrospectively tainted.

The Peruvian diplomat, Javier Pérez de Cuéllar, who succeeded Waldheim, was a distinct contrast: soft-spoken and with deeply sensitive aesthetic tastes. He had to try to cope with sudden eruptions of military action at both the beginning and end of his two terms of office: the Argentine invasion of the Falklands Islands and the Iraqi invasion of Kuwait. Throughout most of the decade he also had the administrative worry of the UN's virtual bankruptcy because of non-payment by several members, notably the USA and USSR. Nor was he an efficient administrator by inclination. However, by encouraging more flexible forms of UN diplomacy he helped to ease the problems of the Iraq–Iran war, Afghanistan and Namibia. Pérez de Cuéllar was succeeded by the Egyptian Dr Boutros Boutros-Ghali (see pp.175–6).

By the nature of his office the Secretary-General must be a solitary figure. It is almost impossible for him to appear right in the eyes of all UN members. Either excessive activity or inactivity may be equally criticised. He must be politician, diplomat and civil servant in one. It is thus an office that it is impossible to fulfil to the satisfaction of all.

THE STAFF

The most difficult question that arises concerning an international Secretariat (and this includes the specialised agencies as well as the UN proper) is how its staff shall be chosen. Article 101 of the Charter lays down that 'the paramount consideration in the employment of the staff and in the determination of the conditions of service shall be the necessity of securing the highest standards of efficiency, competence and integrity'. This seems to imply that employment shall be mainly on the basis of merit. But the same Article then goes on: 'Due regard shall be paid to the importance of recruiting the staff from as wide a geographical basis as possible'. This introduces a second principle: now usually known as 'equitable geographical distribution' (a phrase that does not occur in the Charter). Even so, the Article as a whole seems to imply that efficiency is more important than geography. Unfortunately, the balance has increasingly been reversed: the second condition has often been taken as more important than the first. This principle even operates at the highest level. It is quite possible, for example, that the elderly Boutros-Ghali would not have been chosen in 1991 were it not for the insistent arguments of the African countries that it was the turn of their continent to fill the post.

It is useless simply to bewail this trend. It is inevitable that there must be strong demands, from all quarters, that the Organisation should maintain a balance of staff roughly corresponding to the balance among the membership as a whole (as we saw, the same demand occurred in League days). In the early years, recruitment took place, predominantly in West Europe and America: partly because these anyway then represented a considerable proportion of the membership, partly because applications came chiefly from there (the Soviet Union and other communist countries did not want representation then) and partly because much of the staff of the League had come from these countries.

When large numbers of new members came in, this was no longer acceptable. But by now there was already a full staff, mainly recruited for life. Though the total required increased with time, the number of vacancies was not sufficient to establish the new balance then needed. Developing countries which had been members from near the beginning were of course strongly represented, since they had been offered many posts in the early days to counterbalance the predominance of the West. These countries, such as India, Egypt and some Latin American countries also had a considerable number of qualified personnel. But the newer countries, though understandably anxious to be given their full share of places, in many cases had few sufficiently competent administrators to be able to spare the best easily from their home administrations. Those they did send were not always of the highest quality (though some are excellent). This still further complicated the task of creating an acceptable balance.

In 1948 the system was established under which each state was given a 'desirable range' governing the number of its nationals to be employed in the Secretariat. The range was based on the budgetary assessment, which in turn was governed by population, national income and other factors: this means of course that richer countries have a larger quota. A permissible variation of 25 per cent above or below this figure was allowed, but any country contributing more than 10 per cent of the budget was not allowed to go above its exact proportionate figure. This applied in the first place to the United States and the United Kingdom, and later only applied to the United States and the Soviet Union. From 1962 the Assembly altered the formula for calculating the number of staff members for which each member state was eligible. Every country was given a minimum range of one to six posts. Population was given a greater weight than before in proportion to national income. This had the effect of increasing the quota available to Afro-Asian and Latin American countries, and reducing it for East and West Europe and for North America. These principles applied to over two thousand professional posts within the Secretariat.[6] Technical staff, translators, clerical and secretarial staffs are engaged without reference to nationality.

As a result of these developments, the first consideration today is sometimes to get somebody of the right nationality rather than get the right person for the job. The nationals of many states are virtually excluded from consideration, because they are already over-represented. Others are eagerly sought. It remains at least in theory an essential condition that a successful candidate should possess the right qualifications to match up to the job. But in practice inevitably standards have declined. Some governments from developing countries are reluctant to spare their best people and sometimes even send the throw-outs from their home or foreign services.[7]

To ask, as is sometimes asked, that the UN should recruit without regard to nationality is to cry for the moon. Under-represented countries will always be concerned to achieve their fair share of Secretariat posts and, if Britain or other Western countries were in that position, they would do the same. The proper subject for complaint is not that this demand is made: it is that those countries which seek better representation do not always produce candidates adequate for the jobs concerned. There is no ground, in other words, for the belief, often put forward in discussion of this subject, that fair geographical distribution and efficiency are always *alternatives*. There are plenty of able people in developing countries. The difficulty is that they are not always those who apply for, or are recommended for, UN posts.

If the situation is to be improved, three things are essential. One is that the UN Office of Personnel should consistently insist on the very highest standards in recruitment, and should not be prepared to relax them for the sake of obtaining required nationalities.[8] A second is that the UN should offer pay and conditions which are sufficient to attract the best candidates: contrary to a widely held belief, this is not always the case, especially in the junior grades, for which most recruitment is made. Yet many of the countries which are most insistent on the need for high standards are those which most consistently oppose higher salaries: the US and some other Western countries proposed an amendment at the 1970 session of the General Assembly to reduce a suggested increase in salaries, though this itself was barely sufficient to keep up with rises obtained elsewhere. The final requirement is that the Secretariat should in all cases demand a choice, and if possible a wide choice, of candidates for all jobs that become vacant.

Another problem concerns how much influence, if any, governments should have over the appointment of their nationals. Ideally, it was hoped, recruitment should be direct, and entirely uninfluenced by the views of governments. The Preparatory Commission of the UN, which examined the problem of establishing the Secretariat, explicitly rejected, by a large majority, a proposal that appointments to the Secretariat should require the concurrence of the governments of the candidates concerned (an idea that had the support of the Soviet Union and a number of other governments). This was a vital point of principle. Once the idea of concurrence, or even of influence, of governments over appointments is introduced, the suspicion arises that the candidates supported may remain in some way under their influence in working for the Secretariat. Unfortunately it has proved impossible to avoid some degree of influence by governments over appointments. Mr Lie acknowledged that, while he himself took the final decision, he would seek the assistance of governments in checking the records and characters of applicants.

A more sinister type of influence by governments comes in the form of pressure to ensure the *dismissal* of their nationals, of whatever seniority, who are already in the employment of the UN. During the McCarthy period in the US there were accusations that US citizens in the service of the UN had been involved in subversive activity against the United States. These accusations were investigated by the Internal Security Sub-Committee of the Senate Judiciary Committee; and when some of those accused exercised their right to refuse to answer some questions, there were demands that the government should ensure their dismissal from the UN. Mr Lie argued against direct interference of this kind, but he accepted that nobody should serve the Secretariat if there was evidence that they engaged in subversive activity against their own or another state and relied heavily on evidence provided by the US government. The UN would not, however, base action against any of its employees simply on the wish of the state concerned, but would undertake its own investigation and reach its own decisions on such matters.

In theory the Secretary-General has a considerable degree of discretion in the appointment and method of recruitment of staff: he alone is responsible under the Charter. Appointments do not, as in the League, require to be approved by the Council or by any political body. But in practice his discretion has often been hedged about by the pressures of governments, and there is need for vigilance to ensure that this does not lead to the idea that members of the Secretariat are sent to represent their own countries in the same way that governmental representatives are sent to the United Nations for that purpose.

Where the Secretary-General does retain complete discretion is in determining the structure and organisation of the Secretariat and especially its top stratum, the Under-Secretaries who advise him. Because of the range and complexity of the activities of the UN, and the difficulties for the Secretary-General in maintaining a close eye on all of them, these top officials have considerable influence. It is understandable that there is considerable competition among member-states for posts of this kind and they are in fact shared out among states and regions. Lie organised the Secretariat into departments, under eight Assistant Secretaries-General and a number of high-ranking Directors. The system was first reviewed in 1952. Lie then had it in mind to establish three top posts of Deputy Secretary-General, to take charge of Political and Public Affairs (including Public Information), Economic and Social Affairs, and Administration and Conference Services. This idea had a considerable logic, though it would be difficult to find satisfactory allocation of the three posts which did not either discriminate in favour of the superpowers or against them.

Hammarskjöld, however, had views of his own about administration. He appointed thirteen officials with the rank of Under-Secretary-General in the UN building in New York, including the Legal Counsel, the Controller (the chief finance officer of the Organisation) and the Director of Personnel. But he merged the departments of economic and social affairs under a single head.

From 1960, with the Soviet proposals for a troika, there was increasing controversy about the organisation of the top of the Secretariat and some support for the idea of a sub-troika: three Deputy Secretaries-General representing the West, the East and the non-aligned world. Hammarskjöld favoured appointing five of his Under-Secretaries-General, on a broadly representative basis, to advise him on political matters. There were other proposals for six or even seven such advisers. U Thant, after being appointed Secretary-General, announced that he would appoint eight advisers, selected on a wide geographical basis, and said that he would consult them individually or collectively on important issues. Since then there has been some reorganisation at the top levels. In 1967, with the increase in senior posts, U Thant again divided them into two levels, with eleven Under-Secretaries-General and twenty-five Assistant Secretaries-General. He later added (against the advice of the Committee on the Reorganisation of the Secretariat) two posts to the former category. A new post of Under-Secretary-General for Administration and Management was created to supervise the departments of the Controller and of Personnel. At the same time the post of Chef de Cabinet was separated from that of Under-Secretary-General for Assembly affairs. In his turn, Boutros-Ghali again changed the structure of the top echelon of the Secretariat (see p.176).

Perhaps the biggest and most difficult problem confronting the Secretariat is one that is not in its own control. It is the proliferation of meetings, conferences, programmes, documentation and activities of every kind that are wished on to it by the political organs of the UN. We have already seen how some members of the UN believe that the calling of a conference, or the launching of a new study, in itself represents effective action. Responsibility for carrying out such proposals is placed on the Secretariat. The proliferation of activity creates another difficulty and danger for the Secretariat. The difficulty of maintaining standards is intensified by the perpetual addition to the services demanded by member-states.

A final problem concerns whether staff should be taken on for life, or for temporary engagements (usually from government service in their country of origin). On this question also the policy of the UN has changed. In the early days, almost all engagements were permanent. This was the system established in the League, and a system widely thought essential if a genuinely international civil service, composed of real 'international men', was to be created. Unfortunately, when the problem of geographical distribution arose, temporary secondments inevitably increased. Developing countries had only a few really able and trained administrators. They were reluctant to spare these for long. Thus they made it a condition that they should be released after, say, five years. This system did have the advantage of providing greater flexibility. In filling some gaps in this way it was easier to find posts for the newest members of all when necessary. Thus the proportion of seconded personnel has risen steadily. While there is obviously a need to have a career service, composed of people who have shed their own nationality and devoted themselves fully to the international service, this is not likely to cover the whole of the staff for some considerable time.

There are indeed some kinds of post for which short-term recruitment is an entirely suitable policy. This applies particularly in the field of technical and economic personnel, for which sometimes the requirement is fluctuating. Apart from this, there may be value in interchange between the academic world, business or national government and the international civil service. There are some people who even advocate that short-term recruitment should become the general rule, since it has the effect of spreading a knowledge of the UN, and devotion to its purposes, more widely throughout a population. However, short-term recruitment is often applied to some of the posts where it seems least suitable: for example, as we saw, the most senior posts in the Secretariat have been distributed largely on a geographical basis and are filled by most governments by short-term appointments from their own government service rather than from within the Secretariat, even though they may have very able people available there.[9] This is a deplorable habit, which means that, just where UN officials should be least liable to political pressures, or the accusation of it, they are in fact most so. It is also damaging to the morale of senior permanent members of the Secretariat who are denied the most senior posts.[10]

Though the organisation of the Secretariat is supposed to be within the responsibility of the Secretary-General alone, the membership does sometimes seek to exercise influence on such questions. A committee was set up in 1961 to look at the organisation of the senior levels of the

Secretariat: this was largely a response to the Soviet proposal for a troika, and in fact nothing ever came of its recommendations. In 1967 a more wide-ranging survey was undertaken by a small but broadly-balanced Committee on the Organisation of the Secretariat.[11] This recommended a considerable decentralisation of responsibilities and staff. Housing, transport, resources and tourism, as well as local co-ordination and evaluation were to be delegated largely to the regional economic commissions. Better staff development and training should be introduced, more mobility among existing staffs, quicker promotion for the able officials and earlier retirement. The committee wanted regular meetings of the economic Under-Secretaries and a budget review committee under the Secretary-General, to establish guidelines for limiting expenditure by each unit. Of these proposals the last was almost the only one which was accepted relatively quickly by the Secretary-General. All this shows how difficult it is to introduce rapid changes within an international bureaucracy, but it may be as well that the Secretary-General is not subjected to too much external pressure on such matters. Most recently, the Group of 18, set up by the General Assembly, made detailed proposals for many reforms in 1986. As a result the top level of the Secretariat was restructured (see pp.175–6).

The staffs of the UN and the agencies are in certain respects integrated. Although people do not normally move from one organisation to another, there is supposed to be a 'common system': that is to say, common standards of pay, allowances, promotion, pensions and some other matters. The system is more common in theory than in practice,[12] but there exists a Consultative Committee for Adminstrative Questions (CCAQ), with representatives of the UN and all the agencies, to seek uniformity on matters of pay, grading and so on. There is a Joint Staff Pension Board. And there is an International Civil Service Advisory Board (ICSAB), which examines from time to time subjects that are of general concern to all the Secretariats, such as staff–management relations, pensions and so on.

The larger agencies (WHO, ILO, UNESCO, FAO) have their own business efficiency units (usually management units or divisions) designed to ensure each division is accorded a clearly defined task and employs the most efficient methods in the use of staff. Occasionally they commission outside management studies (as the ILO did, for example, by McKinsys). And some radical changes were made in UNESCO by the new Director-General, Dr Mayor, following the crisis of the American and British withdrawal from the organisation in the mid-1980s. In 1968, as a result of a recommendation of the Committee on the Organisation of the Secretariat, the UN too established an Administrative Management Service, under the new Under-Secretary for Administration and Management (since 1992, Administration and Budget). This undertakes systematic surveys on a desk-by-desk basis, of the entire Secretariat to study 'man-power utilisation and deployment' and ensure the best possible standards of efficiency. It also undertakes management surveys on a wider basis: organisational studies and reviews of administrative procedures, career development and other matters. The Joint Inspection Unit of the UN family also examines the efficiency of particular units or operations throughout the UN system. Finally, a system of management auditing has been introduced by which the auditors comment on and criticise administrative as well as financial procedures.

CONCLUSIONS

There are obvious differences between the role of the bureaucracy in international government and at national levels. The authority of the Secretary-General, or of the executive head of an agency, is much greater than that of his opposite number in national service. This is primarily because in international government there exists nothing which corresponds to the minister, the political head of the department who gives guidance to policy, and reaches the ultimate decisions. Such guidance and decision making, in so far as it is given at all, comes from intergovernmental bodies, the Assembly and the Council. But these meet only infrequently, and for much of the time the executive head is in sole control. Moreover, like national bureaucrats, the Secretariat are able to find many different ways of manipulating and managing the political bodies, persuading them to decide what the Secretariat had decided they should decide: in the words of one writer, of practising the delicate art of 'making policy without appearing to do so'.[13] In a way, therefore, the executive head or Secretary-General is himself a minister of a kind, rather than a bureaucrat, and one of a kind unchecked by outside bodies. For while a minister has a cabinet and a parliament, not to speak of a press and public opinion, to keep him in order, the executive head of an agency is mainly free of these constraints, and can to a large degree go his own way according to his own judgement for much of the time. Indeed the degree of personal power deployed by these heads is one cause of the malaise and restlessness which has existed among some staff of these organisations, who might be less constrained if there were some political body which took more interest in staff conditions.[14]

Moreover, the executive head is often able to expand the activities of his organisation and to expand his own power in a way that a national civil servant is never able to do. He is, for example, responsible for preparing the budget and proposing the expenditure for the following year. But this is very much a political act: and though the executive head is supposed to act within the terms of policy guidelines already reached in the political bodies, in practice he enjoys considerable discretion, both in the amount for which he asks, and in its distribution. His authority, in engaging and dismissing staff, and in deciding the internal organisation of the agency, which is almost unlimited, differentiates his position radically from that of even the most powerful bureaucrat at the national level. In addition, a Secretary-General has often quite consciously sought to expand his role: Hammarskjöld, when he was re-elected in 1957, declared quite openly that he considered it 'his duty to use his office, indeed, the machinery of the organisation, to its utmost capacity and to the full extent permitted at each stage by practical circumstances'. As one writer has suggested, 'the executive head is in the key position to maximise . . . opportunities, in other words to interpret the input pressures in such a way as to bring about an expansion of the tasks and of the authority of the organisation'.[15]

There is a third feature of the role of the bureaucracy in international government which differentiates it from that on national level. Not only do they suffer less supervision from the political bodies than their opposite numbers, but the supervision they do undergo is of a far more unsatisfactory kind. For instead of having to serve a central government composed, normally, of a homogeneous party and a recognised political philosophy and programme, whose wishes can be relatively easily understood (whether or not agreed with), they serve a body of 175 governments of widely differing viewpoints and policies, often wholly unpredictable in their decisions. This makes his task far harder: just as a national civil servant prefers a minister with a firm hand and a clear policy to one of uncertain aim, so the international civil servant would find life easier if clear-cut decisions could more easily be extracted from his masters. Between meetings of his Council, it is not easy for him to take any positive action without the danger that he will offend some powerful member-state. But in the longer term this situation strengthens his position: precisely because the political bodies are so divided, uncertain, and above all disorganised, the bureaucrat is left relatively free and can much more easily manipulate them to adopt the positions which he favours.

Traditionally, Western observers have tended to defend the high degree of personal authority accorded to the executive heads in the UN system, and especially the UN Secretary-General. But, if that system is to become better organised, there is a strong case for saying that some more effective political supervision of the activities of the secretariats is required. Since the Assemblies are clearly not capable of this, even if they met more frequently, this role should be performed by the Councils: in the case of the UN mainly by ECOSOC. To do this the Councils need to meet more frequently and to be more continuously involved in the affairs of the organisation concerned. There is everything to be said for according the Secretary-General the maximum possible freedom in *raising* issues, drawing them to the attention of the relevant bodies; and it is arguable that all the UN Secretaries-General should have made more use of their special right under Article 99(2). It is less certain that he should exercise the same degree of freedom in initiating *action*, except in questions where he is clearly proceeding within the terms of a general authority which has been given earlier. Perhaps eventually the councils, both in the UN and in the agencies, will evolve into something like genuine cabinets in their own fields, formulating policies and programmes, providing guidelines for Secretariat action and supervising their execution as cabinets do within states.[16]

Even if such changes were made, the top ranks of the international civil service would still wield a unique influence within each organisation. Though they must be cautious about exceeding their powers, or taking initiatives which may offend particular members or groups of members, they can, if they act discreetly and deferentially, significantly alter the direction of activity of the organisation concerned. They are constantly in touch with the permanent delegations of member-states and influence them behind the scenes with the special authority which they possess. It is said that at one time the Secretariat 'drafted roughly 30 per cent of the resolutions' at an Assembly session and 'had a hand in most all of them':[17] this is certainly not so today, but they are still often consulted, especially on less political questions. They issue annual reports, which sometimes chart the course ahead for the coming year, and they institute organisational changes, or commission expert studies which ultimately have a considerable effect on the organisation's methods or policies.

Doubts have been expressed on how far anyone can ever become in the proper sense an 'international man'. Was Mr Khrushchev right in saying there can be no neutral man, only neutral nations? It is possibly true, as is sometimes claimed, that somebody who has firmly based roots in his homeland may be better balanced in judgement and more able to play a more useful part than the wrong person from a neutral state or the rootless cosmopolitan who has truly cast off every link with his home country on entering into international service. But there is inevitably a tendency, however illogical, to identify the individual with the country from which he comes. So the Secretary-General could not come fom a major power. But in the period of the cold war a Scandinavian could have been pro-Western and a Briton or Frenchman quite impartial. To suggest, as Mr Khrushchev did, that nobody can really be trusted to act impartially and to shake off his national loyalties in international service is to take altogether too cynical a view, which countless examples of the past amply disprove.

The influence of each Secretariat will anyway normally remain relatively neutral only from the fact that it is a mixture of many nationalities. Very often that influence reflects the general institutionalised view of the organisation as a whole; just as government departments within national governments acquire strong attitudes and traditions reflecting their departments' purposes, which are shared by most of their officials, regardless of political sympathies. So there comes to be an ILO view or a WHO view, which becomes increasingly independent of that of its members, or even of individual members of the staff.

Probably the biggest problem facing all these organisations is that of morale among their staffs. The high idealism and sense of purpose of the early days of the UN has been followed by a sense of uncertainty and frustration among many of the staff, which in a few cases, as in UNESCO, has erupted in almost open rebellion. There are a number of causes. There is the problem inherent in all large organisations: the sense of being a tiny cog in a huge machine. This is intensified by the special difficulty of multinational organisations, the lack of a common language or tradition. There are the uncertain career structure, poor promotion prospects, a lack of positive personnel management in many cases, and capricious political leadership. These problems have been looked at a number of times. What seems to be necessary is more rapid promotion in the early years, more mobility among the departments and agencies, more senior posts for career officials, better training facilities, greater use of career planning and modern personnel management techniques, more chance for staff at all levels to discuss policy questions and much greater interest in staff problems among the political bodies. Higher standards of recruitment and the introduction of probation alone would do much to remedy the malaise, since at present some of the ablest members of staff are having to carry passengers on their shoulders. An intersessional Assembly Committee could keep a permanent watch on staff matters. A UN staff college, as proposed in the Jackson report, taking over some training responsibilities, would also be valuable, at least as a final goal, and might help to instil a greater sense of purpose and group loyalty among Secretariat staffs.

The international civil service performs a task of great delicacy and complexity, requiring diplomatic as much as administrative skills. Their situation is different from that of national civil servants because, instead of serving a government composed of members of a single party sharing single and clearly defined aims, they serve an organisation of diffuse aims whose members have often radically conflicting ideas, not only on political objectives in general but about the role and structure of the organisation itself, and especially about the limits of its powers. It is more like serving a coalition government made up of 175 political parties of diametrically conflicting political views. Their own faith in the value of the tasks which the organisation performs becomes then almost the only solid foundation on which they can build their activities.

Given the difficulties of their position, and the problem of working in several languages with staffs of many different nationalities, they fulfil that role with considerable success. Their deficiencies, which undoubtedly exist, might be lessened if more conscious attention was devoted to their problems.

FURTHER READING

S. Bailey, *The Secretariat of the UN* (London, 1964).
J. R. Bingham, *U Thant: the Search for Peace* (New York, 1967).
Carnegie Endowment, *The United Nations Secretariat* (New York, 1950).
L. Gordenker, *The UN Secretary-General and the Maintenance of Peace* (New York, 1967).
D. Hammarskjöld, *The International Civil Servant in Law and in Fact* (Oxford, 1961).
S. Hazzard, *Countenance of Truth: The United Nations and the Waldheim Case* (London, 1991).

G. Langrot, *The International Civil Service: its Origins, its Nature and its Evolution* (New York, 1963).

J.P. Lash, *Dag Hammarskjöld* (London, 1962).

Trygve Lie, *In the Cause of Peace* (New York, 1954).

A. Loveday, *Reflections on International Administration* (Oxford, 1956).

R.I. Miller, *Dag Hammarskjöld and Crisis Diplomacy* (New York, 1961).

T. de Sa, *The Play within the Play: the Inside Story of the UN* (New York, 1967).

S.M. Schwebel, *The Secretary-General of the United Nations* (Harvard, 1952).

D. Steele, *The Reform of the United Nations* (Beckenham, 1987).

B. Urquhart, *Hammarskjöld* (New York, 1973).

T.C. Young, *The International Civil Service: Principles and Problems* (Brussels, 1958).

M. Zacher, *Dag Hammarskjöld's United Nations* (New York, 1970).

6 The Budgetary System: Finding the Money

In every system of government, some of the most difficult problems are those that concern money: the levying of revenues and the control of expenditure. Within national states the power of the purse has been recognised for long as one of the most basic political issues, disputed between king and parliament in Britain, between President and Congress in the USA, between different chambers of parliament elsewhere. Disputes over what taxes are to be raised, and how they are to be spent, remain today as fundamental as any in politics.

International government has produced similar problems. The basic questions have been essentially the same: how 'taxation', that is contributions to international organisations, should be raised and assessed (comparable to disputes within states over progressive or flat-rate taxation); how to ensure payment of the contributions after assessment (comparable to the problems of tax collection and tax evasion within states – though worse, since the international community has no absolute powers of compulsion); and how expenditure by such organisations can be adequately supervised and controlled by the membership (similar to the problems of effective parliamentary control of national expenditure).

All of these problems have become more difficult as the scale of spending by international government has risen. The UN budget, at first very modest, has multiplied several times and now exceeds one billion dollars a year. The increase has become progressively faster, especially with the rapid increase in field programmes. While expenditure for the regular budgets of the UN and the agencies together did not even double between 1950 and 1960 (rising from about $70 million to $130 million), between 1960 and 1970 they tripled (from $130 million to about $500 million). The budget of the UN itself, though it is the largest, at first showed the slowest and most steady rate of increase, but since 1970 has risen more rapidly to $2.13 billion for the biennium 1990–91.

The problem of financing international organisations arose first in the so-called 'public international unions' set up in the nineteenth century. These were such bodies as the Universal Postal Union and the International Telecommunications Union and other bodies concerned with health, narcotic drugs, patents and other matters. The process of assessment was then relatively primitive. In most, the responsibility for assessing and for collecting was placed on a particular supervising government, usually the host government. Because the total sums to be allocated were very small governments usually made little difficulty about payment, but the demands of national sovereignty had the effect that governments usually had to *agree* to be allocated to a particular category of contributors. The supervising government would help in this assessment, and was also responsible for the entire management of the finances of the union. The Swiss government, for example, took charge of the funds of the UPU and the ITU, supervised their expenditure, proposed a budget, and made advances of funds when necessary. Of all the pre-1914 unions, only the Pan-American Union, which had its headquarters in Washington, had a fully independent financial system, with its own Treasury and legal responsibility for its debts.[1]

When the League was founded, little thought was given at first to its financial arrangements. For a time it adopted the same seven-grade system used by the UPU. In 1942, however, a new system of assessment was introduced, in theory based upon capacity to pay. The assumption was made that the resources of a country must be devoted first to providing a minimum standard of living for its people. Accordingly population was multiplied by a minimum subsistence income to give this figure. This was then subtracted from total national income (in so far as that was accurately known) to calculate the assessment. However the system led to frequent disputes, and arrears were normal. There was no provision for suspension of voting rights or expulsion for a country in arrears, so there was little inducement to pay up. The League as a result found itself in perpetual financial difficulty, intensified by the same national distrust, and the same obsession with national sovereignty, which created so many political difficulties for the organisation.

Its total expenses were tiny. The average budget of the League, including all its social and economic activity, the ILO and the Permanent Court together, was only a little over $10 million a year on average. Yet governments made as much difficulty about agreeing the budget as if it had been a hundred times as large. The result was a perpetual paring and cutting of services, and a perpetual state of financial crisis. The economic and social programmes were starved of funds.[2] At times officials of the Secretariat had to offer voluntary cuts in salary. The ILO was occasionally unable even to pay for the publication of its reports.

The League also had difficulty in establishing a satisfactory system of financial control. During the early years there was a perpetual struggle between the Council and the Assembly to exercise control. The latter felt, not unreasonably, that since every new member had to contribute to the budget, all should have a share in formulating it: in other words it demanded no taxation without representation. Eventually, in 1924, the Covenant was amended to give the Assembly sole authority to control and apportion expenses. The system for examining the budget emerged from the Noblemaire Report of 1921. A budget first had to be agreed between the Treasurer and the Secretary-General; it was then scrutinised carefully by a Supervisory Committee; passed with the comments of the latter to member governments; then to the Assembly's Fourth Committee; and finally to the Assembly itself. This succession of scrutinies foreshadowed almost exactly the procedure later adopted by the UN. Because on such questions the unanimity rule of the League could have proved particularly harmful (since any government might have successfully challenged any item of expenditure proposed) there developed a convention that any item that had been agreed in committee (where the veto did not apply) would not be challenged again in the Assembly.

When the UN was founded, it took over, in this field as in so much else, a great deal of the system built up by the League. The UN also made the Assembly responsible for voting the budget and supervising expenditure. It also established a special committee of the Assembly, this time the Fifth, to be responsible for such matters. It also set up an expert body, comparable to the old Supervisory Committee, this time called the Advisory Committee for Administrative and Budgetary Questions (ACABQ).

In one respect, however, the UN learnt an important lesson from the League experience. The difficulty the League had had over arrears arose partly because of the lack of any sanctions against defaulters. The founders of the UN decided to establish a stricter system. It was provided in Article 19 of the Charter that a member in arrears 'shall have no vote in the General Assembly if the amount of its arrears equals or exceeds the amount of the contributions due from it for the preceding two years'. This wording seemed to imply that the loss of vote is *automatic*, and would be applied without any specific decision (though during the UN's financing crisis in 1962–5, the Soviet Union claimed that a vote was required, and that a two-thirds majority would be needed to carry the suspension). In any case only a vote in the Assembly is forfeited by non-payment of dues: the least valuable type of vote any member wields. Thus it appears, on a normal reading of the Article, that members could continue to vote indefinitely in the Security Council, ECOSOC, the functional commissions, and innumerable other forums where votes are more significant even when they had failed to pay their dues for many years.[3] In 1991, twelve, mainly poor, countries were in arrears under Article 19.

PROBLEMS OF ASSESSMENT

These are then the basic features of the financial system established in the UN. Let us now look at some of the chief problems which have emerged in their functioning. One of the major difficulties has inevitably concerned: who will pay how much? However strongly governments may wish to support international organisations (and not all do), none likes to think it is paying more than its fair share of the expenses, and it is therefore not surprising that there have been considerable disputes. These have concerned either the principles that have been adopted, or the way these have been applied.

It was decided at San Francisco not to attempt to lay down in the Charter the exact system for allocating contributions to be used. This was left for the first Assembly. At that Assembly it was decided to establish a Committee on Contributions to recommend the system to be used. This Committee accepted the proposal of the Advisory Group on Financial Questions set up by the Preparatory Committee of the UN that contributions should be based on capacity to pay; and this should be determined by national income, income per head, economic dislocation caused by the war, and ability to acquire foreign currency. But statistics of national income were either inadequate or unavailable. There was uncertainty how much account should be given respectively to each factor, especially to national income and income per head. Economic dislocation caused by the war was impossible to quantify. Above all there was the problem of the economic dominance of the US at that time.

According to the first assessment the US should have paid virtually 50 per cent of the budget (49.89 per cent). The US immediately protested at this high proportion, and sought to secure acceptance of a ceiling, or maximum proportion, to be borne by any particular nation.

Eventually a compromise was reached – the first of a whole series that gradually eroded the logic of the original system. The US proportion was reduced by an arbitrary figure of 10 per cent, so it became 39.89 per cent. Other contributions were adjusted upwards accordingly. But the US continued to protest at its high share, and in particular objected to the lower contributions of the Soviet Union and her allies (which benefited at that time from the provision relating to dislocation caused by the war). The US therefore asked for a ceiling, or maximum contribution for any state, of a third of the budget. There were good reasons for not making the Organisation too dependent on one country. And eventually, in 1957, a theoretical maximum of 30 per cent was adopted, though in practice it was still often exceeded. Much later in the early 1970s, this was reduced again, to 25 per cent.

This stimulated demands by other wealthy countries that they too should be given special consideration. Canada claimed that no country should be made to pay a higher contribution per head than the USA by the concession. In 1948, this principle too was adopted, so that the basic logic of the system was once again impaired.

These special privileges of the rich (which of course weakened the already partial application of the progressive principle) were accentuated by the adoption of a floor, as well as a ceiling, on contributions. It was laid down from the beginning that no country should pay less than 0.04 per cent of the total budget. This had the effect that poor countries paid more than they would otherwise have done. It was a lower floor than had been adopted elsewhere, for example, in the UPU, or the ITU, or the ILO. It has now been reduced, with the increase in membership to 0.01 per cent. The number of states in this minimum category in 1991 was 78. But it was effectively lower when it was adopted in 1946 than it is today, when there are more members, some still poorer states and much higher budgets. With the current budgets of the UN, the floor contribution can represent substantial sums, and a high proportion of national income for a very small state. In any case the effect of the floor was, once again, to counteract the logic of the basic system employed. For a substantial proportion of the membership the complex and carefully worked out principles embodied in the assessment scheme are not applied at all: they simply pay the floor rate. In practice what this means is that they pay more than they otherwise would. And in some cases it means that the highest rate in relation to national income is paid by the very poorest countries of all. Until quite recently the US contribution of 25

per cent was well below the true figure of its wealth as a percentage of
world GNP.

Some adjustments were made to make the system a little more
progressive. A special reduction of the assessed national income of all
countries with an income of less than $1000 a head was made. The
maximum reduction possible is 50 per cent, and the reduction is from 0
to 50 per cent according to the ratio of income a head to $1000: that is,
a country with an income of $500 a head would pay on 75 per cent of
its national income (it would get a half of the possible 50 per cent
reduction). This system was a real attempt to apply the progressive
principle. And it avoided the inequities of having a rigid division
between those who qualify and those who cannot. However, the poorer
60 per cent of countries, who were already on the floor, were
unaffected, so that the advantages of the scale were largely nullified.
And the value of the concession is reduced all the time with the
declining value of the dollar and the rise in national incomes.

This assessment system, despite all its disadvantages and illogical-
ities, remains largely the one in use in the UN today, having been
renewed virtually unchanged for successive three-year periods since
that time. The system is applied with some flexibility. The assessments
are reconsidered by the Committee on Contributions every three years.
This takes into account temporary difficulties (because of national
catastrophes for example). On occasions the Committee has made
'small downward adjustments' in the assessments of countries
experiencing special difficulties in servicing large overseas debts (a
criterion which could be applied to a large proportion of the
developing countries).

Of the principles originally laid down, no account is any longer taken
of dislocation caused by the war. So far as the difficulty of acquiring
foreign exchange is concerned, the main way of meeting this has been
to allow some flexibility in the currency in which contributions are
made. In the original plans for the UN, it was accepted that
contributions should be paid, and accounts kept, in the currency of
the host country (not then known). But the choice of the US as host
country created special problems owing to the universal dollar shortage
in the post-war years. Although the difficulty of finding foreign
exchange was not embodied in the assessment scale, it was proposed
that the Secretariat should be prepared to accept other currencies when
it could make use of them. The scope for this was limited at first, but a
number of developments have eased the situation. UN activities all

over the world make it possible for the Secretariat to accept alternative currencies much more freely.

The system as it has evolved seems to work (in the sense that it has not caused great dispute). But it is complex and obscure. The use of the ceiling and the floor serve to prevent impossibly wide disparities in the proportions of the budget paid but increase inequalities in terms of income per head. And the scale as a whole is actively regressive: in general the poorer countries pay at a *higher* rate in relation to income a head than the richer countries. Even so, the three countries with the highest GNP (USA, Japan and Russia) pay nearly half the total, while the poorest 78 pay little more than three-quarters of one per cent.

Problems remain. There is inexorable pressure on the UN budget as demands for its services increase. Not only are states required to pay their basic 'membership' fee, other requests are occasionally made for supplementary contributions. For example, at the 'Earth Summit' in 1992 the case was put for substantial sums to be made available to protect the global environment; only Japan was really forthcoming, promising $7.7 billion over five years. At the same time, the relative ability of states to pay is likely to change as the US economy performs less well than those of some east Asian countries, and the poorest, especially African, states stagger beneath the burdens of debt and drought.

Anomalies are probably bound to remain. The original desire was to adopt a system related to capacity to pay. National income is a totally irrelevant factor here since it tells nothing of poverty. A fair scale would take account of two quite separate and unrelated factors: the size of the state, and its income per head. A system taking account of the first factor would be one based on population alone: each state would pay in relation to its size (so defined). This would obviously be a non-progressive system, in which the poorest country would be expected to make the same contribution as one of equal population ten times wealthier. To take account of capacity to pay in the second sense, the scale based on population would need to be adjusted to take account of income per head (not GNP). Alternatively, a formula might be devised under which the proportion of national income paid in UN contributions was related, in any desired proportion, to differences in wealth (income per head); for example, the proportion paid by the richest country might be double that paid by the poorest. Either of these would correspond more closely with the type of system used for direct taxation within most modern national states; and would be the most logically defensible and socially just. For example, by using the

GNP per capita criterion Russia would not be one of the top three contributors (see p.132). As budgets increase, and consciousness of their significance rises, there may be increasing demands for the adoption of a more rational system on these lines.

ENSURING PAYMENT OF CONTRIBUTIONS

Even if the problem of assessment was satisfactorily solved, there would remain another problem: that of securing payment by governments. In the early years, so far as the regular budget of the UN was concerned, this did not prove a major difficulty: far less than in the League, and less than most had foreseen. In general governments did not attempt to evade their obligation to pay assessed contributions, even for programmes which they had themselves opposed. The first main exception to this was that, after 1962, during the general crisis over peace-keeping and financing (see below, pp.135–8) the Soviet Union began to withhold payments for certain expenditure related to the Korean War, UNTSO, the UN field service, and so on, which had been placed on the regular budget and which she had paid until that time as part of her normal contributions, as well as her payments for the servicing of UN bonds. Since these items were part of the regular budget, this was a far more serious act by the Soviet Union (though less publicised) than her refusal to pay the costs of the peace-keeping operations themselves, which were contained in separate accounts. It amounted to a unilateral decision concerning what kind of expenses a member chose to pay. If they accumulated to a sufficient sum, they could create grounds for the application of Article 19 and the suspension of the Soviet Union's voting rights in the General Assembly.

It was perhaps the existence of Article 19, and the sanctions it contains, which accounted for the generally good record of UN members in paying their contributions until the mid-1980s. Occasionally poor and small member states have been in arrears, temporarily, beyond the two-year limit (for example, Haiti a number of times, and several small African and Latin American countries). The list of countries in arrears is notified to the Assembly at the beginning of each session. Usually the arrears were paid in a few weeks. By not seeking to vote until they have been able to make the necessary payments, such countries have been able to avoid the imposition of sanctions.

So far as arrears *within* the two-year period are concerned, however, the situation is different. Within that limit, where no sanctions apply, many members are consistently in arrears. China, in particular when Taiwan claimed that name, had a specially heavy burden of contributions since she was assessed on China's national income, and she was almost always heavily in arrears; indeed hers represented a large proportion of the total arrears experienced by the Organisation. Even so the total of temporary arrears rarely exceeded 15 per cent of the total budget. But their existence was highly inconvenient to the Organisation, causing heavy drawings on the working capital fund and other UN funds.

By the mid-1980s a number of states had become lax in the promptness of their payments and some, notably the USA and France as well as the USSR, had refused to contribute to some activities of which they disapproved. However, it was the decision by the US government not to meet all its regular assessed payments which was truly critical: it plunged the UN into deep financial crisis. The reasons for the US action were as follows. Hostility to the Organisation developed because of UN policies and attitudes antagonistic to the USA. This hostility was fanned by a right-wing body called the Heritage Foundation. In 1985, Congress took two actions to reduce American payments. One was the Kassebaum Amendment. This reduced the US contribution from 25 to 20 per cent. The other was the Gramm–Rudman–Hollings Deficit Reduction Act to pare down the huge federal deficit. By 1986 the USA was paying only half of its assessed contribution. By the turn of the decade the American attitude changed (see p.174). Nevertheless, the deficit in the UN regular budget was still $961 million in 1991, of which $567 million was owed by the USA.

There have been a number of proposals for dealing with the problem: the charging of interest on arrears (as is successfully done in the ITU), the use of monthly payments, or freer use of the working capital fund. The first of these is the most likely to do something to deter arrears, and there would be much to be said for its adoption by the UN. In any case the UN may need to be stricter in applying Article 19 in the few cases where it is applicable: in the IAEA eight or nine members which have been in arrears have been deprived of their vote at certain periods. A more radical and controversial means for reducing financial difficulties has been to rely increasingly on voluntary programmes. At first, these were adopted quite simply as a means of financing undertakings for which the necessary degree of support was not forthcoming to place them on the regular budget. But increasingly they were seen by some of the developed countries as a means of evading the unwelcome burden of direct assessment by the Assembly, then increasingly dominated by the developing.

The first of the voluntary programmes was the UN Children's Fund which, though it inherited substantial funds from UNRRA, was financed from the start mainly through voluntary donations from governments. Perhaps because it was seen in a sense as a kind of charity, this seemed a logical method of financing at that time. The same system was used, for somewhat similar reasons, for the UN Relief for Palestine Refugees (established 1948); its successor UNRWA (1949); and for the UN High Commission for Refugees (1950), though the administrative budget of this last is financed from the UN's regular budget. When the technical assistance programme expanded, voluntary financing was again adopted to avoid the risk of direct taxation of the rich by the poor (and because the Communist states opposed such programmes). The EPTA, the Special Fund, and later the UNDP and the WFP, have throughout been on a voluntary basis and represent by far the largest voluntary programmes: UNDP now approaches $700 million a year; and the value of WFP allocations in kind is even larger. As a result of this process, the UN voluntary programmes together are now much larger than the regular budget of the UN. The only countervailing trend was that the *administrative* budgets of UNCTAD and UNIDO have been met from the UN regular budget, much to the disgust of some of the rich countries[4] (Now that UNIDO is a specialised agency, this arrangement no longer applies to it.)

Voluntary financing has also developed to support peace-keeping operations. The early UN observer teams, UNTSO, the observers in Kashmir, Lebanon and so on, were all financed from the regular budget, with little except routine grumblings from those opposed, including the Soviet Union. Even in 1956, when UNEF, the UN force in Sinai, was established, it was generally expected by most that the expenses would fall on the regular budget, but, largely as a matter of accounting convenience, the expenses were in fact placed in a separate account. It is possible that agreement might have been reached on financing from the regular budget if four years later another, and much larger force (ONUC), had not been established in the Congo. The Soviet Union and its allies had had no major complaint on the *conduct* of UNEF, nor did it seriously protest that it was established by the Assembly; but they had major objections to almost everything the Congo force sought to achieve. They were therefore less than ever ready this time to contribute to its expenses. And since, here too, the expenses had not been formally placed as part of the regular budget, they had some reason to hope that they should not face the sanctions of Article 19 in respect of this refusal.

That refusal was not, as is sometimes suggested, based on the fact that the forces were improperly established: by the Assembly, not the Council. The Congo force was in fact set up by the Security Council (though arguably not by the normal procedure for a UN Chapter VII enforcement action). The main complaint was that the method of financing the force should have been agreed from the start, and have been agreed by the Council: this would mean that a permanent member, by use of its veto, could avoid having to pay for any peace-keeping operation of which it had not approved. This was a position that, though a penny-pinching and negative one, could be respectably defended on the basis of the Charter.

The Soviet Union itself demanded in each case that the 'aggressors' should pay the cost of the forces. France's position was not dissimilar. She too held that the operations had not been properly authorised and controlled, and the financing not satisfactorily agreed in advance; and in her case too a strong underlying reason was hostility to the UN, and all it stood for, on the part of her then government. Yet, illogically, she was prepared to pay for UNEF, which had been irregularly authorised (by the Assembly), but not for the Congo force, established by the Council. In addition to these countries, which categorically refused to pay for the forces, there were a considerable number of others, which without disclaiming all responsibility, claimed that they could not pay for economic reasons, or would not until the whole dispute had been resolved. This was not altogether surprising since the cost of the two forces was very high: more than that of the entire regular budget in some years. UNEF's was originally about half that of the regular budget but gradually decreased; ONUC's was far bigger than the regular budget. The two together in 1962 were roughly double. Thus if paid from the regular budget, contributions would have been trebled. For this reason, a special scale of assessment reducing the burden on poor countries was adopted for ONUC.

The situation was still further complicated by the decision in 1961 to issue 200 million dollars' worth of UN bonds, to be bought primarily by governments, the proceeds of which would be used to reduce the deficit for peace-keeping. More than half the members bought bonds, and many felt that this was an ingenious way of overcoming the problem. However it was manifestly an evasion of the issue. It was provided, through a decision of the Assembly, that the amounts spent in servicing the loan would be placed on the regular budget. Although the proceeds of the bond issue were for any 'urgent claims' of the Organisation, and not necessarily only for peace-keeping, in effect members were being asked to pay the cost of the operations from regular contributions by a roundabout route. Not surprisingly the nations opposed to compulsory assessment for the forces protested sharply. And the Soviet bloc countries and France refused to pay the proportion of their assessments corresponding to the amortisation of the bonds.

In an attempt to obtain advice (and a little delay) the Assembly asked for an advisory opinion of the International Court on whether the costs of the forces could be regarded as 'normal' expenses of the Organisation for the purposes of Article 19. The Court advised that they could. The Assembly was not obliged to accept this opinion, which was only advisory (the Court has no authority to give binding interpretations of the Charter). After some debate, it did however decide, by a considerable majority, to 'accept' rather than take note of, the advisory opinion, even if only as an 'extraordinary' measure. It then proceeded to set up a working group to consider the problem; and the President of the Assembly and the Secretary-General set out guidelines on the way the situation might be met. Both suggested greater reliance on voluntary financing in future, voluntary payments to meet the existing deficit, the use of a special scale of assessments for peace-keeping, and the possible establishment of a 'peace fund' from which future operations might be financed. The attempt to enforce the provisions of Article 19 by withdrawing the Soviet Union's right to vote in the Assembly was not pursued to its bitter conclusion, though the whole of one Assembly (in 1965) was virtually washed away in consequence.

There were calls for voluntary contributions to reduce the deficit; and some were made. The entire matter was looked at yet again by an Ad Hoc Committee on the Finances of the UN established in 1966, and in a more general way by the Committee of Thirty-Three, which was set up to look at the whole problem of peace-keeping operations. But after twenty-three years' discussion no solution has yet been found. And the inherited deficit therefore remains substantial.

The questions in dispute were complex and politically highly charged. Perfectly respectable cases could be made out both for the point of view that a collective decision to establish a peace-keeping force was not different in kind from many other collective decisions of the Organisation, whose financial consequences must be borne by all members irrespective of their own views; and for the opposite view that the establishment of such a force, by a procedure and for purposes different from any envisaged in the Charter, could not create obligations for members who were opposed, and that in practice any powerful state finding itself in a minority on a question of such importance would likewise refuse to pay. It can be argued that the Organisation showed considerable good sense, and even political sophistication, in its approach to the problem throughout: in successfully avoiding an open confrontation, and a possible break-down of the entire organisation, in 1965; even in the apparent illogicality of accepting the Court's advisory opinion (so leaving open the option of including future peace-keeping costs in the regular budget), yet in practice not applying it in the case in dispute. It showed less skill in overcoming the financial problem itself, which has remained a millstone round the neck of the UN until the present time.

At all events, the effect of the crisis and the controversy that accompanied it was to make a majority of members for the moment increasingly favourable towards voluntary financing for future peace-keeping operations. When a security force was sent to West Irian in 1962 to supervise the transfer of authority from the Netherlands to Indonesia, it was laid down that this would be financed by the two countries concerned. When the Secretary-General agreed to send a small observer team to the Yemen in 1963 to verify and to deter external intervention, he was careful to ensure that the costs should be paid by the interested parties. And when a third major peace-keeping force was established to keep the peace in Cyprus in 1964, it was laid down from the start that it would be financed by voluntary contributions. But a major breakthrough on this subject occurred in 1973 after the October War in the Middle East. Then there existed a considerable degree of consensus on the necessity for and purposes of two UN forces to police the cease-fire, in Sinai and in Syria. This time, therefore, it was agreed to finance the forces from contributions by all UN members, though these were to be assessed on a special scale. This may conceivably have solved the problem of financing future peace-keeping forces.

Despite the more frequent resort to voluntary financing, a steady rise in the regular budget continued, which became especially rapid from the mid-1960s onwards. One of the effects of this was to cause increasing restiveness among some of the larger contributors. The Soviet Union was consistently among the most bitter critics of rising expenditure and regularly put down resolutions calling for a reduction of the total budget, or the elimination of particular programmes. Britain in the early years, and France later, were almost equally strident in their calls for economy. In the 1980s it was the USA. Such demands were often made in the Fifth Committee, usually without regard to the fact that the government concerned had supported most of the individual programmes proposed in other committees of the UN. The most senseless expression of these calls were the demands for an absolute ceiling on the regular budget. In fact, as the reports of the ACABQ made clear, a considerable part of the annual increases is due to inflation and to the increases in wages and salaries which inevitably follow. The rest has been due to the perpetual rise in the number of programmes, reports, meetings, and conferences regularly called for by massive majorities in the Assembly.[5]

Although reforms were undertaken in the 1980s (see pp.174–5) and fewer complaints have been registered as a result, the UN has still not solved the problem of defaulting and dilatoriness in payments. By mid-1992 the total owing was over $1.7 billion, nearly half of which was for peace-keeping operations.

THE CONTROL OF EXPENDITURE

The rapidly increasing size of the budgets of the UN and the agencies, and the concern it aroused among some governments, brought increasing attention to the problem of securing adequate control of expenditure within the bodies. In any system of government some machinery must exist for the scrutiny of estimates of future expenditure, and for the examination of expenditure already made. In Britain, for example, these two functions are performed respectively by the Expenditure Committee and the Public Accounts Committee within parliament; and by the Treasury and the Cabinet, and by the Comptroller and Auditor-General, within the government itself. After an uncertain start, a somewhat similar system of control has emerged within international government.

Part of the framework for this system was established in League days. A set of Financial Regulations was then drawn up setting out the general principles to be followed on expenditure and its authorisation. The Noblemaire Report recommended, as we saw, that, since it was almost impossible for the Assembly itself to scrutinise expenditure exhaustively and expertly, an expert Supervisory Committee should be

established to examine estimates before they were passed to the
Assembly's Finance Committee. The budget (which included that for
the ILO) was examined in detail by the Supervisory Commission,
which passed its comments to member-governments. It then underwent
further examination and cutting in the Assembly's Finance Committee.
And finally still further changes, almost invariably cuts, might be made
in the Assembly itself. By the time the budget had passed through all
these phases, it was not often overweight; indeed, as we have seen, the
organisation's activities were slashed to the bone.[6]

When the UN was founded, a generally similar system was
established. Here too a set of financial regulations was drawn up,
though they were not finalised until 1949. Here too a Working Capital
fund was established, on which the Secretary-General could draw 'such
funds as may be necessary to finance budgetary appropriations
pending receipt of contributions'. And here too a special committee
was set up to examine the budget in detail and to make available its
comments and recommendations to the relevant committee (the Fifth)
of the Assembly. This was the ACABQ,[7] the most important and most
influential element in the whole financial system established by the UN.
The essential elements of that system, established in 1945–6, though
they have been refined in detail, remain generally unchanged until
today.

The beginning of the process is the call for the initiation of a
particular programme by committees and subordinate bodies of the
UN. Any proposal which will require expenditure, even if it is only a
conference or committee meeting, must go first to the ACABQ and the
Fifth Committee for a report on the financial implications. They in
turn ask the Secretary-General (in practice the Controller or the
Budget Chief) and his staff to give estimates of the cost: according to
the Assembly's rules of procedure:

> no resolution involving expenditure shall be recommended . . . for
> approval by the General Assembly unless it is accompanied by an
> estimate of expenditure prepared by the Secretary-General. No
> resolution in respect of which expenditure is anticipated by the
> Secretary-General shall be voted by the General Assembly until the
> Administrative and Budgetary [Fifth] Committee has had an
> opportunity of stating the effect of a proposal upon the budget
> estimates.

These procedures, however, are not in any sense a check on the
initiating body. They are largely a formality: neither the ACABQ nor

the Fifth Committee ever seeks at this stage to halt a programme initiated by another committee. The only effect is that the Assembly in voting on the proposal, has in its hand, attached to the resolution, a clear statement of the likely cost. This has never been known to inhibit the Assembly in any way.

The resolution itself usually contains a clause requesting the Secretary-General to include a provision in his forthcoming budget for the programme in question. After it is passed, which will nearly always be in December, the Secretariat has to begin to make preparations for implementing it – for preparing a conference, setting up a new centre within the Secretariat, launching a new technical assistance project. In January, the Secretary-General begins to prepare his budget for the following year. This is done by the Bureau of Administrative Management and Budget, under the Controller. He will send out a budget memorandum, asking the heads of departments, offices and services to prepare their estimates for the following financial year. He usually strongly enjoins economy: for example, he may request that the estimate should not be above that for the previous year, except for the so-called 'mandatory' increases resulting from wage and salary awards and price increase. The estimates received are then carefully examined and usually cut by 'examiners', the officers of the Controller's department. The examiners' reports are considered in turn by the budget chief, who makes adjustments and hears appeals on cuts. The resulting overall budget is then examined by the Controller himself, the senior financial officer of the Organisation, who looks at a the total distribution of expenditure in the light of the policies of the Assembly and the views of the Secretary-General. The resulting budget now goes to the Secretary-General, who may, in consultation with the Under-Secretaries-General, and the Controller (he has now established a senior review group of top officials in the economic and social fields to advise him), call for still further amendments and cuts. He will then ask for the final statement of budget estimates to be prepared.

The next stage is for these estimates to be examined in detail by an outside body. This is the task of the ACABQ. The ACABQ is intended to be an expert committee (under its terms of reference it is to include at least three financial experts of 'recognised standing') and many of its members are representatives of the Treasury or Auditor-General's department of their home government. For something like two months, in May and June every year, this committee, meeting full-time, goes through the budget in meticulous detail. It also looks at the budgets of

The United Nations

the specialised agencies, though since the UN Assembly has no *direct* authority over these (it can only pass recommendations), it devotes less attention to them. As a result of its examination, it draws up detailed reports on the UN budget and on the budgets of the agencies. It invariably recommends some reduction in the UN budget, usually of the order of 2 or 3 per cent a year. It also examines the accounts for the past year and issues a report.

When the Assembly meets in the autumn, the budget is considered by the Fifth Committee, in the light of the ACABQ's comments. The Chairman of the Advisory Committee traditionally attends the Committee's meetings, and plays a considerable part in the proceedings, and his advice is listened to with respect. The Secretary-General introduces his budget, and justifies as best he can any increases, stating where he accepts the ACABQ's recommendations for a reduction, and where he rejects them. The Chairman of the ACABQ then speaks, explaining why the committee felt that reductions were necessary. There is a 'first reading' debate, in which the budget is considered in detail, and agreed in so far as this is possible, but in which delegates express their views on the items which they believe should be reduced, without any attempt to finalise any item at this stage. In the second reading debate, final decisions must be reached on all items, involving the taking of votes on many of the estimates. To some extent these debates degenerate into straight fights between the developed and the developing, or rather between high budget and low budget delegations. The Russians invariably propose large reductions on individual items, and sometimes a symbolic cut in the whole budget: these have become so habitual that they are no longer taken very seriously. In general, however, the committee manages to reach something like a consensus eventually. Occasionally the committee will support the Secretariat in recommending the restoration of an original estimate; and very occasionally the Advisory Committee itself will have second thoughts. But the final decision tends to be close to the recommendations of the ACABQ.

The Fifth Committee's proposals then go to the Assembly itself in the form of a resolution embodying the budget authorisation. This may be debated, and delegations have the opportunity of riding their pet hobby-horses. But by this stage the Assembly is drawing to its close, delegations are anxious to get off for Christmas, and in practice the budget proposals have never been altered by a vote in the Assembly (whose composition is of course always the same as that of the Fifth Committee).

A vital problem concerning the budget, which has never been fully resolved, is how far the Fifth Committee can vote on the estimates in such a way as to nullify the purpose of a decision by another UN committee or body, supported by the Assembly, to initiate or to extend a particular programme. How far is the committee concerned with policy, or only with economy in implementing policy? The issue was debated in the early days of the UN, and it was then decided (if somewhat ambiguously) that the Fifth Committee had unlimited financial powers, and therefore could take a decision that would in effect frustrate the decision of another committee. In practice, however, the committee virtually never does this. Nearly all the cuts which it proposes are decisions not to allow the Secretary-General to create so many new posts (70 per cent of the budget goes on staff costs), or to be so lavish in equipment or accommodation as he would like. That is, they restrict the way he *fulfils* certain commitments; it does not, in practice, say that certain commitments should not be met at all. Nor does the Assembly itself do this in considering the recommendations of the Fifth Committee.

The budget that is approved provides the financial basis on which the Secretariat must operate for the year concerned. But in practice, inevitably, unforeseen needs arise, costs go up more than expected, members fail to pay their contributions in time and additional provision must be made. So supplementary estimates are voted.

As we have seen, a Working Capital Fund was set up in 1946. The Secretary-General may draw on this pending the receipt of contributions, but this must of course normally be only within the terms of the approved budget. Beyond that, he is given authority in a special resolution passed each year, to spend up to a given ceiling in any financial year, even without authority from the ACABQ, if he certifies that the expenditure relates to the 'maintenance of peace and security', a phrase that has proved conveniently vague. He may also make limited disbursements for unforeseen expenses of the International Court, or for emergency disaster relief. He must of course report all disbursements made under this authority to the ACABQ and the Assembly; and the Fifth Committee and the Assembly must, in the light of a report from the Advisory Committee, then vote the necessary funds. In practice he can usually find persuasive reasons why he needed the money for the stated purposes. The Secretary-General has also authority to undertake larger outlays than this 'to meet unforeseen and extraordinary expenditures' (such as those involved in maintaining a peace-keeping operation, for example) so long as he does in this case obtain *prior* authority from the ACABQ. Here too supplementary estimates must be voted *post hoc* by the Assembly.

This procedure too has proved to be quite unsatisfactory. In time the Secretary-General came to authorise almost any type of expenditure as 'unforeseen and extraordinary'. Over the years the ACABQ complained over and over again at the fact that it had been asked to approve requests for 'unforeseen and extraordinary expenses', when these should not have been unforeseen, and were certainly not extraordinary. As a result, almost every year there were supplementary appropriations of one to two million dollars a year, occasionally more. Various ways of overcoming this problem have been proposed (for example, the Secretary-General was to give a 'certification' that failure to provide the supplementary estimate would cause 'serious detriment' to the UN) but not one has yet been accepted as satisfactory.[8]

Another questionable practice arose from the fact that, in some cases, for a number of reasons it was difficult for the Secretariat to make any valid estimate of the cost of a particular programme, perhaps because the controlling body had not yet made a final decision on the form it should take. In these cases, the Secretariat inserted in its estimates an extremely tentative 'pro-memoria' sum or even sometimes left a blank. These items together may amount to as much as 5 per cent of the total budget. When, later, final figures are inserted, they have thus never been properly scrutinised by the appropriate legislative bodies, and may substantially exceed the amounts provided for. This system too has come under increasing attack.

There has long been awareness in the UN of deficiencies in its financial system. For years the Advisory Committee called for various improvements; better machinery for coordination and long-term planning, the rationalisation of the conference and meeting programme, consolidation of premises and services, better coordination in the field, more flexibility in the use of staff and funds, and so on. For long this had only marginal impact. With the rapid increase in the budget, and the financial crisis that occurred in the mid-1960s, there developed increasing concern about the system of budgetary management. A movement to reform the system began.

The main and glaring defect was that the decisions to *launch* programmes, and so to commit expenditure, which were made by the committees and other subordinate bodies, were largely divorced from the general control of expenditure itself, wielded by the ACABQ and the Fifth Committee. There was no major policy-making body (other than the Assembly itself) to decide on overall levels and distribution of expenditure. ECOSOC has neither the power nor the will. The Assembly is not equipped or capable of imposing priorities or a rational overall programme. The effect is that the authorisation of funds, conducted by the Fifth Committee, have never been integrated with each other. This has left the Secretariat with the difficult conundrum, as the Secretary-General reported in 1967, of 'reconciling the work programme as determined by resolutions of the main legislative organs of the UN, and the total resources which member states are prepared to make available for its implementation':[9] two quantities which rarely matched. The ACABQ frequently expressed its dissatisfaction with the fact that individual bodies of the UN were free to pass resolutions calling for expenditure, on a piecemeal and uncontrolled basis, and that, in the final resort, the Fifth Committee had little option but to find the money as best it could. This made it difficult not only to control the volume of new expenditure, but to co-ordinate the programmes of the various authorising bodies.

For these reasons, in the late 1960s, the UN embarked on a reform of its financial procedures. In December 1965 'an Ad Hoc Committee of Experts to Examine the Finance of the UN and the Specialised Agencies' was established. This was partly designed to examine the state of the UN's finances as a result of the peace-keeping crisis (pp.135–8 above). But it was also intended to improve financial procedures generally. Its second report thus contained over forty recommendations for the reform of the financial system in the whole UN family. Its conclusions were generally endorsed by the Assembly. And for once, instead of allowing the report to be forgotten and filed away, the Assembly waged a sustained campaign over several years to ensure it was adequately implemented. Eventually, a substantial proportion of the proposals were put into practice.

One important recommendation was for the establishment of a Joint Inspection Unit, to examine the expenditure of funds by any programme of the whole UN system (not including the IMF and World Bank), if necessary by unheralded spot checks. More important, this unit made general studies of the whole financial and administrative system. It was to consist of not more than eight highly qualified experts in financial and administrative matters. They were to make on-the-spot investigations of any of the services of any of the organisations, and they would have broad powers to investigate: in other words, no body could try to impede investigation by concealing the books or preventing adequate surveys of the methods employed. The new unit came into existence on 1 January 1968, and has proved one of the most important agents for reform in the system. It has produced a series of first-class reports both on individual operations (to take an example, all UN technical assistance activities in sample countries): and on more general matters (for example the influential Bertrand Report on the planning and formulation of programmes in the UN system as a whole, a report on the organisation of the General Assembly and another on recruitment and personnel).

Secondly, there was an attempt to get a grip on the proliferation of conferences, meetings, documents and reports. This had been a subject of concern for some time. The number of normal meetings, both in New York and Geneva, had doubled in six years: to two thousand in New York, and to over four thousand in Geneva, with over a thousand elsewhere.[10] The new reforms had some impact. Each major organ of the UN reviewed its meeting programme and considered reductions; for example, a number now meet every two years instead of every year. Subsidiary bodies were not to increase the length and number of their meetings without authority. Documentation was significantly reduced. Less success was achieved over conferences. A Committee on Conferences was set up to review the whole question and to help the Secretariat in reducing meetings. But, after three years' work, the committee had made no significant impact on the number of meetings and abandoned the effort.

But the most important of the new recommendations concerned the procedures for long-term planning and budget formulation within the UN system. Moves were already beginning for better planning systems within the UN itself and in some of the agencies before (the WHO had been formulating five-year plans since the early 1950s). The Ad Hoc Committee now proposed a more ambitious system. It wanted every agency to adopt a system of two-year, four-year and six-year planning, with harmonisation of the periods used by each agency. These should include broad goals, priority objectives, and the specific courses of action to achieve them. The agencies should establish the necessary procedures and staff units for this purpose. Individual budgets would be closely harmonised with these long-term programmes. The details of this plan were not adopted. But in the years since both the UN and the agencies have substantially improved their procedures for long-term planning, and there is now not a single agency which has not embarked on such a system in one form or another.

Budgetary procedures were also improved. Because they had developed largely independently, the agencies had evolved quite different forms of budget presentation. This hampered comparison and coordination.[11] The Ad Hoc Committee recommended greater standardisation of budget format within the UN system. Later it was decided that at least each agency should produce information about their budgets which was compatible, so as to make comparison and coordination easier. There has been progress in achieving a common budget terminology among the agencies (previously the same words were used by the different agencies in different senses in their budgets). But the proposal that all the agencies and the UN should adopt two-year budgets ran into problems. Some of the agencies refused point-blank to change. The UN, after years of hesitation, has eventually adopted a two-year budget cycle.

The UN also finally adopted at the end of 1972 a system of programme budgeting, with two-year budgets, formed on the basis of six-year plans framed by each programme-formulating body. Both six-year plans and two-year budgets are scrutinised by the ACABQ, ECOSOC and the Assembly. This procedure should in theory make possible better long-term planning of programmes. Whether it does so depends on how far the two-year budget is genuinely related to the usually vague and amorphous six-year programme. If the budget continues to represent simply the sum total of the individual programmes authorised by each subordinate body to conform with every passing whim, with little regard for the theoretical 'plan', the new procedure will not really represent a very significant advance. It is the decentralisation of programme formulation, and the lack of effective control at a higher level, which is at the root of the problem. In 1990 a measure of control over the budget was achieved by the member states as part of a reform package devised by the General Assembly (p.175).

Slowly, therefore, in these various ways, the system of budgetary control within the UN system has been improved and strengthened. The UN now has a sophisticated and rigorous system of control: beginning with the examiners, the Controller and the review groups, then successively by the Secretary-General, the ACABQ, the Fifth Committee, and finally the Assembly. As a US Senate Foreign Relations Committee (not a body likely to be lenient in this respect) reported in 1954: 'The UN budget probably is given as careful a scrutiny as any budget of a similar size anywhere in the world. Representatives from member states in the General Assembly often spend days debating relatively modest sums which would be considered by some national legislative bodies in a matter of hours, or even minutes.'[12] A later US study, conducted in 1964 on behalf of the Brookings Foundation, described the UN regular budget as 'probably the most carefully approved in the world'.[13] The UN has many problems, but it is doubtful if, as is often believed, inadequate care in scrutinising expenditure is one of them.

CONCLUSIONS

Thus the problems of finance, of levying revenues and controlling expenditure, have proved as critical and contentious within the UN system as in other forms of government. The most striking feature has been the rapid rise in budgets in all the major UN organs, despite the financing problems. The total of the regular budgets of the UN and the agencies (including the administrative budgets of the World Bank and the IMF), and of the voluntary programmes, is about two and a half billion dollars. Loans by the financial institutions are additional to this sum. In the biennium 1990–91 the World Bank and the IDA lent nearly $23 billion.

Within the total budget there has been a considerable shift in the direction of expenditure during recent years. Both within the UN itself, and within the agencies, there is increasing emphasis on economic and social activities. Among types of expenditure, most goes on health, education, agriculture and labour and vocational training. Development assistance of course is still larger. (Though by the early 1990s expenditure on peace-keeping operations had substantially increased to overtake development expenditure.) Thus international expenditure is distributed in much the same general proportions as that of national governments; the highest expenditures going on education, health, and development infrastructure. There are not of course, in the international system, the large expenditures on defence, which usually take up such a large share of national budgets; though the commitments for peace-keeping forces might be reckoned within this category, and at times, as we have seen, were a heavier commitment than any other single item within the UN proper.

But if the types of expenditure of international government are generally comparable to that of national governments, the problems of controlling it are entirely different. The basic problem has arisen from the diffuseness and decentralisation of decision making within the UN system. Even within the UN alone, the effective decisions on whether or not a new programme shall be introduced continue to be those of committees and subsidiary bodies, acting largely independently of each other. It is true that these decisions require endorsement by the

Assembly, but as we have seen, until 1990 this was to a large extent a formality. The cuts in expenditure made by the Fifth Committee are invariably cuts in the way a programme is implemented; never cuts of the programmes themselves. In other words the budget is not really a set of plans for expenditure, which may be accepted or rejected, as elsewhere; it is a statement of how decisions on expenditure that have already been made may be carried out.

What is wholly lacking, and which exists in most national systems, is a central decision-making body, which makes the final, overall decisions about the policies and programmes to be implemented. In this respect the UN is different from almost any other political system in the world. In local government, each committee of a council makes proposals, and submits estimates, often highly inflated; but these are then severely scrutinised and pruned by a finance or policy committee, which may cut out entire programmes and imposes overall control. Similarly, at national level, public expenditure programmes of departments are examined and cut back, first by the Treasury and ultimately by the cabinet. In both cases the reviewing body undertakes in that very act, the vital policy-making rule: a selection of priorities. This does not take place within the international system. The ACABQ grumbles and protests, and sometimes cuts a little here and there off the estimates. But it never seeks to impose an overall direction on the programme, nor cuts out a single individual proposal. Nor does the Fifth Committee. The General Assembly could do so in theory, but it has not; and in any case it certainly is not equipped to undertake this role. ECOSOC and its Committee on Programme and Coordination (CPC) have a theoretical role in coordinating the programmes, but in fact exert little influence.[14] And the Secretary-General, though he has been asked by the ACABQ to undertake the same task, and if necessary make representations to the authorising bodies in practice has little impact. He certainly cannot cut out the programmes altogether. The UN must be the only system of government in the world in which spending authorities make their own proposals for expenditure in virtual certainty that the proposals will be implemented in some form.

There is thus a vital need for some intergovernmental high-level body to perform the important, scrutinising, policy-making role. In theory it could be played by the CPC, in the examination which it now gives to the preliminary budget programmes before detailed estimates go to the ACABQ. But the CPC is not a body of sufficient weight or authority to perform this role effectively. It could not excise a programme already agreed on by the previous Assembly, and is unlikely to cut a new proposal either. It may suggest reductions here or additions there, but it is basically a question of patching and pruning, not of planning and programme formulation.

A second possibility is for ECOSOC, as a more high-powered body, to take over the twin roles of planning and financial control. At present it is too inexpert, too large and too overburdened with other tasks for this. Possibly a representative group of the Assembly called together by the President, to consider together during the Assembly all resolutions calling for additional expenditure before they go to the plenary, could provide the necessary system for choosing priorities.

But the third, and better way still, would be for some high-powered coordinating group to formulate the budget as a whole *after* the Assembly, but only on the *basis* of the resolutions passed, without any strict obligation to ensure that each one was implemented. The primary Assembly decision would then be on the overall level of expenditure proposed, rather than on the individual resolutions coming from each committee (which it is impossible for them to judge in relation to the UN's programme as a whole). Unfortunately, the UN does not have a high-level policy-making body at the centre which can guide actions by the Assembly in this way, comparable to the Governing Councils in the agencies. Only the development of some such cabinet system could finally solve the problem of adequate financial control.

An equally strange feature of the UN's financial system at present is the total exclusion of the voluntary programmes from the procedures for control and evaluation. The ACABQ has from time to time commented upon this, and suggested a greater uniformity between the administrative and budgetary arrangements of the UN and its voluntary programmes, and more centralised control. Considering that the UN voluntary programmes together, including UNDP, are now about twice the regular budget, it is strange that there has not been a demand to scrutinise their budgets and administrative expenses more rigorously. It is true that this could scarcely be done by precisely the same bodies or procedures as the regular budget, because some members of these bodies, particularly the Communist countries, did not contribute to the voluntary programme, while one or two countries are not UN members. But there is a need for some comparable system of control: either by establishing a separate body for the task from among the contributors, or by commissioning the ACABQ, with or without representatives of the non-contributors, to perform the task. The conclusions of such a committee would then be considered by a meeting of the contributors as a whole.[15]

Then there is the uncertainty of the voluntary programmes. These have certain obvious advantages. It may be possible to launch some which otherwise would not be launched at all. There need be no limit on the amount or proportion paid by one country (the US has paid consistently up to 70 per cent of some).[16] Non-members of the UN can contribute to them (West Germany was a large contributor to UNDP before she joined the UN). They help to overcome the problem of securing consensus, since controversial programmes (such as the population programme or peace-keeping operations) can be undertaken without splitting the Organisation. For some causes, such as the 'charities', more money can be raised, by placing most of the burden on the richer countries.

Some of these arguments can be contested. If a majority agree that a certain programme is valuable, it may be better that all should be obliged to contribute, and so increase the total funds available. Special scales could be devised for particular programmes (as has been done for peace-keeping) even if obligatory. If poor countries find it hard to contribute, the scale of assessment for all programmes could be altered. And so on. But eventually one always comes down to the difficulty of securing *consensus* on particular levels or types of expenditure. To insist on regular programmes only could reduce the total sums that would otherwise be raised.[17]

The financing of international government differs from that of national government in one vital respect. It cannot in the final resort be extorted by enforcement. If pushed completely to the wall, the unwilling contributor will leave the system altogether and its contribution will be irretrievably lost. While this remains the case, the majority must show some discretion. The fact is there is room for increases in both voluntary and regular programmes. The former act to some extent as safety-valves for the latter. Big contributors may be more willing to accept big increases in the regular budget if they still have the feeling that there are some expenditures at least which they can control. What voluntary programmes do not provide (and what some seek to secure from them) is justification for resisting increases in regular budgets as well.

Given the rapid increase in the budgets of the UN and its agencies, the surprising thing is not that there have been disputes, but how *few* serious disputes have occurred. This is a healthy sign. It would obviously be impossible to run any international organisation effectively if members were free to pick and choose which of its programmes they were prepared to pay for. The readiness of nations to pay for international programmes whether or not they supported them individually is the only objective test of their commitment to the international system as a whole. Judged by that standard, UN members have shown a considerable, but not unlimited, commitment. Most people pay most of the time, despite rapidly rising budgets. The majority has so far shown considerable good judgement in not forcing the pace: in deciding not always to demand compulsory assessments for peace-keeping forces, even though a majority had expressed the belief they would be legally justified in doing so; in deciding on voluntary programmes where there would be strong resistance to compulsory ones. There will continue to be disputes about which programmes should be put on the regular budget and which outside; and, above all, about the overall scale of expenditure. Such conflicts are inherent in any political organisation, which must reflect the conflicting interests of its members. As budgets increase, the disputes will grow in intensity. Poor countries will continue to want more expenditure and rich ones less. All this means is that, in international society as in domestic systems, one of the central political issues will be the scale of government demanded and the degree of redistribution this should bring about.

An alternative and more imaginative way to ease the UN's financial difficulties would be to introduce completely new methods of raising funds. A number of suggestions have been made. These include taxing the revenues derived from oil, the sea and Antarctica. Although there is much good sense in such proposals, there is little hope in the foreseeable future that any such scheme will be adopted.

7 The Fundamental Political Problems

Many of the political conflicts that have manifested themselves in international organisations resemble those that have been fought out in political institutions from time immemorial, and about which political philosophers have debated and dissented for centuries: disputes between liberals and authoritarians, conservatives and socialists, believers in big government and in little government. Though often wrapped up in the cruder warpaint of national rivalry and ideological conflict (just as within states the conflict of abstract principles is often transmitted into the slogans and platforms of individual parties or classes), almost identical principles have been involved.

One of the most fundamental of all political struggles has always concerned the degree of centralisation of authority. This has usually been associated with conflicts over the *amount* of authority, or government, desired. The struggles between the rising monarchs and the bad bold barons of medieval Europe, or between a federal government and individual states, as in the United States, Switzerland and other systems, or between advocates of freedom for market forces and supporters of a mixed economy today, are all different manifestations of this fundamental political conflict. Centralisation and big government were demanded first as a means to power by the sovereign authority against local magnates. But more recently they have often been supported equally by liberal and egalitarian forces, which sought more government as a means of achieving more justice, equality or other social purposes within the territory as a whole. The conflict was then between those who saw the increase in central authority in terms of the enhanced welfare it could provide, and those who saw it in terms of the threat to liberty and independence it might represent. In other words it partly concerned the purposes of government.

This same division has been reflected in international organisations. How large should they be, how powerful? Attitudes to this have

153

depended on whether they were seen as a threat to national freedom or a means to national welfare. This lies at the root of many North–South conflicts in the UN. Poor states want more international government as a means to equality. Rich states want less, to preserve their freedom of action.

But the belief in centralisation does not depend only on the purposes it is thought able to procure. It depends also on who controls the central authority. The higher bourgeoisie in Elizabethan days was not against a powerful monarchy when it performed objects which they supported; but when the monarchy used it in ways it rejected in Stuart days, they thought it necessary to turn and subdue it. Conservatives in Britain and Prussia in the nineteenth century favoured a powerful state machine when they were able to control it and use it for purposes of which they approved; but opposed it in the next century when it might be controlled by popular forces desiring to use it in ways they disapproved. Communists favoured the withering away of the state when they themselves were in opposition and saw the state as a threat to freedom, but they have sought to strengthen its power and authority almost indefinitely when they themselves controlled it. So in international organisations too: attitudes on the fundamental question – how much power should such organisations have in relation to the nation-state? – have been partly determined by whether a nation, or a group of nations, could expect to be in the majority within such organisations and so control the purposes it promoted. This was once at the root of many East–West conflicts in the UN. Communist states consistently opposed any growth in UN power for fear it should be used against them. Western states wanted a strengthening of UN so long as they controlled it. Third World states wanted it, and the West opposed it, when the Third World won a dominant voice in the General Assembly.

For the first twenty years of the UN's history, the most important political division was the cold war between East and West. This was reflected there in such intense form that at times it almost seemed the entire edifice might be shattered from the reverberations. That this never happened was some indication of the solidity of the original foundations. Some recognition probably persisted, even at the height of the cold war, that the mutual interests of all were served by the continued existence of a body in which divisions could be discussed and debated with words and resolutions, rather than fought for with more dangerous weapons. In an age of ideological warfare, moreover, an international organisation whose debates were relayed and reported across the world could represent at least a valuable pulpit for both sides. The dais of the General Assembly was the soap-box which could be used by skilful orators to proclaim a creed, and win converts in all parts of the world.

In their use of the UN as a vehicle for propaganda, the two sides in the cold war resembled each other. But in their attitude towards the UN's role they differed totally, in representing majority and minority groups. The eruption of the various individual cold war issues in the UN – Iran, Syria and Lebanon, Greece, Indonesia, Czechoslovakia, East Europe, Berlin, Chinese representation and finally Korea – was accompanied by a related series of differences about the political structure and powers of the UN itself. The minority group (the communists) were concerned to preserve their veto power, oppose new programmes, reduce budgets, and in other ways to neutralise the UN. The majority group (the West) demanded a series of institutional changes to strengthen the UN, to make the organisation more active. Over some questions, the majority group were able to use their voting power to get their way. As we saw earlier, successive establishment of the Interim Committee, the by-passing of the Security Council on various issues, the passage of the Uniting for Peace resolution, all of these were successfully introduced by Western majorities. Their effect was to strengthen the powers of the Assembly, in which the West's strength was most pronounced. All were resisted by the Soviet Union for the same reason.

In the 1950s the position remained little different. The West supported the despatch of UN forces, even if controlled by the Assembly, and wished a strong role for the Secretary-General; the Communist states opposed them. The differences that arose around 1960 about the structure of the Organisation reflected the same basic interests of the two groups. In resisting the delegation of power to the Secretary-General in the Congo crisis, and in proposing the establishment of a troika system, the Soviet Union was seeking not merely to ensure that the UN was not used to further Western interests; but to weaken the power of the UN as a whole. The West favoured 'leaving it to Dag', not merely because they had confidence in the political discretion and judgement of Hammarskjöld, but because they favoured a strong and effective role for the UN as a whole (since they could control it). The Soviet Union refused to pay peace-keeping costs, not only because she disapproved of some of the specific acts which were taken in the UN's name; but because she rejected a principle (compulsory assessment) which might increase the capacity of the

UN to embark on peace-keeping action by majority vote (that is, against her interests) in the future. The West took the opposite view, not merely because they believed in a strong UN, but because a strong UN was likely to be strong on behalf of the West.

Slowly, as the balance in the UN changed, the attitude of the West too began to change. As developing countries secured a majority, the West were less inclined to support an increase in UN power. This still illustrated the same basic principle: the majority forces are always likely to favour an increase in power for the central authority, the minority to resist it. The attitude of a minority group towards the development of international authority has been accurately described by a Polish writer:

> The Socialist states . . . probably will continue to display a tendency to resolve . . . institutional questions at the lower level of possibilities. This rather cautious attitude reflects their fear that since they are a numerical minority, their risks are greater at a higher level of resolution and their past experience confirms this . . . In view of their experience with the UN Secretariat the Socialist states will approach any expansion of the competence of administrative bodies carefully, particularly in the areas of political power and operational functions in the field of economic and technical assistance.[1]

On the distribution of authority within international organisations the same writer stated: 'The Socialist states have repeatedly proposed that the seats in limited membership organisations [that is, the Councils and other bodies] be distributed between the main groups of states in such a way that each would receive a portion of the seats roughly corresponding to its actual importance (in general, approximately one-third for the Socialist states)'.[2] In other words a strengthening the power of the minority representation quite out of proportion to membership, numbers or population is demanded. Similar attitudes have been expressed towards the specialised agencies. A textbook on international law used in the Soviet Union stated that the specialised agencies 'not only do not guarantee peace between states, but themselves frequently reflect and experience the effect of contradictions and conflicts between states, which become particularly acute when capitalism entered its imperialistic stage. It should also be borne in mind that many of these organisations were dominated by monopoly capital, which has secured control over the bourgeois state machine and directs and guides its activities'.[3]

The political benefits that could be won by the majority in an international organisation are of a number of kinds. First, on many political issues the UN could provide the luxury of a voting victory, and so at least the illusion of a victory in the cold war itself. Second, by skilful tactics, other delegates, especially uncommitted nations, might be manoeuvred to their own side; for example through the support shown for the UN and its programmes, which poor states also demanded. Third, and most important, the UN might be induced to take specific actions in particular directions, which might not only promote the purposes of the UN, but also the political objectives of the West: the despatch of a commission to Greece to deter intervention in the Greek Civil War, the decision to support South Korea against attack from the north, the attempts to investigate violation of human rights in East Europe. All of these were perfectly justifiable initiatives; but they undoubtedly served to promote Western, rather than Eastern political interests.

But over the years the West's dominance steadily declined. In the early days of the UN, of the thirty-odd Third World delegations twenty were Latin American, and the overwhelming majority were favourable to the Western cause. Even after the big influx of new members in 1955, a majority remained pro-Western. It was only with the admission of a large group of African states in the early 1960s, and some changes in government elsewhere, that the balance began to change. Some competitive bidding for support was made by both sides. The Russians, in particular, for example during the visit of Mr Khrushchev to the UN in 1960, gave every possible emphasis to anti-colonial issues, in an attempt to win the support of the Afro-Asians. The Soviet-sponsored resolution, Resolution 1514, calling for the end of colonialism and a timetable to bring this about, was a striking example of that strategy. So were the many, often unrealistic, disarmament proposals. The USA too, though in somewhat less strident tones, sought to show its devotion to Third World causes, especially on development questions and on southern Africa: the foundation of the IDA is known to have resulted largely from such competition.[4] Britain was constrained to abandon its original practice of opposing all resolutions on apartheid, as violating the provision of Article 2(7) of the Charter. So a basic feature of the UN political process was revealed: as always, competition brought a convergence (in favour of popular causes). The Afro-Asians were quite sophisticated enough to be sceptical of the blandishments offered by both sides. On the whole they continued to be neutral on all cold war issues. They had interests of their own, on Africa, the Middle East, development and other matters. Thus the majority of resolutions were Third World resolutions acceptable to neither superpower: for all the manoeuvring, both the superpowers found themselves in the majority considerably less often than the average state.[5]

In the specialised agencies the East–West battle was also fought out, if less stridently. The belief once widely aired that functional organisations can be insulated from political pressures has not been borne out in practice. The Soviet Union, especially, has frequently raised political issues there. For example, in 1960 she introduced in WHO a resolution on general and complete disarmament (in support of the campaign she had been pursuing elsewhere), claiming this would 'open up wide opportunities' for the organisation (something of an understatement). The following year she called on it to support a UN resolution in favour of the liquidation of colonialism in all parts of the world: a proposal that was equally irrelevant to the organisation's aims and was politely but firmly rebuffed by African delegates. Later the Soviet Union several times sought to raise the Vietnam War in the WHO ('the epidemiological situation in Vietnam in connection with US aggression in South East Asia'). In UNESCO the Russians promoted resolutions on peaceful coexistence, the granting of independence to colonial countries and peoples, and the 'barbarous war in Vietnam'. In general, Western delegates have not attempted in such organisations to retaliate in quite such blatant terms (this may be partly because they are usually technical experts rather than Foreign Office delegates): an attitude which has perhaps done more to win support from Afro-Asian representatives than the crude propaganda of the Communist powers. But they too have not been above raising questions on which the Soviet Union was particularly vulnerable to score political points.

However, UNESCO has been the centre of an unhappy quarrel which highlighted the difficulties involved in running parts of the UN system including some of the specialised agencies. The accusations, voiced especially by the USA, included administrative incompetence, misallocation of funds and 'politicisation'. This last word was used to describe the straying away of UNESCO from its technical and professional purposes into politically contentious areas of policy. In protest the US withdrew from membership in 1984 and the UK followed suit the next year.

In general East–West issues had come to play a less and less important role by the late 1970s, both in the UN and the agencies. This is partly because that struggle had itself lost some of its original intensity. It was partly because of the increasing recognition that, especially in the agencies, the majority of listeners and potential converts only became bored and irritated with the injection of such issues into debates where they had no natural place. But it was perhaps above all because the differences between the two superpowers and their allies were increasingly overlaid by another more fundamental division: that between rich countries and poor. And, as the issues of development started to play a larger role, so the whole pattern of politics altered. The two superpowers, and the cold war alliances as a whole, found themselves increasingly pressed on to the same side, in resisting the demands of the developing world: the first and second world increasingly came into alliance against the third.

This had a somewhat paradoxical effect. The West was converted, by the influx of new members, into a minority, part of the larger minority of the developed. As we saw earlier, the division between the majority and the minority must always be the major division in the UN. The effect is that the West became increasingly constrained to adopt precisely the same strict constructionist arguments about the Charter and the limits of the Organisation's competence which in the 1960s they were resisting. They too became inclined to see a danger in increasing the powers of the Assembly, in weakening the safeguard of the veto, in strengthening the role of the Secretary-General; and clung to the sanctity of the Charter in preventing such developments. The Communist powers became more uncompromising than ever in resisting the demands of those, now the poor countries, who favoured internationalist, and even supranationalist solutions. By the early 1990s these trends had been reinforced by two developments. One was the collapse of communism and the ending of the cold war; the other the increased indebtedness and relative poverty of many Third World countries. The major conflict is now between the majority and the minority on the major issue of the day: those who want a radical increase in the UN activities, for development and other purposes, and so an increase in budgets, and those who oppose this.

NORTH–SOUTH POLITICS

The political division between rich and poor is distinguished from the former dissension between East and West in a number of important ways. It is not associated with an individual contest between two superpowers, who are the protagonists on each side: the developing have no major power to speak as their acknowledged representative (though China perhaps seeks to fill that role). It is not associated in a close sense with strategic issues, with whether there shall be peace or war, as the cold war was. It is not in the proper sense a difference of ideological viewpoint, associated with divergent political philosophies, as that was; it is rather a difference of material interest, associated with divergent standards of living. It is not even a competition for votes or for converts.

A number of consequences follow from these differences. Because it is not associated with a major power struggle, it does not take the form of bitter personal duels between the major protagonists, but of confrontations of groups of nations of varying shapes and sizes. Because it is not associated with strategic issues, it is less tinged with the fear and hysteria that characterised the cold war in its heyday. Because it is primarily a difference in material interest rather than political viewpoint, it cuts completely across traditional ideological divisions; and arises mainly in the economic rather than the political debates and institutions. Finally, because it is not a competition for votes, the tactics are quite different: it is not a question of cajoling and canvassing to win support among the bystanders, but of confrontation and negotiation between large organised groups together comprising the whole membership.

Although the struggle between rich and poor plays a far more dominant role in the UN today than in former times, it began to emerge almost from the beginning of the UN's existence. Even then about half its members were developing countries, at that time mainly from Latin America. It was largely at Latin American insistence that at San Francisco the Economic and Social Council was given an equal role with the Security and Trusteeship Councils among the 'principal' organs of the UN. It was in response to their demands that in 1948 the Technical Assistance Programme was first started. And the Latin Americans were increasingly joined by other developing countries, newly independent. (India especially took the lead on such questions in the early days.)

One of the main weapons used at first (when votes were lacking) was the systematic mobilisation of reports and resolutions. Groups of experts were appointed to produce them. These provided the ammunition for the developing countries. In 1950 a report on 'National and International Measures for Full Employment' proposed an expansion of the activities of the World Bank, and better commodity schemes.[6] In 1951 a report on 'Measures for the Economic Development of Under-developed Countries' proposed the establishment of 'an international development authority to assist the under-developed countries in preparing, coordinating and implementing their programmes of economic development' and 'to distribute to under-developed countries grants in aid for specific purposes'.[7] The next year ECOSOC was asked to prepare a detailed plan for establishing 'a special fund for grants in aid and for low-interest, long-term loans to under-developed countries'. In 1953 a Committee of Nine produced a further report recommending the establishment of a Special UN Fund for Economic Development (SUNFED).[8]

Against such an array of reports and recommendations, the rich powers had to devise their counter-proposals. In 1953, President Eisenhower proposed that the savings which could be achieved by internationally supervised disarmament might be devoted to a fund for assistance to developing countries: this both made clear that large-scale assistance was not likely to be available without disarmament, and also shifted responsibility on to the Soviet Union for failing to accept international inspection for disarmament. In the UN the rich countries said they could accept the preparation of a 'plan' for a fund, but not a 'scheme'. The developing secured the establishment of yet another committee; but the developed ensured this would only 'collate' their views. When this committee proposed the establishment of a fund, the developed demanded a new *ad hoc* committee: but not to make dangerous recommendations, only to 'report' the views it found. When a new committee was set up to propose the legal framework of the fund, the developed countries held that it should not recommend a particular framework but only put forward possible alternatives. And when ECOSOC, finally, voted in favour of a fund with only three dissentients (including the USA and Britain), the rich countries made it clear they were not prepared to contribute to it.

But despite this sustained and skilful rearguard action, the pressures had their effect. Although SUNFED never came into existence, the Western countries were constrained to put forward alternatives. The USA eventually proposed a more modest fund, financed entirely by voluntary contribution, to be devoted to pre-investment surveys and training: this Special Fund, though very far from what the developing countries wanted, was an advance over what they had had before. The World Bank, which had previously been hostile to an independent fund on the lines proposed, put forward ideas of its own for an International Development Association, which would be under its own auspices (and therefore subject to the voting system used within the Bank). As the President of the Bank himself subsequently said, 'the IDA was really an idea to offset the urge for SUNFED'.[9] This demonstrates an important feature of UN politics: a process of sustained pressure conducted on a systematic basis may eventually, even if it does not achieve its original objective, finally lead to evasive action, make necessary some concession, or the production of an alternative proposal. The dreadful bogey of SUNFED was frequently brought up as a reason for agreeing to some alternative. As Paul Hoffman put it, 'You can't fight nothing with nothing.' And it is reported that the US Secretary of the Treasury in advocating IDA perpetually reiterated 'the spectre of SUNFED if IDA were not established'.[10] So a sustained campaign, even if superficially unsuccessful, can achieve some results.

None the less, in the final resort there were points beyond which the North would not be pushed any further. This was clearly illustrated by the next stage in this particular history. The developing countries, not satisfied with the establishment of the Special Fund and the IDA, continued to demand the establishment of a capital development fund. Because the developed still resisted, they finally had to content themselves with the establishment of a fund with only voluntary contribution. And to this in general the rich countries refused to contribute. At pledging conferences for the Capital Development Fund only derisory sums were offered. That outcome perhaps convinced the poor countries that on some issues it was better to negotiate for an agreed solution, however modest, than to bulldoze proposals through which would never come to anything much.

For this reason the procedures of UNCTAD, when it was set up in 1964 emphasised negotiation and consensus as the means of securing progress. A conciliation procedure was established to make possible the compromise that would be necessary if a complete refusal to co-operate by developed governments was to be avoided. Under this, voting was delayed for a period while attempts were made to resolve the issues at stake. That conciliation procedure has in fact scarcely ever been used. But none the less informal meetings of representatives of the leading countries usually succeed in achieving agreement on a compromise text where necessary. And a similar procedure was successful, after long negotiations, in securing agreement on the system for generalised preferences for developing countries and some movement towards acceptance of the Common Fund idea. But the method does not always work: on other occasions, the developed countries have simply dug in their heels, as when many refused to name specific target-dates for achieving particular levels of aid during the second development decade or when all refused to give generalised debt relief.

Block politics are thus inevitably promoted over North–South issues. Such questions are almost the only ones on which there is any close identity of interest within the various blocks. They are thus the ones on which regional groups consistently vote together. Even here there are exceptions. Such countries as the Scandinavian, the Netherlands and Ireland quite often break ranks with the other rich states. Similarly, among the developing, there are divergencies between the less and the least developed. Even here, therefore, the block system counts for less than is often supposed.[11]

North–South politics became an even more pervasive problem in the mid-1980s. There were several reasons for this. First, with the ending of the cold war, this issue no longer diverted attention from Third World poverty. Second, the public became increasingly conscious of the horrendous suffering caused by this poverty as disasters like the Ethiopian famine of 1984 were portrayed on television screens. Third, in spite of (in some ways because of) aid programmes, the wealth gap between the North and South was widening. For example, in 1960 the richest twenty countries had incomes thirty times that of the poorest twenty countries. By 1990 the ratio had doubled to 60 times. Many poor countries had incurred such crippling debts that the sums paid both to private banks and to the IMF and the World Bank exceeded the sums being received. In the words of the UN Secretary-General in 1991, 'The external debt of capital-importing countries, which was less than $600 billion in 1988, has reached $1.2 trillion.'[12]

The fourth reason for the intensification of the North–South division has been the realisation of the interconnectedness of development and environmental matters. Industrialisation has caused environmental degradation, yet the North is unwilling to lower its standard of living and the South desires the benefits which the North has enjoyed. Each side accuses the other of straining the ecosystem: for example, the USA produces 25 per cent of the world's carbon dioxide, which is causing global warming; equatorial states such as Brazil and Malaysia are responsible for clearing the 96 000 acres of rainforest which are lost every day, UNCED sadly revealed the depth of the divisions more clearly than any willingness to co-operate.

OTHER POLITICAL DISPUTES

So far we have examined only the two most general political divisions
which have affected international organisations. There are other types
of dispute which regularly recur. International organisations inevitably
mirror the world outside, so that all external disputes tend to find
expression there. An example concerns the problems of Southern
Africa, perhaps the issue most bitterly and long fought out both in the
UN and in the agencies. We saw earlier how a substantial part of the
agenda of the political bodies of the UN, of the Human Rights
Commission, and other bodies was for many years regularly taken up
with these questions.[13] Special programmes of education and support
for refugees from the ex-Portuguese colonies, Namibia and Rhodesia,
were established. Moral or practical support for freedom-fighters has
been called for. The same trend has affected the agencies. There have
been demands in UNESCO for special educational programmes to
assist refugees from this area, in WHO for special health programmes,
in the World Bank for special development. Conversely, there have
been increasingly urgent calls on the agencies to cease all operations in
Southern Africa. (The World Bank, in seeking to resist this call, has
fought a prolonged rearguard action to resist the claims that the UN
can give direct instructions to it to cease operations in a particular area,
especially after such a programme has already begun.)

One of the most frequent forms in which such issues arise is over
representation. Questions of representation or membership are
inherent in the life of an international organisation. Most are intended
in theory to be universal. They are open to all states that ratify its
Convention, accept its basic aims or (as in the case of the UN) are
'peace-loving'. But in practice, whatever the theory, arguments can
always be found for the exclusion of any state that may be held
objectionable. The classic case is that of mainland China, kept out of
all UN bodies for twenty years for purely political reasons. If China
could be excluded for twenty years on such grounds, it is scarcely
surprising that alternative arguments have been found in other cases:
for example to exclude South Africa on the grounds of her apartheid
policies.

In the early years of the UN, South Africa became a member not
only of the UN itself, but of most of the agencies. With the influx of
African members in the early 1960s there were increasingly strenuous
demands for the expulsion of South Africa from many of the agencies,
and occasionally from the UN. In 1961 Nigeria, then recently

independent, proposed a resolution in the ILO, declaring that South Africa's continued membership was not consistent with the aims and purposes of the organisation, and asking the Governing Body to 'advise her to withdraw until apartheid had been abandoned' (the constitution at that time did not permit expulsion). Later there was a mass demonstration by the African delegations, which prevented the South African representative from speaking at all. In 1964, the Governing Body proposed constitutional amendments which would permit any state to be expelled because it had been expelled from the UN, or to be *suspended* for 'flagrantly and persistently pursuing . . . a declared policy of racial discrimination'. A month later South Africa voluntarily withdrew: the outcome many countries had been hoping for all along. Somewhat similar events took place elsewhere. In 1963, the African delegates walked out of the FAO Conference when the South African delegate spoke. A resolution was passed, excluding South Africa from meetings in Africa (which the African delegates had said they would boycott anyway if South Africa attended). But there too South Africa herself withdrew from the organisation. Similarly, in WHO, African delegates boycotted a regional committee in 1963 because of the attendance of South Africa, and the whole conference had to be abandoned. Again, South Africa eventually decided to withdraw. None the less, South Africa at present remains a member of some of the agencies, notably WHO, ICAO and IAEA.

Within the UN itself no move has ever been made for the total expulsion of South Africa.[14] In the early 1960s she withdrew from the Assembly for a few years but later returned.[15] In practice her representatives have been partially ostracised within the Organisation, in the committees and in social activities. But from 1970, South Africa's presence at the UN has been raised in a different form. In that year the African states proposed an amendment to the report of the Credentials Committee; this accepted the report 'except with regard to the credentials of the representatives of the government of South Africa'. The legal counsel of the UN submitted a statement, saying that suspension of the rights and privileges of membership through the rejection of credentials would be 'contrary to the Charter': in other words such a suspension required a specific vote, probably demanding a two-thirds majority (as for expulsion). The President of the Assembly, addressing the Assembly after the vote, said he interpreted this as a 'very strong condemnation' of the policies of the South African government and 'a warning to that government as solemn as any such warning could be'; but it would not mean that the South

African delegation was unseated and it would not affect the rights and privileges of membership of South Africa. Similar episodes have occurred since and the effect to be given to the vote depends each year on the President's ruling. Since the Algerian President's ruling in 1975 South Africa has taken no part in Assembly discussion, while remaining a member of the Organisation.

The Middle East dispute has also sparked off disputes on representation. In the UN itself Israel has virtually no hope of being elected to any of the committees or representative bodies. She does not belong to any regional block responsible for the elections. She is thus in a highly isolated position. As in the South African case, the issue has been raised first in the agencies. There has been a long-standing dispute about the organisation of WHO's regional activities in the Middle East. Because of Arab opposition, Israel is not included with other parts of the Middle East and West Asia, but in a group of European countries. Israel has sought to get this position changed, so that she is recognised as a country with a stake and a permanent position in the Middle East. In 1969 the Arab delegation threatened that if the position was changed, they would boycott any meeting which Israel attended. As a result it was decided to maintain the existing position. Similarly in UNESCO Israel has sought to be classified as a part of Asia, as geographically she clearly is, but this too has been resisted; in 1976 she was permitted to join the European group. The Middle East dispute has of course been raised in many other ways within the agencies: for example in resolutions in WHO, deploring 'deficiencies of health conditions in occupied territories in the Middle East', and in UNESCO, denouncing the acquisition by Israel of cultural objects and antiquities in the occupied areas as a result of 'imperialist Zionist aggression'. Most dramatically, in 1975 the General Assembly passed Resolution 3379 declaring that 'Zionism is a form of racism'. It was repealed in 1991.

Probably the most bitter and protracted dispute concerning representation and admission have been those affecting China and East Germany. Both of these were closely bound up with cold war politics. The China question was complicated because it was not a matter of *admission* of the Chinese People's Republic, but of deciding *which* government was to occupy the China seat that already existed. Although the procedures governing admission are clearly laid down, those governing representation are not. At first it was widely held that the Security Council could rule which goverment should occupy the seat. Later, it came to be accepted that it was for the Assembly to make the decision. For ten years the Assembly, at US instigation, decided 'not to consider' the China question. For ten years after that, from 1960, it was decided that the matter was 'an important question', and so required a two-thirds majority. When, in 1970, a simple majority in favour of a change in representation was obtained, this was still not sufficient to bring about the transfer of the seat. Only in 1972, despite an ineffectual plea at the last moment that Taiwan was not part of China (though for twenty years the same government had kept her in the UN on the sole grounds that she was part of China and so entitled to the China seat), was the mainland government finally seated. The corollary has been that Taiwan does not have a seat.

On the German question the position taken (which in theory concerned qualifications for membership, the representation of divided countries and 'universality') depended in practice largely on political predelictions. For long there was no serious move for the admission of either half of Germany as full members: the admission of West Germany without that of East Germany would inevitably have been vetoed. As a result other methods were used to achieve almost the same effect. Even during the fifties West Germany was admitted, with the support of Western states, to membership of some of the specialised agencies. But West Germany was also given observer status at the UN; she had, for long before she was admitted, a permanent UN mission, which was active behind the scenes. Other ways were found to bring West Germany closer to full membership, without risking being vetoed on admission: for example she was elected to the Governing Council of UNDP and other bodies. Only when a general relations agreement covering mutual recognition was agreed between the two states in 1972 was it possible for both to secure membership free of veto by supporters of the other.

Today, hostilities have eased and the theory of 'universality' of UN membership is almost entirely reflected in practice (see p.188).

CONCLUSIONS

We have only been able to sketch here particular *types* of conflict in the UN system. There are some obvious distinctions between the political life of international organisations and that of national states. The political process in national states is concerned not only with politics, but, above all, with the process of acquiring the power which alone enables the policies to be carried out: indeed some political writers consider that politics is concerned *essentially* with 'power' – the means of acquiring and maintaining it. Certainly, both in democratic states, in the struggle for electoral support, and in authoritarian states, in the contest between factions and personalities, the political process is *partly* concerned with winning power; the most idealistic programme cannot be implemented unless power is obtained to do so. In international organisations this whole aspect of the political system is missing; for there are no seats of power to be won. Everybody occupies seats in the UN and its Assembly. Almost everybody occupies seats in other bodies too at some time, according to a rotational system. There are disputes about the *degree* of representation of particular countries or groups within such bodies; but there is not yet an organised struggle by particular groups to win total control, such as exists within states. Exclusive occupation of the seats of power never occurs. All share power in all bodies all the time.

There are a number of consequences of this. First, in most cases, because many factions of widely differing views are represented, and because at least a simple majority, and often more, is required for action, no single group can normally get its way. None can freely put into practice their own political philosophy and purposes, as dictators and small minority groups (as well as majority parties) can within states. A number of different groups must be satisfied. All must bargain and trade. Compromise is the essence of the system. This is not always consensus. The compromise agreed need not be equally acceptable to all groups. It may be a deal between two or three groups at the expense of another.

Even this will not always suffice. Because the entire fabric is fragile, because in the final resort a group may refuse to cooperate altogether, even withdraw from the Organisation on the most important issues, caution must be exercised. If the system is to operate at all, no major groups can be antagonised or excluded. This is one of the reasons why, as we saw earlier (p.48 above), so much of the political process in international bodies takes place in the corridors, in informal negotiation rather than formal discussion and debate. On both the major political controversies we have examined in this chapter, concerning the *degree of authority*, and the *volume of expenditure*, by international organisations, there has been no outright victory. For outright victory would involve outright defeat. And this might involve the destruction of the whole Organisation. Both parties have to give something all the time.

The absence of any organised power within international bodies, and the consequent need for compromise, accounts partly for what is believed to be the distinctive feature of the UN: that it is all talking and little doing. This is a largely erroneous view, based on those aspects of UN activity which receive most publicity. As we saw in Chapter 3, there is a great deal of activity in the UN system as a whole, involving total expenditure of billions of dollars a year. But it is true that there is also a fair amount of talking. This results inevitably from the characteristics we have just noted: the need for compromise and agreement on most issues, among a very large number of different governments, before a decision can be taken. Talk is necessary before the doing can begin. The talking is not directed mainly at persuasion, any more than debates in parliament are aimed at persuasion: nobody in UN bodies really expects that their opponents are going to be so overwhelmed by the persuasiveness of the argument that they will immediately concede the point. It is directed at a systematic presentation of the position of each party after which a compromise reconciling each may be drawn up.

Another feature of the political system of international organisations is connected with this. Discussion is virtually never directed to general objectives, still less to the political philosophy on which policies should be based: for example, to discussing what the general aim of an organisation's policies should be, still less whether supranationalism should be extended or reduced. It is devoted to very specific proposals for action: the establishment of a particular programme, the setting up of a peace-keeping force, what should be done about global warming. This is one reason why alliances are usually ad hoc over a particular issue, rather than over a wide range of issues as under a party system.

There is one further characteristic of the politics of international organisations which differs from that of national states. Because there is no party system, there is no initial commitment by each delegation to support a particular proposal when it is made, in the way that a parliamentary representative is in some way already committed to the policies of his own party. Every delegation has to reach its own decision anew on every proposal which comes before it. It is this which makes necessary the intensive process of consultation, lobbying, persuasion and arm-twisting described earlier. Compromise inevitably involves much huddling away from the set-piece speeches. Attitudes on a wide range of issues are determined not by commitment to the party but by a number of types of pressure, sometimes conflicting. The regional block may take up a position which, other things being equal, its members will be expected to support. Ideological convictions may influence a member-state in some other direction, possibly altogether different. There may be pressures from individual states, especially those with which the country concerned has very close relations; or from a superpower on which it is especially dependent. Finally, and by far the most important, there is a national interest, which may not coincide with any of these. It is understandable that, in these circumstances, the process of reaching agreement by the Assembly may be much more complicated than in a national parliament; and certainly much more complicated than the stereotype of 'block politics' suggests.

The regional blocks have influence only on a comparatively small proportion of issues. A large number of them do not even discuss at all. The EC is today probably closer to reaching joint decisions than any other group and even its members sometimes fail to agree. Most countries formulate their own policies, normally in their own capital, on each individual issue. All the larger missions, and many of the smaller will obtain instructions from their capital about their voting position on almost every resolution, and even on individual clauses and sub-clauses. The mission may make their own recommendations, but these are not necessarily accepted (invariably the mission wants a position more pro-UN, or closer to the majority than the government in the capital).

In so far as countries frequently vote together, therefore, it is rather because of common *interests* than of common politics. This makes for loose and perpetually shifting coalitions. This is particularly true in the vital function of initiation; putting forward proposals. Initiatives come usually from *individual* governments, rather than the regional groups (for example the proposal for an anti-terrorism Convention put forward by West Germany in 1976). The groups meet to *respond* to initiatives rather than to make them. They discuss particular issues but not general ones. And they have no policies, in the sense of long-term strategies to which all their members are expected to conform. A genuine party system does not yet exist, therefore.

How about the political *means* employed in this system, the strategies used by a state to get its way? These vary widely. The powerful state has means of influence of which most members do not dispose. For many years the US could rely on support from the Latin American countries (and had therefore in effect twenty votes virtually in its pocket) because of its powerful influence with their governments. This was less true in the agencies, and is scarcely true today even in the UN. The Soviet Union, on the other hand, had ten votes which remained until 1989 more reliably at her disposal. France to this day retains a considerable sway over the votes of some francophone countries in Africa, which are dependent for economic, and often military, support from France. Other countries have had special forms of influence. India for long, despite the fact that she was not associated with any particular power grouping, held a special place as a spokesman of the Afro-Asians, and as one of the largest, most educated and sophisticated of the developing countries. The Scandinavians have a voice disproportionate in weight to their numbers or power because they are neutrals, regarded as 'respectable' partners by both developed and developing alike, as well as floating voters, whose support may therefore be worth bargaining for.[16]

Many votes, however, are to some extent influenced by the majority views in regional or economic blocks. Here the small nation has some say. Sometimes the influence of individual nations *within* each regional group can largely determine the way the whole block goes. For a decade from the mid-1960s, Tanzania and Algeria were the most powerful and influential voices among the Afro-Asians. Usually they advocated the most extreme policies and so won the competition in militancy; few within the group dared to risk the transgression of appearing moderate. In the 1970s, other African countries, Nigeria and Senegal, though more moderate, probably had equal influence.

Thus the block system works in an extremely haphazard way. On many issues it does not operate at all. On others, such as development and other economic issues, groups vote together but because of common interest not the group system. In time, as economic differences among the Third World countries emerge, geographical groupings may be increasingly replaced by genuine interest groups, based on stages of development and political philosophy alone. When voting becomes sufficiently consistent on this basis, something like a genuine party system will emerge. Only then will the institutions of international organisations begin to reproduce something like the political pattern as it exists in national states.

At present the politics of international society remain those of the eighteenth-century parliament in Britain, with individual actions and groups giving or withholding support for particular proposals, rather than an organised parliamentary system as in modern democratic states. This may not remain the case in the future. Economic issues increasingly dominate the scene; and here common interests are most common and most immediate. There may then emerge a more systematic organisation, with coalitions formed on that basis, with much greater consultation on strategy, and with far higher discipline in voting. The eighteenth century may give way to the nineteenth.

8 Conclusions: A New Lease of Life?

THE END OF THE COLD WAR

When the 1980s opened the UN was in a parlous condition. The efficiency and morale of the Secretariat were at a low ebb because of Waldheim's style of management. Animosity between the USA and USSR was tense during this so-called 'new cold war' period, a condition scarcely conducive to collaboration in the Security Council. The Reagan government was pursuing a policy of positive hostility to the UN system. And, because of the withholding of funds by several states, including the two superpowers, the Organisation teetered on the edge of bankruptcy. Yet by the end of the decade the scene had changed to one of hope and creative activity. The purpose of this chapter is to outline how the UN acquired this new lease of life and to indicate the agenda of the early 1990s for further improvements.

Throughout the whole of its history the UN and particularly the Security Council had been stymied by the cold war confrontation between the USA and the USSR. With the advent to power of Mikhail Gorbachev this bitter hostility and suspicion rapidly dissolved. Soviet spokesmen soon revealed that 'new thinking' was producing a more flexible and collaborative foreign policy. A combination of the impossibility of maintaining a huge military expenditure and Gorbachev's personal worry about world instability lay behind this revised posture.[1]

In due course, a positive and co-operative demeanour in the UN became evident as part of this Soviet 'new thinking'. The boring denunciations of the Organisation as an 'imperialist' body and the obstructionist tactics of Soviet representatives were discontinued.

Gorbachev made two key statements in which he showed his belief that a more peaceful and stable world was dependent on the powers working for an enhanced role for the UN. The first was an article written in September 1987; the second was a speech in the General Assembly a year later. His article urged a much greater use and strengthening of the UN in very many spheres of international political

173

and economic life: the environment, Third World debt, combating
terrorism, protecting human rights, monitoring the use of nuclear
energy, arms control and peace-keeping operations. He argued too for
a more effective use of the Security Council. In his speech, primarily
devoted to announcing substantial unilateral arms reductions,
Gorbachev signalled the new constructive policy by expressing regret
that the UN had become 'for many years a field of propaganda battles
and for cultivating political confrontation'.[2]

That Gorbachev's statements were more than just conciliatory words
was made evident in the most helpfully tangible way – by the USSR
starting to pay some of its debts. In 1987 payment was made both of
the arrears in regular contributions and nearly two hundred million
dollars previously withheld from the bills for peace-keeping operations
of which the USSR had disapproved.

Although many Western governments quickly welcomed the Soviet
'new thinking' and its implications for the UN, the USA remained
suspicious for a while. However, a certain mellowing of attitudes in the
Reagan administration towards the UN had already been evident
before Gorbachev's conciliatory gestures. And as it became increasingly evident that these gestures were not a mere smokescreen for more
trouble making, the American change of stance on the UN accelerated.

The US had vented its displeasure regarding the UN by refusing to
pay its full assessed contributions. The argument was twofold: that the
Organisation wasted money and that it was unreasonable for
Americans to fund a body which repaid them in the currency of
propaganda vilification. However, by 1986–8 the USA was finding it
increasingly embarrassing to hold to these arguments: as we shall see
below, the UN was reforming itself to some effect; other defaulters,
notably China and France, as well as Russia, were paying their backlog
of dues; and the European Community was exerting pressure on the
USA to pay up for fear that the Europeans themselves might have to
meet the shortfall in order to rescue the UN from bankruptcy.

INTERNAL REFORMS

The UN was in better shape in the late 1980s than formerly to respond
to and take advantage of the warmer relationship between the two
superpowers and between them and itself. Furthermore, the momen-
tum of reform continued into the early 1990s, spurred on by the feeling
of 'being wanted' and by the appointment of a new Secretary-General

determined not to allow the opportunities for improvements to grind to a halt.

From 1985 to 1988 the Secretary-General, Pérez de Cuéllar, wrestled with the Organisation's financial troubles, induced largely by the shortfall in American payments. He instituted economy measures in 1986 and 1987, reducing conferences, meetings and travel allowances and economising on staffing by freezing appointments and promotions. But the sums saved were petty in relation to the debt. The UN was helped in 1988 by the American agreement to pay $664 million, some of it immediately.

This eventual turnabout in the US attitude was largely due to the work of the '18-member Group of High-Level International Experts'. This team was established by the General Assembly in order to draw up recommendations for administrative and financial reforms for the Organisation. It reported to the Secretary-General in 1986. The report was comprehensive. There were wide-ranging suggestions for retrenchment. These included fairly substantial staffing reductions, most severe at the senior levels, together with departmental restructuring. The group strongly advised reductions in the number of conferences and meetings and the bulk of documentation. They also had important comments to make on the way in which the UN budget was devised.

Since quarrels over financial contributions, especially the American, were both significant causes and effects of the crisis in the UN in the mid-1980s, reforming the budgetary process was of central importance. As a result of the work of the Group of 18 and subsequent General Assembly deliberations a new system was introduced. The old method (see pp.146–7) gave individual governments no voice in the allocation of funds under the various heads of expenditure. The arrangements agreed in 1986 rectified this. The task of drafting the budget was allocated (as from 1990) to the Committee for Programme and Co-ordination (CPC), a body of thirty-four members and a sub-committee of ECOSOC (see p.149). The CPC arrives at decisions by consensus. In effect, therefore, this new budgetary procedure provides the representatives of states such as the USA who disagree with any allocations the opportunity to shape the budget according to their priorities. Hence the relaxation in the American mood and the start, in 1988, of paying off its debt.

As for the reform of the top management recommended by the Group of 18 this task fell to Boutros-Ghali. It is perhaps ironic that the first major shake-up of the Secretariat structure should have been

The United Nations

undertaken by a Secretary-General the manner of whose appointment was so widely criticised. When, in 1991, a replacement was needed for Pérez de Cuéllar, the African states were persistent in their claim that it was 'their turn' to supply a Secretary-General after three Europeans, an Asian and a Latin-American. Yet they had no acceptable candidate, so Dr Boutros Boutros-Ghali, an Egyptian, was agreed upon as an approximation for the Africans and as inoffensive to the major powers. Commentators who were perhaps looking for a dynamic Hammarskjöld-like figure to lead the resuscitated Organisation regretted not only the lack of *positive* reasons for his appointment, but also his age: he admits to being born in 1922, though it has been put about that he is in fact a few years older. Boutros-Ghali, a Coptic Christian, was trained as a lawyer, has academic interests and served the Egyptian government as minister and diplomat. He accepted the UN post in full consciousness of the opportunities presented by its new-found life. 'If I was offered the job five years ago, I would have turned it down,' he declared. 'The UN was then a dead horse, but after the end of the Cold War the UN has a special position.'[3]

Soon after assuming office Boutros-Ghali announced a rationalisation of the structure of the Secretariat as a first phase of projected reforms. He reduced the number of departments from twenty to eight and the number of first- and second-level posts from forty-eight to thirty-two. The eight departments, each headed by an Under-Secretary General, are: Political department dealing with Africa, Asia and the Middle East; Political department dealing with Europe, Latin America, disarmament, the General Assembly and the Security Council; Peacekeeping operations; Economic department; Legal affairs; Disaster relief; Information; Administration and budget. It is notable that peace-keeping and disaster relief are allotted special departments of their own, indicating the importance attached by Boutros-Ghali to these UN activities. It was also notable that the principle of the geographical distribution of appointments was abandoned. Only two Third World countries, China and Sierra Leone, featured in the list of Under-Secretaries-General. One American and five Europeans filled the other posts.

The highlighting of peace-keeping by making it a separate department was much welcomed. Nevertheless, this facet of the UN's work depended on a more harmonious and efficient handling of business by the Security Council than had been the case during its first forty years. Here, too, there was a welcome change of heart and procedures. (It is symptomatic of the new mood that no veto has been cast since May 1990.) Four improvements from the mid-1980s may be noted. One has been the much greater willingness of the members, released from the cold war tensions, to work together for solutions to regional crises and conflicts. Secondly, the institutionalising of informal meetings (see p.18) has been shown to be beneficial: there has been less temptation to allow rhetoric to impede problem solving. Thirdly, a start was made to build into the programme of the Security Council 'periodic' meetings of foreign ministers so that discussions and even decisions could involve governments directly in addition to their permanent representatives. (In fact, the first ever heads of state and government meeting of the Security Council was held in January 1992 – important also as a symbolic gesture of the commitment of all states to the UN.) And fourthly, much better co-ordination became evident, at least, until 1992, between the Security Council and the Secretary-General.

As an indication of the activity of the Security Council, the following topics were handled in its 69 meetings in 1990: Middle East and related questions (25); Iraq's invasion of Kuwait (15); Central America, especially the activities of ONUCA (8); Iran and Iraq (4); Cyprus (5); peace-keeping operations in general (1); Afghanistan (1); Western Sahara (1); Cambodia (1); admission of new members (4); appointments to the ICJ (2); termination of trusteeship status for four Pacific territories (1); general business (1).

The fruit of the Security Council's more constructive mode of working was indicated by Pérez de Cuéllar in 1991. He wrote about the period since 1988 that

> never before in the history of the Organization were so many new insights gained about the varied tasks of keeping, making or building the peace in areas riven or threatened by conflict. Never before were such precedents set as has been done, in different ways, in Namibia, Haiti, Angola, Nicaragua and now, most notably, in Central America, particularly El Salvador. Indeed, today, the Organization is conducting some missions that were unthinkable in the previous era.[4]

And it must be remembered that Pérez de Cuéllar was a Secretary-General not given to hyperbole.

ACTIVE DIPLOMACY

Once the cold war had come to an end the UN could help resolve the conflicts which had dragged on for so long in Afghanistan and south-western Africa. Moreover, the Organisation was able to display its usefulness and expertise in these diplomatically challenging problems. For most of the 1970s Afghanistan was in a condition of chaos. A Communist government came to power in 1978. The following year Soviet forces invaded the country to support one of the leaders of that government and with a view to stabilising the régime. The result was civil war and cold war by proxy. The Soviet Union found itself in a situation analogous in miniature to the American in Vietnam a decade or so earlier.

The UN was soon involved in trying to secure a peaceful settlement. The Secretary-General's representative, Cordovez, engaged in lengthy and patient negotiations as mediator. Gorbachev's arrival on the scene in 1985 gave increased hope of a settlement. But the negotiations dragged on. The diplomacy was complex, involving the Soviet Union and its client government in Kabul, on the one hand, and Pakistan and the USA, supporting the *Mujahidin* Muslim guerrillas, on the other. Eventually a series of accords were signed under UN auspices in Geneva in 1988. These did not solve the Afghan internal problems; but they did allow the withdrawal of Soviet forces with some saving of face and removed one obstacle to the healing of the rift between the two superpowers. In these ways the UN had performed a valuable service.

Eight months after the Geneva Accords two agreements were signed in New York to stop the fighting in Namibia and Angola. This was another regional problem which had become entangled in cold war politics, in this case because of the involvement of Cuban forces with Soviet backing in the Angolan civil war. Angola had been a Portuguese colony, but, since its independence in 1975, had been wracked by civil war. Namibia had been governed (under the name of South-West Africa) by South Africa since the end of the First World War, contrary to UN demands since 1967 that it should be given independence. The two problems became intertwined because the fighters for Namibian independence operated from Angola.

The Angola/Namibia Accords of 1988 were the result of activities undertaken by both the USA as a mediator and the UN. The UN established the ground rules for a settlement in the late 1970s and provided a neutral institutional framework in which the various contending parties could honourably reach agreement. The accords provided for the withdrawal of Angolan forces, while in return South Africa agreed to concede independence to Namibia.

In both the Afghan and Angolan/Namibian cases the UN followed up its diplomatic achievements by sending in the 'blue berets'. A small

UN Good Offices Mission in Afghanistan and Pakistan (UNGOMAP) was in place from 1988 to 1990. A similar-sized contingent monitored the withdrawal of Cuban forces from Angola (UNAVEM). A much larger UN Transition Assistance Group (UNTAG) helped to ensure fair elections in Namibia.

In many ways the conflicts in Afghanistan and south-western Africa were relatively self-contained. In the case of the two Gulf wars (1980–88 and 1990–91), however, the interests of so many states in ensuring uninterrupted oil supplies from the region rendered the conflicts potentially more dangerous. Moreover, the interventions of the UN in these wars are more interesting than in the issues just reviewed.

The Iraq–Iran war, which broke out in 1980, was often likened in style and horror to the First World War. At first the UN was ineffectual. Circumstances had changed by 1987 and, with the superpowers co-operating, the Security Council was able to pass Resolution 598. This was couched in terms of Chapter VII of the Charter: the threat of sanctions or even military intervention therefore lay behind the demand that the two belligerants cease fighting. But it was a year before Iran accepted the terms of the resolution. The UN Iran–Iraq Military Observer Group (UNIIMOG) was then despatched to ensure compliance with the cease-fire.

Two years later the world community was faced with the problem of what to do about a most blatant act of aggression. Iraq's invasion and seizure of Kuwait. This crisis and its aftermath presented the UN with a number of serious questions. How could Kuwait, a sovereign member of the UN, be liberated? How could the Iraqi people, whose human rights had been violated by the dictator Saddam Hussein, be protected? (The most vulnerable were the Kurds.) What action could be taken to deprive Saddam of his nuclear and chemical-weapon capacity? And how could actions taken in pursuit of these objectives be justified if they involved the UN sanctioning the violation of Iraq's sovereignty?

On 2 August 1990, Iraqi troops crossed the Kuwaiti border. The Security Council convened in emergency session and demanded an immediate ceasefire and withdrawal of Iraqi forces. This was the first of numerous Security Council meetings during the crisis. Subsequent sessions agreed to wide-ranging sanctions and, with Resolution 665, authorised the use of military action to enforce the economic embargo if necessary. In November, Iraq having remained recalcitrant, Resolution 678 was adopted. This authorised the use of 'all necessary means' to liberate Kuwait. The following January multinational armed forces, predominantly American, launched the counter-attack.

The economic and military campaigns against Iraq were powerful demonstrations of what the UN could achieve in the post-cold war diplomatic conditions. President Bush spoke of the dawning of a 'new world order'. However, sceptical commentators pointed out blemishes in this apparently immaculate picture of international law enforcement. Should the economic sanctions have been given longer to bite? Did President Bush exert pressure to conduct a war more for his own personal and national interests (notably an assured oil supply) than for the sake of international order? Was not the virtuous justice of the war tarnished by the perception of many Arabs at the time and since that it was a new Christian crusade against Islam? What credence could be given to the argument that the whole world community sanctioned the use of force when China abstained and Yemen and Cuba voted against Security Council Resolution 678? But at least it was a more universally acceptable operation than the Korean War, which had had UN backing only because of the fortuitous absence of the Soviet Union from the Security Council.

Nor did UN concern about Iraq end with the aggressor being driven from Kuwait. Following precedents in so many other trouble spots, an observer force was deployed on the border – UNIKOM, the UN Iraq-Kuwait Observation Mission. Other activities were quite novel. By virtue of a series of resolutions adopted throughout 1991 the UN engaged in the most intrusive activities against a sovereign state in the history of the Organisation. The objectives were to exact reparations, destroy Iraq's nuclear, biological and chemical war potential and relieve the suffering of the civilian population. The methods used have been the imposition of economic sanctions, offers of their relaxation under strict monitoring, and the inspection and destruction by UN-appointed experts, of weapons and production facilities. Two resolutions were particularly significant. One was 706, which allowed Iraq to sell some oil (its main source of income) for the purpose of buying supplies under supervision and strictly for humanitarian purposes. Resolution 715 authorised the weapons inspectors to search anywhere in Iraq for forbidden stocks and factories and without any specified time limit. In some ways, the creation of UN demarcated 'safe havens' for the Kurds in northern Iraq was the most significant move: it was the first time that the Organisation had interfered in the internal affairs of a sovereign state without its consent.

From the perspective of early 1992 the UN Secretary-General and, especially, the Security Council had extended and deepened their effective diplomatic and peace-keeping activities well beyond what would have seemed feasible a mere five years earlier. Apart from the perhaps special circumstances of disciplinary proceedings against Iraq, the increased scope of activity was notable. In January 1992 the 'summit' meeting of heads of government at the Security Council declared that 'UN peacekeeping tasks have increased and broadened in recent years. Election monitoring, human rights verification and the repatriation of refugees have . . . been integral parts of the Security Council's efforts to maintain peace and security.'[5]

FAILURES AND UNRESOLVED PROBLEMS

Lest the enthusiasts for the UN become too euphoric in reading this catalogue of recent successes, it is as well to remind ourselves that there have also been recent failures and that many a problem remains unresolved. The second Gulf war revealed the Organisation's limitations as well as its new-found strength. We have already noticed that the UN backing for the use of force against Iraq has not been without its critics. After the war the Iraqi government broke the UN-imposed economic blockade and had some success in obstructing the UN teams working on the demolition of weapons of mass destruction. Moreover, the Iraqi regime has been as much condemned for the way it has made its own people suffer as for the seizure of Kuwait. It is therefore a melancholy irony that, despite the war, Saddam Hussein remained in power while, as a result of the war, the sufferings of the innocent Iraqi people increased – by war casualties, the effects of the economic sanctions and the brutal policies pursued by the government against the Kurds in the north of the country and the Shi'as in the south. Indeed, the UN High Commission for Refugees was quite unprepared for the scale of the problem presented by the displacement of so many of these Iraqi citizens from their homes. Furthermore. when the scheme to protect the Kurds by the delineation of an 'exclusion zone' was brought forward by the British government, the UN Secretariat reacted with little enthusiasm and by mid-1992 the operation had been wound down.

A similar lack of decisiveness marked the UN response to the bloody disintegration of Yugoslavia, in particular the civil war in Bosnia–Herzegovina. True, in this case the failure to act promptly and firmly was caused by the reluctance of either the USA or the EC to commit armed forces to the task. The agony of Sarajevo in 1992 therefore served to prove the truism that the strength of the UN is dependent upon the resolve of its members.

If the events in Iraq and the former Yugoslavia in 1991–2 laid bare the limits to the revival of the UN in its peace-keeping role, the anti-climax of the 'Earth Summit' in Rio confirmed the weakness of the commitment of the world's nations to effective policies of sustainable development. This largest-ever gathering of world leaders produced documents listing bland statements of principle while the speeches and avoidance of effective commitments emphasised the continued priority of national economic growth rates. If anything, the conference deepened the gulf between North and South because of the evident refusal of either side to concede the evil of its own ways and the justice of the other's. An agreement was reached to establish a Sustainable Development Commission to monitor the environmental impact of projects funded by various UN agencies. However, even that arrangement has its negative side: it involved the creation of yet another body in the UN system already confused by the proliferation of so many; and it reports only indirectly to the General Assembly, via the feeble ECOSOC.

By the middle of 1992 criticism of the UN and of the Secretary-General in particular was gaining in force. Saddam Hussein was defying the UN in his treatment of the Kurd and Shi'ite populations of his own country and of UN personnel endeavouring to implement Security Council Resolutions. The civil wars in the former Yugoslavia had generated the biggest refugee problem in Europe since the end of the Second World War (some three million). UN personnel there could not keep the peace because there was no peace to keep. And they had neither the authority, manpower nor weapons to *enforce* a peace in a horrendously complex situation of interethnic hatred.

Meanwhile, in Cambodia, although that country was enjoying a semblance of peace through exhaustion, the UN was equally unsuccessful in brokering an effective settlement. After the experience of American bombardment during the Vietnam war, the maniacal policy of slaughter by the Khmer Rouge regime, and the charitable invasion by Vietnam, peace seemed within grasp by 1991. On the understanding that all factions were willing to collaborate, the UN established a peace-keeping force (UNTAC) to help stabilise the country and prepare for elections. It has been a massive and costly operation: by the summer of 1992, 14 000 troops, 1500 police and thousands of civilians were ready for this ambitious task when the Khmer Rouge made it clear that they were not in reality going to honour the cease-fire.

Boutros-Ghali suffered criticism on grounds of his bad working relationships and failure to grapple with these crises. In his defence it must be recognised that the Cambodian and Yugoslav problems were exceptionally difficult and complex; that the UN was not equipped to cope with such problems; and that the appalling civil war and famine in Somalia needed greater UN attention, as Boutros-Ghali urged, than the major powers were willing to allow.

These instances of the failure of the UN to make much progress in resolving the most dramatic problems it faced in 1991–2 may be simply interpreted as the continued tension between supranational idealism and the reality of state sovereignty. The Organisation is based upon the principle of the 'sovereign equality' of its members (Article 2(2)). And yet if the UN is to tackle current problems such as nuclear proliferation, human rights violations, civil wars, threats to the environment, threats to health (for example, AIDS, drugs trafficking), then its agents must have access to and authority within states. In so far as that authority might be exercised independently of and even against the interests of the individual state, that state would suffer a diminution of its sovereignty. A start has been made along these lines in the destruction of Iraq's nuclear war potential by officials of the IAEA. Whether this precedent can be built upon remains to be seen.

One of the reasons that state sovereignty remains largely untrammelled is the weakness of international law. The parallel between the medieval development of 'the king's peace' and the need to develop a 'world peace' has often been remarked upon. The most formidable prospectus for the reform of the UN system was indeed entitled *World Peace through World Law*.[6] Yet, in the words of Sir Brian Urquhart, 'There is little or no machinery for monitoring respect for international law, let alone for enforcing it.'[7]

The founders of the United Nations were well aware that they were not creating, indeed could not create, an ideal organisation. Mindful of the failure of the League of Nations, they put their faith in the collaborative power of the 'Big Five' to maintain world peace. That the cold war rendered that design inoperable is not the point at issue now, at the turn of the century. The point now is the perceived obsolescence of the 'Big Five' dominance in the context of the world's environmental and economic problems and the tensions they are generating between the states of the northern and southern hemispheres. The Security Council worked reasonably effectively, as we have seen, in resolving military conflicts in the late 1980s. But it has little relevance for the resolution of stresses deriving from development, trade and ecological problems.

Yet it is precisely in these areas that the continuing weakness of the UN system is most serious. The acceptance of the autonomy of the specialised agencies and the frailty of ECOSOC have led to the chronic problems of the multiplication of organs, their overlapping of functions and failure to co-ordinate their programmes. The kind of authoritative leadership displayed by the Security Council in assisting the diminution of conflict in the late 1980s needs to be paralleled in the economic-social environment spheres. Although this confusion has occasioned frequent and bitter complaints, the will for the radical institutional reform that is required seems utterly lacking. Boutros-Ghali, it is true, is alert to the problem: 'The UN,' he declared in 1992, 'is still in the Middle Ages, where the king [the Secretary-General] is quite weak and the barons [the heads of the Specialised Agencies] stronger than the king.'[8] It remains to be seen whether his determination to make the agencies 'better synchronised' can overcome the in-built inertia. An even bigger problem of the same nature concerns the relationship between the UN proper on the one hand and the IMF and World Bank on the other. With the support of Western powers these institutions have made themselves increasingly independent and trespassed on the economic, social and economic functions originally intended to be performed by the UN itself.

Matters of detail also remain unresolved. For instance, neither the USA nor the UK have resumed their membership of UNESCO. More seriously, the financial condition of the UN continues to be insecure. When Pérez de Cuéllar compiled his last report as Secretary-General in September 1991 he noted sadly that only forty-nine member states had fully paid their annual subscriptions and that the total amount owing in outstanding contributions was nearly $1.3 billion. The General Assembly had still not agreed to his comprehensive plan for correcting the problem. Yet, given the demands on the Organisation, it needed more rather than less than the assessed funding. Despite the marginal validity of the complaints about wastage of money, those who urge the UN to achieve more might do well to remember the truth of the adage that you get what you pay for.

THE WAYS AHEAD

The resuscitation of the UN has by no means led to complacency. The failures and continuing problems are well-known causes for concern. The restored morale and revived hopes have rather produced a greater interest in further reforms. If the Organisation is not going to die after all, it is worthwhile planning new ways to make it even more effective. Four main ideas may be noted.

First, and fundamentally, questions are being raised about the very nature and purpose of the UN. In so far as it sometimes seems to be floundering in pursuit of so many different objectives, perhaps it is because the membership has not fully thought through what its objectives should properly be.[9] Given the resources which the member states are willing to allocate, what is reasonable to expect the UN to be able to undertake with efficiency? If the answer to this question is still a wide-ranging agenda, then a more co-ordinated 'unitary United Nations' should be constructed. (In 1992 the Secretary-General initiated work on integrating various UN activities and identifying one senior official in each country as his local Representative.) If, on the other hand, it is felt that some functions might more usefully be undertaken by other, specialist or regional, agencies, then it is necessary to specify what must remain quintessentially UN tasks. These are, of course, big issues and they certainly will not be resolved in the near future. In comparison, however, the other three ideas for improvement are minor.

The second idea could nevertheless have significant effects. It is the belief that a world organisation which stands for peace and justice should be seen to be committed much more overtly than it is to democracy. This belief has three facets. One is the view that the UN itself should make provision for a popular representative institution. This idea is expressed in the proposal for a 'Second Assembly' composed of representatives from International Non-Governmental Organisations (INGOs). By introducing a measure of popular participation the UN could come to enjoy weightier popular support than it has in the past. For is it not paradoxical that an organisation whose Charter opens with the words 'We the *peoples* of the United Nations' should be an organisation of states and not in fact of the peoples of which they are composed? The second aspect of the democratic argument is the view that the international community as a whole should be 'democratised' in the sense of involving all states more fully in collaborative ventures and bringing non-UN organisations to co-operate in specific programmes with the UN. The third face of the democratic argument is that the UN should use its best endeavours to promote liberal democracy as a form of government. Clearly such a policy would need to be pursued with delicacy. Nevertheless, if a state is willing to accept advice concerning the conduct of elections or the organisation of political parties, there is no reason why that advice should be considered any more intrusive than, say, the work of the IMF. The Organisation has already had experience in monitoring the fairness of elections in Haiti. The extension of such services would be consonant with the Organisation's commitment to human rights.

The matter of sharing international work with other, particularly regional, bodies needs further comment, as the third major idea for rendering the UN more effective. It is related, of course, to the notions already outlined both of shedding some responsibilities in order to rationalise the international system and of sharing some responsibilities in order to democratise the international system. Both Pérez de Cuéllar and Boutros-Ghali have favoured the more active involvement of other bodies in the kind of work undertaken by the UN in the field of peace-keeping. Chapter VIII of the Charter in fact specifically commends the use of regional arrangements or agencies for the resolution of disputes. Where the concept of a network of regional organisations complementing the work of the UN was somewhat hypothetical for Pérez de Cuéllar, it assumed a practical urgency for Boutros-Ghali, faced with the chaos of a disintegrating Yugoslavia. The EC claimed particular interest in the situation: it was a dangerous condition on their doorstep; they took the initiative in recognising the independence of Croatia and Slovenia; and they appointed a mediator, Lord Carrington, to try to stop the fighting. Yet, complained Boutros-Ghali, they fumbled the job, half expecting the USA or the UN to make the decisive interventions. In such circumstances, argued the Secretary-General in effect, it is Chapter VIII of the Charter that should be considered the most pertinent.

The fourth idea concerns pre-emption. This relates to the readiness of both the Security Council and peace-keeping forces to prevent the outbreak of violent conflicts. As early as 1982 Pérez de Cuéllar was urging that the Security Council should develop a mode of working which would embrace the identification of potential trouble spots. It should then adopt measures to prevent the tension degenerating into violence. Since it is so difficult to persuade warring parties to lay down their arms, the principle of prevention being better than cure seems as valid in international affairs as in other spheres of life.

But would not a UN attempt to pre-empt the outbreak of fighting require the readiness of the Organisation to introduce its own armed forces into unsettled regions? Peace-keeping would surely need to be supplemented by peace-*making*. In 1992, Dr Boutros-Ghali, at the invitation of the Security Council, produced a report recommending that the Organisation be given stronger and more flexible armed forces with pre-emption as one of the main objectives.[10]

The scheme distinguished between preventive diplomacy, peace-making, peace-keeping and post-conflict peace-building. It involved the ear-marking by states of contingents of volunteers to be specifically trained and on permanent standby for deployment in peace enforcement units. In order that such a force might be a deterrent against the outbreak of war by its very existence and be effectively able to act as a buffer against the quarrelling opponents, it would need to be more heavily armed and equipped than the traditional peace-keeping forces. It should be remembered that, although this plan seemed daring when produced, it did little more in effect than recommend the activation of Article 42 of the Charter (see p.11).

Whether any of these ideas for improving the effectiveness of the UN are implemented or not, there can be little doubt that the world would be even less happy, peaceful and just without the Organisation. It is the only truly universal organisation there is in an age which is witnessing a bewildering multiplication of problems quite beyond the competence of separate states to deal with. Moreover, the committee rooms, corridors and cafeterias of the UN headquarters provide unique opportunities for face saving and creative diplomacy. The facilities for secret and extended discussions and negotiations ultimately sanctified by the UN imprimatur, provide possibilities for conflict-resolution often unavailable in any other forum.

Not only is the United Nations the one such universal body in existence but it is a body which may make some claim to impartiality. This impartiality has often been doubted, and sometimes with good cause. None the less, as long as it can hold to the ideal and the Secretary-General especially be seen strenuously trying to be impartial in all his words and deeds, then respect for the Organisation and willingness to use its good offices have a chance to grow.

The United Nations cannot be properly understood outside a broad historical framework. It is the culmination of theoretical plans from Dubois and Dante in the Middle Ages through Saint-Pierre, Bentham and Kant in the eighteenth century until the League of Nations gave the vision of a peace-keeping body some form of reality. All the designs, whether the myriad hypothetical schemes or the flesh-and-blood League and UN, reflected the preconceptions of their times. The League failed to adapt to markedly changed circumstances and foundered on the twin rocks of American isolationism and Axis aggression. The UN Mark I, it may be argued, was badly holed by the unforeseen East v. West cold war. Running repairs and renovations may be in the process of converting the original model to a more seaworthy Mark II.

Realists (or pessimists, if you will), recognising the stormclouds of a new cold war – of North v. South – must pin their hopes on the refitted UN. And they must hope in particular that the ideas for pre-emptive planning and action on the tactical level will be matched by far-sighted adaptability at the strategic and structural levels to cope with yet more unfamiliar situations. Evidence emerged in 1992 of plans being drafted in the USA for new nuclear weapons and a Nuclear Expeditionary Force 'primarily for use against China or Third World targets'. These plans were compiled in response to the fearful realisation in the USA that 'the growing wealth of petro-nations and newly hegemonic powers is available to crazies and bullies'.[11] At the same time the virtual failure of the Rio Earth Summit revealed the dangerous drifting apart of wealthy North and impoverished South on all the crucial global issues.

The impartiality, hope and idealism for which the UN stands will be desparately needed in the decades ahead.

EPILOGUE

Although the reader has been introduced to much historical background, the purpose of this book is also to explain the UN in a contemporary context. Yet the 'contemporary' is a constantly shifting point. The updating of the text has been undertaken during the summer of 1992 in the midst of events in which the UN was controversially embroiled. From the perspective of September, as the final touches are being made to the manuscript, a few additional comments seem necessary.

By that time the membership had risen to 179 states. The pressure for amending the membership of the Security Council was mounting. The claims of Japan and Germany were becoming increasingly difficult to deny; not to mention the cases of Brazil, Nigeria and India on grounds of Third World representation. The second and third largest contributors to the UN budget (after the USA) were now Japan and

Germany (cf. p.132). Japan's constitutional amendment to allow the despatch of troops overseas led to that country's first contribution to a peace-keeping force (in Cambodia) in September. Meanwhile, Germany was discontented with the way Britain and France were presenting the EC position in the Council.

Criticism of UN inefficiency became an unfortunate feature of the operations to relieve the famine in Somalia. One of the problems was the perennial issue of lack of co-ordination among the various agencies. Another was the matter of the safety of UN personnel.

This difficulty was highlighted in three ways in September. First, in Somalia, effective government had all but broken down and rival warlord armies, it was feared, would not be inhibited by the UN flag from seizing food supplies by force. Second, the published suggestion that Hammarskjöld had been killed by Belgian-employed mercenaries gave an historical warning of the perils threatening UN officials in regions of civil turbulence. Third, attacks on UN-protected convoys in Bosnia led to the sanctioning of UN peace-keeping forces there returning fire in self-defence.

Moreover, the problems of the relative priority to be given to Bosnia and Somalia and the financing of UN activity in the former area led to friction between the Secretary-General and the Security Council.

As the break-up of Yugoslavia continued its violent course, more peace-keeping troops were committed to that theatre – an increase from 1500 to over 7000. The diplomatic search for a solution was formalised as a joint UN–EC effort. Yet neither peace-keeping (or rather peace-making) efforts on the ground nor diplomacy in Geneva appeared likely to produce early solutions. The costs of the peace-keeping forces were rising inexorably. The total UN peace-keeping bill for 1992 would be in the region of $3 billion. Yet hundreds of millions of dollars of arrears remained unpaid.

Meanwhile, the UN agreed to an air-exclusion zone in southern Iraq in an attempt to protect the Shi'ite population from Saddam Hussein's persecution.

To summarise the position of the UN in the autumn of 1992: there was widespread agreement that its work was crucial; widespread discontent with its inefficiency; and widespread reluctance to finance and staff the agencies and forces adequately. New events were confirming the old picture.

Notes

Introduction: Has the UN Failed?

1. For figures and further analysis, see E. Luard, *Conflict and Peace in the Modern International System* (Boston, 1968) ch. 6. Also J. Laffin, *The World in Conflict. War Annual: contemporary warfare described and analysed* (London, 1987–).

1 The Security Council: Keeping the Peace

1. From 1970 to 1978, 18 vetoes were cast by the US, nine by Britain, seven by the Soviet Union, four by France and two by China. From 1946 to 1991 the figures were as follow:

USSR	114
USA	69
UK	30
France	18
China	3

2. The Security Council held 136 meetings in 1947, 61 in 1950 and only 22 in 1955. In 1960 the figure had again risen to 70 and the average number of meetings has remained about 65–70 since that time. In 1990 it held 69 meetings, of which 44 focused on either Israel or Iraq.
3. No attempt is made here to describe in detail the actions taken by the Security Council in individual cases and their result: those who are interested are referred to the author's *A History of the United Nations*, 2 vols (London, 1982, 1989). Here our concern is to analyse *how* the Council operates rather than what it has done.
4. The allocation does vary. For example, in 1990 there were three African members (Ethiopia, Ivory Coast, Zaïre), one Asian (Malaysia) and one Arab (South Yemen).
5. On the other hand, Secretaries-General have written to the Security Council on occasion about dangerous situations without formally invoking Article 99.
6. These have been increasingly used since the early sixties. They are officially recognised, and published, as 'decisions' of the Council. See S. Bailey, *Voting in the Security Council* (Bloomington, 1969) pp.75–83.
7. In his 1991 Report the Secretary-General explained: 'Instead, the Council authorized the use of force on a national and coalition basis. In the circumstances and given the costs imposed and capabilities demanded by modern warfare, the arrangement seemed unavoidable' (p.8).

8. For a description of the financial crisis which resulted from the creating of these forces, see pp.135ff. From the start of the system until January 1992, 528 000 military, police and civilian personnel served at the cost of 800 lives and $8.3 billion. The arrears in payments for the forces were over $800 million in 1992.

9. In rare cases, the Security Council itself becomes the forum for negotiations. This was the case over the negotiations on the Suez Canal crisis in October 1956, when six of the 11 members, including the permanent members, were represented by their foreign ministers in discussions chaired by the Secretary-General.

10. The degree to which it is possible to arrive at a consensus is often underestimated. In 1967 (for example), the Council adopted altogether eleven resolutions (seven on the Middle East, two on Cyprus and two on a complaint by Congo against Portugal), every one of which was adopted unanimously, without even abstention. Over the Congo, in 1960–4, though there were sharply conflicting views and one resolution was vetoed, six other resolutions were passed without any dissentient votes. Over the Middle East, for all the differences, agreed resolutions were passed in 1967 and again three times in 1973 (when only China abstained). In 1991, thirty-six of the forty-one resolutions were passed unanimously.

11. The Charter itself provides for 'periodic meetings at which each of its members may, if it so desires, be represented by a member of the government or by some other specially designated representative' (Article 28(2)).

12. See p.100.

2 The General Assembly: Discussion of World Issues

1. For a discussion of proceedings over South Africa's credentials, see p.165.

2. The continuing expansion of the agenda without any corresponding increase in committees means of course that there is less time to be devoted to any one item. The following table shows the increase in agenda items and resolutions passed between 1947, the first normal Assembly Session, and 1976:

Year	Agenda items	Resolutions passed
1947	62	76
1955	66	87
1960	92	94
1965	108	124
1976	125	208

The figures for 1990 were 158 agenda items and 268 resolutions.

3. For many purposes states have been clustered into recognised regional groups. These are: African, Asian, Latin American, Eastern Europe, Western Europe and others (includes Australia, Canada, New Zealand, USA).

4. For well-informed accounts of this process at work see J. Kaufmann, *United Nations Decision Making* (Rockville, MD, 1980); R. O. Keohane, *Political Influence in the General Assembly* (New York, 1966).
5. For example, R., Hovet, *Bloc Politics in the UN* (London, 1960); H. R. Alker and B. M. Russett, *Political Influence in the General Assembly* (New York, 1966).
6. Delegations which have received no clear instructions also seek to be among the majority to avoid trouble later. When a vote begins to be taken, not all hands in the Committee rise at the same time.
7. The degree of detail varies greatly from delegation to delegation. The delegates of some developing countries receive little instruction and guidance, and so enjoy considerable discretion in voting.
8. All of this again is far more difficult for the tiny missions of smaller countries. It is difficult enough to keep all the committees manned; still more difficult to maintain a large volume of communications with the home capital. In consequence the Ambassador in such a mission consults far less: and takes more decisions himself. They also have less background briefing on issues.
9. These are described in the author's *A History of the United Nations*, 2 vols (London, 1982, 1989).
10. See p. 71.
11. For a description of the Human Rights Commission see pp. 71ff.
12. The degree to which resolutions are 'forced through' by machine majorities in these debates is often exaggerated (like so much else) by the press and mass media. At a typical Assembly in the 1970s, of over 150 resolutions or decisions passed, more than two-thirds passes without *any* contrary votes; on none were there more than 50 votes against; on only three more than twenty; and on two others more than ten contrary votes.
13. This has affected the Trusteeship Council (set up to discuss territories made over as Trust Territories) even more; only one such territory now remains: the Pacific islands of Micronesia, which is not supervised by the Council but by the Security Council. The Trusteeship Council is thus now without duties.
14. Some of the Committees, or sub-committees from them, might also have sessions outside the General Assembly: this would make possible more specialised attendance.
15. Report of the Joint Inspection Unit (JIU) A/8319 of 2 June 1971.
16. A system of weighted voting was formally proposed by Italy in 1969 (A/7690 of 9 October 1969).

3   The Economic and Social Institutions: Securing a Fairer World

1. These agencies are described in more detail in the companion volume to the present, *International Agencies: The Emerging Framework of Interdependence* (London, 1977) and are only briefly mentioned here.
2. Co-ordination in the UN system is described and discussed in Chapter 17 of *International Agencies: The Emerging Framework of Interdependence*. See also M. Hill, *The United Nations System: Co-ordinating its Economic and Social Work* (Cambridge, 1978).

4 The Legal Institutions: Laying Down the International Law

1. The distinction between the 'development' of new law and the 'codification' of rules where there already existed a substantial body of practice, precedent and doctrine, though laid down in the Commission's statute, has in practice now been largely abandoned.
2. For an account, see I. Brownlie, *International Law and the Use of Force* (Oxford, 1963).
3. Usually the monarch so approached would entrust the task to advisers, sometimes international lawyers.
4. Cf. H. Lauterpacht, *The Development of International Law by the Permanent Court of International Justice* (London, 1934) p.5.
5. One or two countries which are not members of the UN today – Switzerland and Nauru, for example – have become parties to the Statute.
6. The method of drawing base-lines has since been defined legally in the 1958 Convention on the Territorial Sea and Contiguous Zone.
7. Introduction to the Secretary-General's Annual Report, 1970.
8. Partly for this reason there has been a move in the UN, led by the Latin Americans (always strong upholders of legal procedures), to re-examine the role of the Court. In 1970 nine states asked that a review be undertaken 'of obstacles to satisfactory functioning' of the Court and additional possibilities for its use, but this has not led to any significant change.
9. The UN has undertaken a considerable programme to spread knowledge and understanding of international law, especially in developing countries, through fellowships, regional seminars, advisory services of experts, the improvement of library facilities, assisting in the teaching of international law and in other ways. The UNDP provides some assistance in the development of international law.
10. See I. Brownlie, *Principles of Public International Law* (Oxford, 4th edn, 1990) pp.26–7.
11. This contained seven principles: the prohibition of the use of force; the peaceful settlement of international disputes; the duty not to intervene in matters within the domestic jurisdiction of another state; the duty of states to cooperate with one another in accordance with the Charter; the principle of equal rights and self-determination of peoples; the sovereign equality of states; and the principle that states shall fulfil in good faith the obligations assumed by them in accordance with the Charter.
12. So far only twenty-one advisory opinions have been asked for against twenty-seven by the Council of the League between 1922 and 1935 (thirteen years).

5 The Secretariat: Running the Organisation

1. See S. M. Schwebel, *The Secretary-General of the United Nations* (Cambridge, 1952).
2. This chapter is concerned mainly with the UN Secretariat, though much of what is said holds good equally of the specialised agency secretariats.
3. See above, p.52.

4. For accusations of inefficiency and demoralisation of lower-ranking staff, see S. Hazzard, *Countenance of Truth* (London, 1991).
5. Cf. this comment on the UNCTAD Secretariat: 'On the assumption that a good expert study can often exert an important influence on the policies of governments, the Secretariat has made its studies and reports a basic policy weapon of the organisation' (B. Gosovic, 'UNCTAD, North–South Encounter', *International Conciliation*, May 1968). Much the same holds of the UN itself.
6. The idea of weighting posts according to seniority has been mooted but rejected.
7. Most of the agencies have similar provisions to the UN. For example, the WHO constitution provides in Article 35: 'The paramount consideration in the employment of the staff shall be to assure that the efficiency, integrity and internationally representative character of the Secretariat shall be maintained at the highest level. Due regard shall be paid also to the importance of recruiting the staff on as wide a geographical basis as possible.' Article VIII of the constitution of FAO provides that: 'In appointing the staff, the Director-General shall, subject to the paramount importance of securing the highest standards of efficiency and of technical competence, pay due regard to the importance of selecting personnel recruited on as wide a geographical basis as possible.' The financial agencies, such as the World Bank and the IMF, are those which have maintained most rigorously the insistence on highest standards of ability in recruitment. As a result they have probably the most highly qualified staff of all agencies, though with a high proportion from Western countries. They have, however, made a considerable effort, without sacrificing their high standards, to recruit more of their staff from developing countries, and so to reduce the heavily Western image which they have. Similarly, UPU, which had a high proportion of Swiss staff originally, later also recruited a more geographically balanced staff. The only UN body which has been almost entirely uninfluenced by all considerations of nationality has been UNDP, which has consistently recruited so far as possible exclusively on grounds of ability, and without regard to geographical distribution.
8. A proposal by Norway in 1969 that the Secretary-General should give preference to under-represented countries only when their qualifications were equal to those of other available candidates was defeated in the Fifth Committee.
9. For example, the permanent members of the Security Council used to have posts of Under-Secretary-General permanently reserved for them, and in effect made the appointments themselves. For changes made in 1992, see p.176.
10. Britain set a good example in 1974 by nominating the most senior and experienced Briton in the Secretariat, Mr Brian Urquhart, to the post of Under-Secretary-General.
11. Report of the Committee on the Organisation of the Secretariat A/7359, of 27 November 1968.
12. A Special Committee for the Review of the UN Salary System in 1971–2 examined long-term principles and criteria governing salaries, allowances, grants, superannuation and other benefits throughout the UN family.

13. H. G., Nicholas, *The United Nations as a Political Institution* (Oxford, 5th edn, 1975) p.175.
14. The ICSAB has considered there was no need for staff representatives to have direct access to legislative bodies.
15. R. W. Cox, 'The Executive Head', *International Organisation*, spring 1969, p.213.
16. For further discussion of this question, see p.177 below.
17. S. M., Schwebel, *The Secretary-General of the United Nations* (Harvard, 1952), pp.78–9.

6 The Budgetary System: Finding the Money

1. See J. G. Stoessinger, and associates, *Financing the United Nations System* (Washington, 1964) pp.35–7.
2. F. P. Walters, *A History of the League of Nations* (London, 1952) p.131.
3. Most of the agencies founded after 1945 adopted systems similar to the UN's. They mainly use a similar, and sometimes the same, assessment formula. Usually there are sanctions, either permissive or automatic. But as in the UN, these sanctions have scarcely ever been used, even when members have been in arrears. Some have voluntary programmes in addition to regular budgets. For example the WHO has funds for medical research, malaria eradication, community water supply and so on, to which governments can contribute if they wish. It has also raised a small amount of additional revenue for itself by the sale of stamps (for example malaria-eradication stamps). The FAO also has voluntary programmes as well as the regular budget; and it raised some money by Freedom from Hunger stamps. The ILO, because it was originally established long before the UN, uses a system which at least in its details differs from that of the UN and most other agencies. Its minimum contribution was 0.12 per cent (instead of 0.04 per cent) and the maximum 25 per cent (now adopted also by the UN). Thus the system was rather less egalitarian. It also possesses stronger sanctions, in the form of the right to deprive a defaulting government of all voting rights (not just those in the Conference). As in the UN this is supposed to be almost automatic: the Government Body has standing orders to 'inform' the General Conference when a member has lost its voting rights. The sanction was applied in the case of Hungary in the mid-1950s, but on other occasions the claim that there are special circumstances, beyond the control of the member, has been used to avoid imposing them.
4. The administrative (including headquarters) costs of work undertaken by the agencies on behalf of UNDP are reimbursed to the agencies by UNDP. Most of the agencies believe that the amount they receive is inadequate to make up the full overheads involved and this question has been the cause of serious disputes.
5. The Ad Hoc Committee on the Finances of the UN at the Specialised Agencies in 1966 explicitly turned down the suggestion that a ceiling should be placed on UN expenditure.
6. See F. P. Walters, *A History of the League of Nations* (London, 1952) p.133: 'The budget of the League was subjected to a series of controls for which it would be hard to find a parallel.'

7. Originally this was to have had the same name as the League (Supervisory Commission), but it was eventually decided to alter the name, to emphasise that the real responsibility for supervision lay with the Fifth Committee and the Assembly: the Committee's role was to advise in this task. However in practice the Committee is the only effective supervisory body.

8. There is still another form of supplementary estimate; that which becomes necessary because of the authorisation of new programmes after the budget has been first formulated (that is any time after May of each year) but before it is finally approved. The ACABQ disapproves of these last-minute propositions but provides reports on all requests and in practice there is little choice for the Assembly but to vote to provide the necessary funds.

9. UN Assembly Document A/6705/Add 2.

10. The work and expense of each meeting is huge in providing conference facilities, interpretation, a very large volume of documentation and reports (one ECOSOC meeting alone is said to have required eleven thousand pages) which not only need considerable labour and preparation, but have to be translated into all working languages (the same ECOSOC meeting cost half a million dollars for translation alone). In 1966, 500 million impressions of documents were being produced a year in New York, and 333 million in Geneva. Altogether something like $26 million dollars a year, or about 20 per cent of the UN budget, was being spent on conference activities.

11. Some classified expenditure by objects of expenditure (staff, equipment, transport and so on); others by programmes of activities (with staffs and other costs for each individual programme kept separately). The UN itself had a hybrid system, basically adopting the former method for the Secretariat itself, but presenting separate chapters altogether for the International Court, the High Commissioner for Refugees, UNCTAD, UNIDO and so on.

12. Senate Staff Study No. 6, p. 161 of 1954. The same study suggested that the Assembly should be given direct control over the budgets of the specialised agencies.

13. J. G. Stoessinger, and associates, *Financing the UN System* (Washington, 1964) p.96.

14. For an examination of coordination in the UN family, see Evan Luard, *International Agencies: the Emerging Framework of International Interdependence* (London, 1977), ch. 17. See also p.175 above.

15. The UNDP Governing Council has considered establishing some kind of finance committee, or making greater use of the services of the ACABQ. The Committee of Experts on the Restructuring of the UN recommended the integration of the voluntary programmes within the UN's general development programme.

16. The rich countries have consistently supported more use of voluntary programmes. Yet in fact the rich pay a larger, not a smaller, share of such programmes. Moreover, since 1950 UN voluntary programmes have increased more, and not less, rapidly than the regular budgets. So expenditure is not necessarily curbed by these means. The preference of

the developed no doubt results from the fact that they have greater control over what they give in voluntary programmes.

17. The first major crisis over financing in the UN's history, over peace-keeping finances in 1965, demonstrated the dangers of seeking to impose compulsory assessment for controversial purposes. The Soviet Union and other countries, though not justified in seeking to determine unilaterally which UN expenses they felt legitimate, were in effect being asked to accept a tripling in their dues to pay for a controversial operation, outside the normal range of activity, of which they totally disapproved. Until commitment to the Organisation is much greater than it is now, the majority will be wise not to press such issues to the final extreme. This does not mean that future peace-keeping operations must depend on ad hoc voluntary contributions. Provided the Security Council is responsible for authorisation and control, and for determining financial contributions, all members may be willing to contribute in most cases even if under a special scale (as for the Middle East forces). The essential point is that the arrangements for financing should be known from the beginning.

7 The Fundamental Political Problems

1. W. Morawiecki, 'Institutional and Political Conditions of Participation of Socialist States in International Organisations', *International Organisation*, spring 1968.
2. Ibid., p.501.
3. F. I. Kozhevnikov, (ed.), *International Law* (Moscow Foreign Language Publishing House, 1961).
4. J. H. Weaver, *The International Development Association* (New York, 1965) p.28.
5. R. O. Keohane, 'Political Influence in the General Assembly', *International Conciliation*, 1966, p.120.
6. E/1584 of 22 December 1949
7. E/1986 of 3 May 1951.
8. E/2381 of 18 March 1953.
9. J. H. Weaver, *The International Development Association* (New York, 1965) p.28.
10. Ibid., p.90.
11. According to one study, on all types of issue (including development) 'significant divisions were apparent within the major regional groups except for the East European one. ... Cross-regional coalition was very much in evidence on a number of issues', including social and economic questions. (R. O. Keohane, 'Political Influence in the General Assembly', *International Conciliation*, March 1966, p.12).
12. J. Pérez de Cuéllar, *Report of the Secretary-General on the Work of the Organization* (New York, 1991) p.15.
13. See p.45 above.
14. Under Article 6, a member which has 'persistently violated the Principles contained in the Charter may be expelled from the Organisation by the General Assembly upon the recommendation of the Security Council'.

15. The question of South African membership of UNCTAD was raised and strenuously debated in 1968. The issue was a complex one, because UNCTAD is not a specialised agency (which could take its own decisions according to its own constitution) but an integral part of the UN, of which all UN members are automatically members. It is also extremely comprehensive in membership, including even some members who have not been members of the UN. It was argued by Africans and others that it was open to the UN, in establishing such an organisation, to designate its membership, and so to make any exceptions it chose from the normal membership of the organisation. Others, including the UN's legal counsel, argued there was no constitutional provision for this in relation to subordinate bodies of the UN. The vote for expulsion did not obtain a two-thirds majority; and a procedural vote declared the question an important one demanding such a majority.
16. For an examination of various types of influence, see R. O. Keohane, 'Political Influence in the General Assembly', *International Conciliation*, March 1966, pp.40–2.

8 Conclusions: A New Lease of Life?

1. See J. Haslam, 'The UN and the Soviet Union: new thinking?', *International Affairs*, autumn 1989; and G. R. Berridge, *Return to the UN* (London, 1991) ch. 3. Some of the material in this chapter is heavily dependent on the latter.
2. Quoted in Haslam, p.683.
3. Quoted in the *Observer*, 24 November 1991.
4. *Report of the Secretary-General on the Work of the Organization* (New York, 1991) p.4.
5. Quoted in *Keesing's Contemporary Archives*, 38744.
6. G. Clark and L. B. Sohn, *World Peace through World Law* (Cambridge, Mass., 1958).
7. B. Urquhart, 'The United Nations in 1992: problems and opportunities', *International Affairs*, April 1992, p.318.
8. Quoted in the *Guardian*, 23 May 1992.
9. See P. Fromuth, (ed.), *A Successor Vision: the United Nations of tomorrow* (Lanham, MD, 1988).
10. B. Boutros-Ghali, *An Agenda for Peace* (New York, 1992).
11. Quotations from Paul Rogers' report in the *Guardian*, 2 July 1992.

Index

199